The History of the Coptic Orthodox Church in the United States

From the Land of the Pharaohs to the United States of America

E. M. GABRIEL

ISBN 978-1-0980-5282-9 (paperback)
ISBN 978-1-0980-5283-6 (hardcover)
ISBN 978-1-0980-5284-3 (digital)

Christian Faith Publishing, Inc.
832 Park Avenue
Meadville, PA 16335
www.christianfaithpublishing.com

Scripture quotations from The Authorized (King James) Version. Rights in the Authorized Version in the United Kingdom are vested in the Crown. Reproduced by permission of the Crown's patentee, Cambridge University Press.

Printed in the United States of America

To our children and grandchildren:
the baptized Generation X, millennials, and Generation Z
of St. Mark's Coptic Orthodox Church of America.

On the occasion of celebrating the church's golden jubilee
in the United States, October 6, 2018.

CONTENTS

ACKNOWLEDGMENTS

I would be hard pressed to think of an author who needed more help and received it in greater measure of support than I did in the writing of this book. First and foremost, I would like to thank my wife and both of my daughters, who encouraged me to write this history for posterity's sake and who prayed for this purpose. I am especially grateful to my wife for her devotion to this project and her invaluable editing. Her excellent suggestions, care, and sensitivity enabled me to really focus not only the writing of this book but my other publications as well.

I owe special thanks to HH Pope Tawadros II, HG Bishop David, and Hegomen Fr. Mina Yanni, whose sacrificial love and tireless efforts both assisted and honored the Coptic Christian pioneers who made history when they arrived in the United States of America. I am grateful to Hegomen Fr. Roufail Youssef for his prayers and unwavering dedication, as well as many other members of the clergy for their support—I would love to name them all but fear to miss any. Last but not least, thanks to all those who prefer to remain anonymous—without their prayers, this task would not have seen the light of day. Finally, my heartfelt thanks to St. Mary and St. Joseph, whose presence, protection, and intercession became ever more real for me as I thought about and wrote this book.

Acknowledgment also is due here to the support of (the late) His Grace Bishop Samuel, bishop of public, ecumenical, and social services, who was instrumental in sending Fr. Rofael Younan Nakhla of Montreal, Canada, to the United States. Father Rofael celebrated the first Holy Liturgy at Riverside Church at 475 Riverside Drive and West 120th Street, New York City. The Mass started at 10:00 a.m., Sunday, June 30, 1968. He celebrated the Holy Liturgy for the second time at the General Theological Seminary at 175 Ninth Avenue, Chelsea, New York City, on Sunday, November 10, 1968, from 11:00 a.m. to 1:00 p.m.

These beginnings were the seeds that paved the way to establishing St. Mark Coptic Orthodox Church in Jersey City, New Jersey. The church was incorporated March 6, 1970, in the state of New Jersey. Following Father Rofael service in New York he served the first mass in Philadelphia.

A member of the Coptic American Association (CAA) was relocated to Philadelphia, Pennsylvania, in September 1969. While in New York, he would join Father Rofael for home visitations of Copts who were newly arrived in New York. Father Rofael, upon finding out about the member's intended move to another state, was very supportive and promised to come and visit. He gladly did, and during that visit he met with a few families who recently immigrated and lived in the Philadelphia area. He then encouraged them to join other members in New York for the monthly Holy Liturgy he had been conducting there. Some of us attended the service every time Father Rofael celebrated the Holy Liturgy in New York and continued to do so for almost a year. Many, however, were not able to make the trip to New York but yearned that he would come and celebrate mass with them in Philadelphia.

Father Rofael then planned a second visit to Philadelphia and celebrated the Holy Liturgy at the Central Presbyterian Church on Broad Street near city hall in Philadelphia in October of 1969. The numbers of Coptic families did not exceed more than six families, of whom three families were of another denomination. We were joined by many members from the New York area, and it was a joyous day to remember. This beginning was the seed that paved the way to establishing St. George Coptic Orthodox Church in Philadelphia. The following day, the Sunday *Philadelphia Inquirer*, a well-circulated newspaper in the state of Pennsylvania, announced that "History Is Made: Coptic Mass Celebrated in Philadelphia."

The rest is history. However, this history has been recorded in an objective reality and ontological manner, not a subjective one. Published records of this history are here to be offered on behalf of the first immigrants to His Holiness Pope Tawadros II. It consists of:

- The first Coptic Church constitution and bylaws ever was drawn according to federal law, US Code Section 501(c) for nonprofit organizations. Published by His Holiness Pope Kyrillos VI, December 3, 1969. (A copy of the bylaws is included.)
- Part of this history has been preserved in the US Library of Congress under the title of *The Exemplary Leadership of Pope Kyrillos VI & Pope Shenouda III*. (A copy of the book is included.)
- The third phase of this history was a response to a kind request by His Grace Bishop David. A textbook was written for the massive influx of Copt immigrants to know how to raise their children and preserve family life in a secular humanistic culture and in the face of permissive society. The title of this textbook is *The Exemplarily Upbringing of the Child & Transformational Stages toward Perfect Maturity*. (A copy of the book is included.)
- The fourth is "A Well-Thought-Out Proposal" in response to Your Holiness's inspired call during your visit to Canada in 2014 encouraging efforts to explore and plan the church's catechism activity in the next fifty years. This proposal was built on a summary of input and statement of need from thousands of participating Coptic youth in the West through digital communication. Project activities and outcomes, evaluation, and dissemination were prompted and shared with His Grace Bishop Suriel while he resided in the Diocese of New Jersey, then later was handed to His Grace Bishop David, the Patriarchal Exarch at the Archdiocese of North America in Cedar Grove, New Jersey, at that time. (The proposal is included.)

- This history will not be complete without including the writings of the Very Reverend Fr. Tadros Yacoub Malaty in a book titled *The Church in the Land of Diaspora*, dated June 1972, and his popular message, "The New Pope and the Power of the Communal Repentance," dated November 2012. (A copy of the original title page of the book and copies of the message, in both Arabic and English, are included.)

- Finally, Your Holiness will be pleased to know that the rich history, treasures, traditions, and theology of our Coptic Orthodox Church are also recorded and preserved in almost every university's religious department in the nation under the scholarly magazine *Coptic Church Review*, established and edited by the late Dr. Rodolph Yanney and a board of scholarly writers and theologians. (A special copy of *Coptic Church Review* on the subject of the Eucharist sacrament in the Coptic Orthodox Church is included.)

Last and not least, we are greatly thankful and eternally grateful to His Grace Bishop David, the Very Reverend Hegomen Mina Yanni, and all those who planned and toiled behind the scene. Through their sacrificial love, they orchestrated this magnificent celebration and made it possible to honor the first immigrants, to entice and enlighten Coptic generations to follow the path of their contribution in establishing the Coptic Orthodox Church in the United States of America more than fifty years ago.

PREFACE

⬥⟨•••⟩◆⟨•••⟩⬥

I
t all started with a presentation delivered before His Holiness Pope Tawadros II, pope of the Coptic Orthodox Church of Alexandria.

Soon after I delivered my speech on October 6, 2018, in the presence of His Holiness the pope, their graces, the bishops, and other church clergy and dignitaries, I was approached by several dignified guests and dear friends. They expressed a deep desire to have me write the history of the Coptic Church in the United States as it was witnessed by those who took part in its founding. In particular, Mr. Nassif Banout, a leading servant and member of St. George Church in Brooklyn, New York, and Dr. Farid F. Shafik, a devout thinker, the celebration's moderator, and a spiritual son of the late Very Rev. Fr. Gabriel Abdelsayed, both expressed their zeal for preserving the history of the Coptic Orthodox Church in America.

Mr. Banout is a very close friend. Our relationship goes back to our youth and dedicated service at St. Mark Church in Shoubra and Archangel Michael Church in Toson, Cairo, Egypt. We also served at St. John the Son of Thunder's weekly college meetings. There, we met an outstanding group of pious graduate and undergraduate students from elite universities throughout Cairo. Many of them became successful professionals in a variety of scientific and medical fields, and a majority of them later immigrated to the United States. These wonderful faithful servants were the bedrock of the establishment of many Coptic Orthodox churches in America.

My friends and colleagues were not the only ones who wanted me to write this history. Their children and even my own family demanded that it be recorded in English by the ones who witnessed it. Even if some segments of this history were already written in Arabic, many felt a complete book in English would be worthwhile to add to the picture and enhance its fullness.

I was approached for this important task because I was one of the early settlers who witnessed and experienced the inception of the Coptic Church in the United States. I was a member of the first and only Coptic association in the US, the Coptic American Association (CAA). In addition, I had moved early on to the state of Pennsylvania where, along with a few others, I helped establish the first Coptic Orthodox church in the City of Brotherly Love, Philadelphia, in 1969. My long-time association with our church in America made me the ideal candidate to record these historical events for the benefit of future generations of Christian Copts living or born beyond the borders of Egypt.

We believe it is essential to keep track of this history. Christian Copts treasure their ethnic origin as the direct descendent of the pharaohs. Our ancestors are the original inhabitants of the great land of Egypt, one of the cradles of civilization. But more importantly, Coptic Christians are proud to be the direct beneficiaries of their faith, adhering to their spiritual path by walking in the footsteps of St. Mark the Evangelist. He is the author of the Gospel of St. Mark and the founder of the Church of Alexandria, one of the most important sees of early Christianity.

During the early years of the Coptic Orthodox Church in the United States, a visiting dignitary from another denomination expressed his surprise and admiration when he noticed that one of our churches in New Jersey was full of young worshippers. During the service, the dignitary turned to His Grace Bishop David and asked, "What do you do to keep your youth in the church?" He related that church leaders in America were worried about the dwindling numbers of Christian youth, and he was curious about these young Copts who appeared to be enjoying their spiritual experience. He entertained the idea that, rather than abandoning Christianity, some young people were joining more traditional liturgical denominations.

It is true. Young Coptic Christians are involved in every aspect of church life. The worship, doctrine, and tradition are an integral part of the life of the community of believers as members of the body of Christ. Besides the fact that the Coptic Church is part of their ethnicity, our children are spiritually elevated by the liturgical beauty they encounter every time they are in the church.

Such is not the case in other parts of America, where young people are known to be leaving churches in droves. According to a Public Religion Research Institute poll, 55 percent of self-declared "unaffiliated" youth identified with a religious tradition when they were younger.[1] It is believed that some young people are joining more orthodox churches for their deep, rich tradition of spirituality and faith. Indeed, many members of the millennial generation are exploring new horizons and seeking the meaning of faith. Many of them feel an emptiness or a lack of purpose, and nontraditional churches apparently cannot fill that spiritual void. It is a search for meaning that goes to the heart of finding a destiny and purpose for life beyond worldly pleasures.

* * * * *

St. Pope Cyril VI, the 116th pope of Alexandria and patriarch of the See of St. Mark (May 1959–March 9, 1971), in his first papal message to the churches of America, stated:

> How we need to live the spiritual life at a time when materialism, atheism, and digressive ideas are prevailing the world. How do people need to see Christ in our life and sense this sweet smell in us? The Church has a crucial duty at this stage that the world has reached. The Church has to strengthen faith in all hearts, spread virtue, and give peace and tranquility to all tired souls. By this, it will provide stability and increase happiness.
>
> The Message of the Lord Jesus Christ is to give a better life to people. "I have come that they may have life, and may have it abundantly." It is

the immaculate, pure, and quiet life that makes the good productive citizen and the active member of the Church, who knows how to be always honest to God, his nation, and to human society, dealing with all in a brotherly love and nobility of the spirit.

The pope's first papal message can be seen as a prophecy! He says that the church has a crucial duty to proclaim the message of the Lord Jesus Christ to give people a better life. One wonders, was he thinking only of people within the See of St. Mark or people everywhere as well? Little did we know that his prophetic words would take a firm hold across the Atlantic during His Holiness's reign, recalling the words of ninth-century abbot Bishop Sawyers of Nstroh about St. Mark the Evangelist: "That great saint who had not only shined over the land of Egypt but also shone over the whole world."[2] Would the newcomers to the United States play a role in fulfilling the prophecy of Pope Cyril VI? Would they take part in reflecting that shining light that illuminates the whole world as Bishop Sawyers spoke of St. Mark?

After five decades, we have witnessed what took place, and therefore we can attest to the wonderful work of the Holy Spirit in this land. The establishment and expansion of the Coptic Church in America and all over the world has been evident. We trust it has been part of the divine plan and that the Holy Spirit has led the first pilgrims to pursue that very plan.

The past is prelude; the present and future are subject to the inspiration and guidance of the Holy Spirit. We know that the Holy Spirit is active in the world. He does many things in the lives of believers (John 14:26). He enlightens, guides, strengthens, and consoles them. The Holy Spirit comforted the first immigrants to the United States and continues to fill them with fellowship and joy in a sometimes hostile world.

* * * * *

Esmat M. Gabriel
Montgomeryville, Pennsylvania
May 1, 2019
Blessed Feast of St. George

CHAPTER 1

The Plight of the Coptic Christians of Egypt

The gallant person will always consider the
world with a smile of toleration,
and his own doings with a smile of honest
amusement, and Heaven with a
smile which is not distrustful being thoroughly
persuaded that God is kinder
than the genteel would regard as rational.

—James Branch Cabell

Egypt and the Christian Copts

Egypt is one of the cradles of civilization, and Egyptians love their country. It is a well-known fact that they are one of the most sedentary ethnic groups in the world, rarely emigrating from their homeland.

But this is not true of all Egyptians. Due to lack of religious freedom and restrictive government policies, Coptic Christians—the largest minority in Egypt—have experienced gradual and systemic marginalization. Islamic extremists have targeted the Coptic community with hate crimes and terror. Churches and homes have been burned, young girls have been kidnapped, and even murder has become, sadly and painfully, a devastating daily occurrence. When life became unbearable, and once an opportunity presented itself, many Coptic Christians left the country of their birth.

At the time, I was living comfortably in Alexandria and was well compensated working for the international company TECALEX. A Finnish company, TECALEX built galvanized-steel transmission towers that supported high-voltage power lines. These lines in turn transmitted electricity throughout the entire country from its primary source at the Aswan High Dam in Upper Egypt.

Nonetheless, I was one of those Copts who yearned to leave the country and be liberated from endless discrimination in every field. In 1966, I applied for immigration at both the Canadian and American embassies in Cairo. At first the latter declined to accept my application, not yet having opened its door for Egyptians. I asked if I could fill out an application to be kept on file just in case, and the embassy worker politely agreed, sensing that I was a desperate candidate.

To my utter surprise, I was notified a few months later that my application for immigration had been considered, and a meeting was set at the American Embassy in early 1967. Unexpectedly, the Six-Day War broke out on June 5, and Egypt broke off diplomatic relations with the United States due to American support for Israel, causing the US to open an interests section in the Spanish Embassy in Cairo. For that reason, I was not able to leave the country until July 15, 1968, arriving in New York on July 16. The American Embassy in Egypt would not open again until 1974.

Copts before the Immigration and Nationality Act of 1965

When I first settled in Manhattan, I eventually met some Coptic Christians who had been there prior to the Immigration and Nationality Act (INA) of 1965. Most, if not all, of them were in the United States on scholarships and/or pursuing their graduate studies. A few had settled and had no intention to return to Egypt. They occupied prestigious jobs as educators, librarians, mathematicians, and scientists.

The INA (enacted June 30, 1968), also known as the Hart-Celler Act, changed the way immigration quotas were allocated by ending the National Origins Formula that had been in place in the United States since the Emergency Quota Act of 1921. Representative Emanuel Celler of New York proposed the bill, Senator Philip Hart of Michigan cosponsored it, and Senator Ted Kennedy of Massachusetts helped promote it. The 1965 act marked a change from past US policy that had discriminated against non-Northern Europeans. By removing racial and national barriers, the act would significantly alter the demographic mix in the United States.[3]

The new law restricted the number of visas to 170,000 per year and maintained per-country limits, but it also created preferential categories that focused on immigrants' skills and family relationships with US citizens or residents. Thus, there were no restrictions for immediate relatives of US citizens and "special immigrants."[4] Apparently I was considered a part of the second category.

A Journey into the Unknown

The following is essentially a personal story that reflects on what happens when one leaves his or her own country for good. I had spent three decades of my life in a secure family with loving siblings and wonderful, supportive friends. How could I ignore wise people who were tripping over their own feet to do me favors and prevent me from leaving Egypt? How would I feel about missing weddings, christenings, graduations, birthdays, and yes, funerals—milestones I would never experience because my life was planted elsewhere?

For a Coptic Christian, Egypt is the land of the martyrs, the home of orthodoxy and the faith of the desert fathers. It is the land where St. Mark the Evangelist proclaimed the Good News. How could I leave the birthplace of Coptic Christianity and have a "lavish" life overseas? How dare I cut my very self from feeding at the table of the Lord by traveling to unknown lands? Waiting for me there was the secular, immoral, and pagan world where the Coptic Orthodox Church did not exist—at least not yet!

The Story of Coming to the United States

The story, though, is not only about me, nor is it about the culturally painful feelings of separation. It is neither about the views of others, nor about challenging prevailing wisdom. It is about how the good Lord plans our lives and the Holy Spirit leads if we resign to His will. I am sure that every immigrant to any country in the world has his or her story. The circumstances and details may be different, but in the end, it is divine providence that plans every step of the way.

* * * * *

In 2010, I received an email from my daughter while she was on duty during the US war in Afghanistan.

> Subject: Happy Father's Day!
> Cc:
> Bcc:
> Sent: Sat., Jun 19, 2010 03:20 PM
>
> Hi, Dad,
>
> Although I lose track of even what day of the week it is, I could not forget that today is Father's Day.
> Happy Father's Day to the number 1 dad out there (and grandfather for that)! I hope you have a good Sunday and that you get to spend some time relaxing or at least with Mary and her family. You work hard and deserve some time off.
> If you're in the mood to do any more writing, you should write me the story of you coming to the USA. I have a guy who was born in Canada although his family is from Trinidad. He wants to become a US citizen, and as the legal officer for the squadron, I get to do the interview, make the

recommendation, and submit the paperwork. It's a real treat as opposed to only interviewing people who get in trouble. Anyway, he had it easy compared to the challenges you faced.

Thanks for all the time and love and care. Hope you know how proud I am to have you as my father and how evident it is to everyone around me what a great father you truly are.

July 4, 2010

Dearest daughter,

Thank you for your lovely and kind words and for your interest to know the story of my coming to the USA. It has been over forty years since this chapter of my life began. It is still fresh in my memory as if it happened just a short time ago, which make life events move with the speed of light—something you are very familiar with because every day you fly.

How Did It Happen?

In the mid-1960s, I began to think about emigrating from Egypt as I realized I had no future in the culture and environment of the time. Although clergy and other church leaders considered it anathema to leave Egypt and dwell among "satanic" worshippers and the immoral culture of the West, I always believed that the God of the East is the same in the West. As the psalmist once wrote, "The earth and its fullness are the Lord's; the world and all that dwell in it." (Psalms 24:1)

In Egypt, I spent time in confession with my father, Fr. Mikhail Ibrahim, who always advised to pray and leave it in the hands of the Lord. As I mentioned, at that time I was working in a prestigious and well-paid position as an authorized communication officer at

TECALEX, a Finnish company headquartered in Helsinki. The company specialized in building high-voltage towers for the Aswan High Dam project, or *Saad el Aali* in Arabic. The project extended from the dam and Lake Nasser in the south all the way up the Nile River to Alexandria in the north. As a highly trusted officer at the company, I was privileged with numerous perks, including an imported company car, lodging at first-class resorts wherever I went, and monetary incentives dispersed on a quarterly basis.

I was the company's representative to the highest levels of governmental agencies. These agencies had the authority to prioritize demands and oversee the timely progress of the Aswan Dam. In 1965, I applied to the Canadian and Australian embassies for permission to immigrate. The Canadian Embassy soon notified me that my application was initially approved, contingent on a final meeting with the immigration consul who would evaluate my professional credentials in light of Canadian needs. After I announced my intentions to TECALEX, the Finnish staff, their spouses, and many others celebrated with me. They all, without exception, thought that it was a golden opportunity and a courageous, smart, and daring step in the right direction. They knew that the company would fold its operation once the dam project was completed.

In addition, I did not want to lose the opportunity to invest in my profession as a psychologist. I was hoping to pursue my graduate studies abroad as it became quite clear that doing so would be my best chance for professional advancement. In Egypt—the land of the religiously "chosen," where everyone else is considered an infidel— there was not even a slim chance to succeed in one's field of interest based on merit alone. However, I adopted a motto: "Work and invest in the land of Egypt as if you live there for good; prepare and be ready to leave the country as if it will happen the next day."

Moving Along!

Consequently, when a governmental position opened up that matched my credentials, I resigned from TECALEX and took it. I was appointed as a psychologist with the Ministry of Industry in

Alexandria. I took a substantial salary cut, losing 60 percent of my income and all the perks I had enjoyed at TECALEX. However, my hopes were high that it was only a matter of time and—God willing—I would leave it all behind sooner or later.

The first day I arrived at the Ministry of Industry in Alexandria, I felt sad and quite disappointed. I experienced my first day among other bureaucrats, and it was drastically different than working for an elite Western corporation.

Feeling devastated, at the end of the day I took the first scheduled train from Alexandria back to Cairo. When I arrived home, everyone was surprised by my sudden return. After speaking with my uncle Morcos, I felt better about the new job and eventually returned to Alexandria. After all, disregarding or quitting a governmental job meant abandoning a ministerial appointment, hence losing any future right for employment with the government. Many people thought that I was fortunate to have the position in the historical city of Alexandria. So I did return, although I knew it would only increase my motivation to immigrate sooner than later.

In the governmental Department of Psychology, I was worked with the best professionals in the country. They all appreciated my leaving a rewarding job in the private sector to start in such an entry-level position in the government. The general director at TECALEX even paid my department a surprise visit. Meeting with the regional director and key personnel, he spoke highly of his experience working with me and how my unexpected resignation was considered a shocking loss to the company. He added that I was "a unique and dedicated person and an asset to any organization that he would work for."

After that visit, the director of the department took me under his wing. He was a cousin of the prime minister of Egypt at that time, Zakaria Mohieddin, who was one of the commanding officers of the 1952 Egyptian revolution led by Gamal Abdel Nasser. The department head helped me find an apartment—a rare commodity in Egypt, let alone the beautiful city of Alexandria—and gradually I settled in.

In the summer of 1965, I decided to pursue my graduate studies in the fall at the Institute of Psychological Sciences at Alexandria University. There, I met my future wife. We were distantly related but had lived in different cities and had not been in contact for years. In fact, when I introduced myself to her, she thought I was a stranger! However, with an understanding smile, she listened to my description of our family tree and the names that connected us and proved that we were indeed relatives.

Eye on the Ball

Although my time was divided between work, studies, serving the youth in churches, and organizations such as the YMCA and summer camps in Alexandria, my priority was to pursue my dream of going abroad to complete my graduate studies. Finally I was able to return to Cairo and submit an application to the Canadian Embassy and eventually to meet with the Canadian consul in 1966. A sharp-witted woman with a quick and discerning intellect, she was willing to grant me an entry visa on one condition: that there was no guarantee for working in a professional capacity. The demand at that time in Canada was only for skilled labor. I hesitantly agreed, but she sensed my disappointment and gave me six months to make up my mind. She added that she was concerned that my "decent" appearance and credentials might be an obstacle in finding work in a nonprofessional capacity. I left the Canadian Embassy, and my mind was set to visit the nearby US Embassy in Garden City, Cairo.

In the American Embassy

Visiting the US Embassy in Egypt over five decades ago was an entirely different experience than today, with its armed security guards and long lines of applicants. The place was very elegant, and there was not a single soul in the charming, well-furnished lobby. The minute I walked in, an interior door opened and there appeared a welcoming face with an attractive smile and almost whispering voice asking, "Can I help you?"

When I made my wish known, she responded that the United States had not opened the door for Egyptians to immigrate to the US. Undeterred, I kindly asked if I could fill out an application to be kept on file just in case things changed. She went back behind closed doors and returned with someone else—a tall, very formal lady with a dominant presence and determined look who wanted to find out exactly why I was there.

I politely explained my situation and my recent experience at the Canadian Embassy. When I noticed my interviewer was listening attentively, I elaborated by expressing my wish to further my studies and enhance my career. I had embarked on a profession that was considered unessential and unnecessary to the needs of Egyptian society at the time.

To my surprise, the woman had her assistant bring me an application to fill out, although she could not commit to any present or future action. As she handed me the application, she asked an unexpected question: "Where in the United States are you planning to go?" Without missing a beat, the response came: "New York." She smiled widely and left me to complete the application. When I was done, I expressed my appreciation for her time and kind cooperation.

Family and Clergy Opposition

Leaving the country on a scholarship to earn a degree abroad was (and still is) a welcome and honorable undertaking that many Egyptians pursued. Candidates usually went through a selection process by educational committees and applied for governmental approval for financial support. Applicants had to sign an affidavit to commit to returning to Egypt and serve the country upon earning the intended degree. On a more personal level, however, immigration was a foreign concept at that time, unacceptable to families and friends and not supported by the Coptic Church. There was a strong belief that once out of Egypt and away from her churches, the immigrant would be like a fish out of water in the permissive and immoral society of Western culture. To dare to think of venturing out of Egypt would surely—in the view of spiritual leaders—lead to spiritual demise and the corruption of one's soul. Since there were no Coptic churches available to the faithful in other countries, the popular belief was that there was no salvation. It was better to remain within the boundaries of the Holy See of St. Mark to avoid being exposed to overwhelming temptations in foreign lands.

On the other hand, if the Coptic Church was going to expand beyond its limited borders, it needed pioneers to establish churches wherever the spirit may lead. Copts were taught all along how a few Coptic monks proclaimed the Christian faith and established the monastic life in Ireland by the end of the fourth century! And there was already a Coptic church in Toronto, Canada, though it celebrated Mass in a rental space. So to a logical thinker, this tradition of allegiance to the land of the martyrs and staying within the bosom of its boundaries was a lame excuse and coercive rationale to remain loyal to a conservative culture that opposed leaving the homeland.

My family was also opposed to the notion of immigration, especially my uncle, who insisted that being with and caring for family was essential. My brother and sister were very young (six and four years old), and they needed someone to look after them. Both of our parents had passed away at a relatively young age. My father was only sixty-four years old when he died. My mother, who had survived a severe car accident, eventually suffered from a bleeding ulcer. Unwilling to be readmitted to a hospital again, she opted out of surgery, which contributed to her death at an early age. You could see why my uncle objected to my leaving the country, at least at that time.

Meanwhile, my older brother was very understanding and quite supportive of my ambitions to pursue my education and career. He was well aware of my relatively high achievement at TECALEX and my ardent desire to earn a higher degree abroad. He knew I could never be a bureaucrat working at a governmental job. To him, immigration was the only way I could fulfill my dreams and attain my goals. He truly was a wise man with deep insight and trust in the Lord. He always felt that prayers were the sure path to God's will revealed in our lives. No wonder he eventually left the second highest position at the Ministry of Finance when he heard the call for priesthood from the mouth of HH Pope Shenouda III.

CHAPTER 2

<···>◆<···>

Immigration Concept: Inexplicable Self-Destructiveness

*The Comedy is always the same. In the first
act the hero imagines a place
where happiness exists. In the second he strives
towards that goal. In the
third he comes up short or what amounts to the
same thing he achieves
his goal only to find that happiness lies a little
further down the road.*

—James Branch Cabell

Alexandrian Priests' View of Immigration

In Alexandria, several well-known priests in the Coptic Church were against the idea of immigration and urged me not to abandon the land of martyrs. Some clearly communicated their opposition from the pulpit. To them, it was a risky adventure and meant the ultimate perishing of the believer's soul. They strongly affirmed their belief, reciting a popular verse in defense of their stand: "For what is a man profited, if he shall gain the whole world, and lose his own soul? Or what will anyone give in exchange for his life?" (Matthew 16:26)

Many other priests had valid practical reasons for their concern. They feared that there were no Coptic churches in the West to attend. They were also worried that more of the faithful might adopt the immigration concept and leave their beloved country and Coptic Church. They wanted to keep the Coptic Christian population intact and the Coptic Orthodox faith preserved in Egypt.

Coptic priests were not the only ones against emigration from Egypt; the president of the country was opposed to it as well. In a national televised speech, President Gamal Abdel Naser attacked the idea of leaving Egypt. He questioned the motive behind it and challenged young men not to abandon their country, wondering, "Who would marry our daughters if our men leave?"

In this modern digital age, persecution of Christians has increased dramatically and is instantly broadcast all over the world. Islamic fundamentalists have a special hatred for Christianity. In the Middle East, Christian communities have long been subjected to acts of savagery and wickedness, and holy historical sites have been burned to the ground. Back then, a few Alexandrian priests heroically defended Coptic Christians from unrelenting persecution. They were even converting non-Christians and restoring faith to those who had abandoned it under threat or fear. Authorities in Egypt discreetly tried to exert pressure on Pope Cyril (Kyrillos) VI to limit the activities of a couple of those priests and curb their efforts to build new churches. Lo and behold, the same priests who fought against the idea of immigration ended up being instrumental in establishing churches in America years later.

A Bright Hope

Early in 1967, I was surprised to receive a letter from the United States Department of Justice's Immigration and Naturalization Service. I was notified that my application had been approved and was forwarded to the US consulate in Cairo, hence I was required to meet with the American consul for further arrangement. I could hardly believe the good news and was ecstatic, but I decided to keep the matter completely to myself until it reached a successful conclusion. By then I had moved from a two-bedroom apartment in Camp Shezar, Alexandria, to an elegant brand-new four-bedroom apartment in Cleopatra Hamamat with a magnificent view of the Mediterranean Sea. It appeared to my family, friends, and acquaintances that I had made it and was enjoying a lavish life preparing to get married. Little did they know I was completing the required documentation for leaving the country.

The decision to immigrate was not easy. I had spent a fortune on my new home, most of my savings from my well-compensated job at TECALEX. The luxurious spacious apartment was located in one of the nicest spots in Cleopatra, Alexandria. I took the time to furnish it exceptionally well with European-style furnishing and adorn its walls with oil paintings that I either bought or painted myself. The fresh air and exquisite beauty of the sea always enticed me to take an evening walk during the hot summer months. When the weather was cooler, I took morning strolls along the lovely Mediterranean beach. But my favorite scenery of all that never failed to capture my heart were the sunsets—just amazing! It always brought to mind the old saying, "Nature is a second Bible!"

I was well recognized and respected in my position with the government. People noticed how I was furthering my graduate education, and I was praised by peers and family alike. Secretly, however, I started to entertain the idea of resigning from my position—something that was seldom done. Once you are a government employee in Egypt, you are expected to retire from there.

One of the required documents before leaving the country was proof of resignation of one's position. Because it was a considerable though calculated risk, I decided to resign once I was absolutely sure I had completed every requirement, including all medical tests and security clearances.

Though no laughing matter then, a funny thing took place around this time. This happened after I was visited by my former boss, an English-speaking director from my old company, TECALEX.

Staff at the office where I worked wondered about the cause of my considerable sacrifice. I had resigned my highly prestigious job with TECALEX to accept a governmental position with meager compensation compared to what I had been making before. They fantasized that I must have been a disguised ranking officer from the Egyptian internal security apparatus who, upon orders, was transferred from TECALEX to a new position at the Ministry of Industry. Most likely, they figured my new job was to monitor the effectiveness of certain branches of the government, especially since the head of my new job was an immediate cousin to the then prime minister of Egypt!

This fantasy among the staff was only affirmed when it was announced in the office that I had received a personal message from the president of Egypt—a "thank you" telegram by special delivery from President Nasser on his official presidential stationary. The telegram was actually in response to my sending the president a "Happy Birthday" note after reading in *Newsweek* that he had been born on January 15. Nonetheless, their belief about my disguised identity was confirmed as an unchallenged reality.

The Six-Day War

When I had almost completed the process and required documentation to leave the country, I still had one more thing to do: submit my resignation letter. I obviously did not want to hand it in until I had received official permission to enter the United States. As I previously mentioned, on June 5, 1967, war broke out between Israel and Egypt, Jordan, and Syria. The United States was accused of supporting Israel, which many claimed was the cause of the Arab countries' defeat. Consequently, popular anger against Israel and the US erupted in the Arab world.

Diplomatic relations between Egypt and the United States was severed, and the American Embassy was closed until further notice. In the wake of these sad events, all hopes for leaving the country to pursue my education and career vanished. But I never forgot my adopted motto: "Work and invest in the land of Egypt as if you live there for good; prepare and be ready to leave the country as if it will happen the next day."

St. Mary Apparition: A Memorable Event and Historic Date

Until this time, I had not revealed my plan to anyone. I could have shared my plans with my older brother—a wise, discreet, and loving person—but I did not want to burden him with my own unfulfilled dreams. Instead, I waited on the Lord and trusted Him completely to show the way, remembering St. Paul's words: "And we know that all things work together for good to them that love God, to them who are called according to His purpose." (Romans 8:28)

In April 1968, a miracle occurred in Egypt: St. Mary appeared in the Zeitoun district of Cairo, which had been one of the stops of the Holy Family while traveling and staying in Egypt. The sightings began on April 2 and lasted for a full year. The magnificent apparitions took place at the Church of the Virgin Mary on Tomanbay Street, and the news traveled all over the world.

Though I was living in Alexandria at that time, I visited the site and spent all night there, witnessing the apparition with thousands of other people of all ages, status, and religions. It remained in full view of the spectators for hours at a time, especially during the night or at dawn. My immediate thought was that St. Mary would facilitate my leaving Egypt if that was the will of God. I petitioned her intercession to resolve the immigration process at the American Embassy that had come to a halt due to the Six-Day War.

A couple of weeks later, miraculously, I received an official letter from the American Embassy in an envelope that carried the Canadian Embassy's logo and address! Remarkably, the letter was apparently hand-delivered (no postage or postmarks) to my mailbox at home. The cover letter that came with the sealed envelope requested my appearance in person at the Canadian Embassy in Cairo at an appointed time and place.

The Return of Relics of the Great St. Mark: A Second Memorable Event and Historic Date

Because of the delays in my immigration process, not only was I fortunate enough to witness the apparition of St. Mary, I also was present for another great and historic event. On Monday, June 24, 1968, in the tenth year of the papacy of HH Pope Cyril VI, the 116th pope of Alexandria, the relics of the apostle St. Mark the Evangelist, the first patriarch of Alexandria, were returned to Egypt. After eleven centuries outside Egypt, St. Mark's body at last was returned to the country where he was martyred. Awaiting the arrival of the relics were Pope Cyril VI; Mari Ignatius Yacoub, patriarch for the Syrian orthodox community; a great number of Coptic and foreign bishops; and the heads of various other denominations and religions. A sea of Egyptian Christians and Muslims sang joyous religious songs while waiting for the arrival of the plane that carried the relics from Rome.

When the plane landed, HH Pope Cyril VI went up the stairs of the aircraft and received the relics of St. Mark from the head of the delegation. Many observers, including those who were watching from the balcony of the airport, reported that they saw three white doves flying over the aircraft. People clapped and cheered as they marveled at the sight of these beautiful birds. The faithful believed it was a sign from the saints welcoming the relics of the great evangelist St. Mark. The head of the Roman papal delegation, Cardinal Léon-Étienne Duval, cardinal of Algeria, was amazed by the joyous reception.

Around this time, a great spiritual revival was taking place in the Coptic Church not seen since the enthronement of Pope Cyril VI. As the day of my leaving Egypt for good approached, I wanted to visit the spiritual mentor of my youth and seek his blessings. So I visited His Holiness, thinking that it might be my last opportunity before leaving Egypt, and asked him to bless the sealed envelope that would be opened by the immigration authorities upon my arrival in the United States.

His Holiness took the envelope and, with a big smile and compassionate heart, blessed it. As I knelt before him in adoration and great respect, he lifted me up by hand, saying, "Ya ibni oumm—lel Rab wahdoh tasgod." That means, "My son, get up. To the Lord only you shall kneel." It is worth noting that I was a regular and welcome visitor at His Holiness's papal palace. Pope Cyril VI was my father in confession long before he was heavenly chosen and enthroned as the pope of Alexandria and the patriarch of the See of St. Mark.

Since the pope's ordination, I was reluctant to impose on his valuable time by visiting or interfering with his newfound burdens and responsibilities. However, one time I was eager to see His Holiness, but not to simply visit with him as I used to before he became pope. Instead I decided to join the multitude of worshippers who went to St. Mark's Cathedral. While he was blessing us with the liturgical incense, he suddenly stopped where I stood and called me by an old nickname from my high school years. (During my youth, I had regularly visited "Abouna Mina," my father in confession, who later became Pope Cyril VI. Father Mina used to call me by a special nickname, as loving fathers often do.) Looking at me, he asked, "Why don't I see you anymore?" I could hardly speak from this unexpected surprise, and as the crowd focused on me, I responded hesitantly: "Saydna [our Lord], your Holiness is overly busy now!"

He answered, "Come, I want to see you," and then, "Ana zay Mana," or "I am still the same." Wow! The monk who became a pope still lived his life as a monk!

A Historical Departure

On July 15, 1968, I left Egypt for good. On the way to the airport, I was accompanied by family members and friends, many of whom were crying or just tearful. A well-educated friend who received his PhD in Europe was convinced that I would be spiritually lost and "enslaved to the almighty dollar." It felt more like a funeral as he and other grieving folks said goodbye to a person they felt they would never see again. From there, I flew to Greece, then to London, where I spent my first night away from my homeland.

On the foggy early morning of July 16, I left London for the United States and arrived at Kennedy International Airport at night on the same day. There was no one waiting to welcome me in the new land, I had no place to go, and I had no idea what I would do from that point on. I collected my luggage and walked through what appeared to the eye of a foreigner to be a huge airport with endless moving escalators and multitudes of people going in different directions. Announcements were broadcasting constantly in different languages, and I wondered which one was in English!

Though I trusted my ability to speak and write fluent English, the American English accent was totally foreign to my ears, so I followed the signs to the immigration office at the airport. There, the officer explained that I needed to notify them with a permanent address so the Department of Immigration and Naturalization could mail a green card. Without the card, I could not earn a living or do anything meaningful in the States.

Feeling exhausted and somewhat lost in the crowded airport, I proceeded to the information booth and asked the official if she could direct me to a YMCA address I had obtained from the local branch in Egypt. With a cursory glance at the address, she handed it back to me, murmuring a few words that did not make sense! When I asked her to explain, she repeated the same thing: "Just take a cab. It will take you there!" *What is a cab?* I wondered! She then realized that I was a newcomer to the country, so she pointed toward the exit door, where I could see a yellow taxi. Aha! That was what she meant by a cab—it was short for taxicab. Good to know!

I dragged my luggage out of the airport terminal and over to where the cabs were lined up. I hopped into one and asked the driver to take me to the YMCA. He obviously sensed that I was not familiar with where I was going, nor did I know the location or the type of accommodation where I would be spending the night. He was a godsend. The driver paused and said, "You don't want to go there!"

I wondered for a moment, why not? The driver suggested taking me to a nearby hotel to spend the night. It was getting late, so I agreed. When we arrived at the hotel and before even unloading my luggage, the driver accompanied me into the lobby to find out whether there was a room available. At the check-in desk, we were told the only room available was at the top of the hotel and that the air conditioner was out of order.

It was past midnight already, and I was exhausted and hungry, so I took the keys to the room. After my luggage was brought in, I grabbed something to eat and went straight to my room to sleep.

Afterward, I found out that the good Lord had an eye on me. Had I went to the address that was given to me, I would have been stripped of all my possessions, including all my money. That YMCA turned to be a den for drinkers and addicts.

That first night in the hotel, I woke up at 3:30 a.m., sweating all over. It was an unbearably hot night, and I regretted renting a room without an air conditioner. I opened the window, but there wasn't even a breeze to cool me off. But the scene from the window was a magnificent sight. I looked up—the sky was clear, and the stars were shining bright. Beneath the beautiful heavenly lights there were the sparkling lights of Manhattan.

So this was it! New York at last! Now, I wondered, what was I going to do under these circumstances? Where would I go? I had no idea! There was not a single person I knew or could call in that vast sleepless city. I lifted my eyes. "Hear me, Lord!" I prayed and asked what the plan was. I received no answer, feeling as if I had been thrown in the middle of nowhere and had no alternative but to wait until morning, when the Lord might lead me through the wilderness of the unknown in my new home.

CHAPTER 3

―‹••›◆‹••›◆‹••›―

Exploring the Unknown

*When you walk to the edge of all the light you have and take
the first step into the darkness of the unknown, you must believe
that one of two things will happen. There will be something solid
for you to stand upon or you will be taught to fly.*

—Patrick Overton

When I had gone to the United States Embassy in Cairo to explore the possibility of immigration, the American representative there asked me, "Where do you want to go in the States?" My response came without a blink: "New York!" Was that answer just a coincidence, or was it the first step in a divine plan? I believe the latter. On Tuesday, July 17, 1968, this newcomer, a make-believe "New Yorker" (a title reserved for someone born and raised in New York City), moved to the Milburn Hotel on Seventy-Sixth Street.

Like all new immigrants, I could not work in the United States until I provided the US Immigration and Naturalization Service (INS) with an address to receive my green card. I spent the first day at the hotel sending my address to the authorities, writing letters to family back home, and reading. Sitting down to write letters was quite a pleasure back then, long before digital communication made it easy to connect instantly anywhere in the world. It would take at least a month before receiving a reply. On top of that, international long-distance calls, or "trunk calls," were quite expensive. One had to reserve time for the call and then take his turn and be connected. Usually it took three days to reach a designated party in Egypt. Calls initiated from Egypt were placed at a central office after the caller had filled out a paper form. Three minutes was the maximum time allowed for international calls.

In the Company of St. Mark

That evening, I opened one of my suitcases and picked my favorite book to read. It was titled *The Apostle Morcos: The Saint and Martyr* by HG Bishop Shenouda and given to me as a gift just before leaving the country. The book was quite enlightening and consoling in its reflection on the life of the great saint. "Morcos," of course, was an apostle of Jesus who wrote the Gospel of St. Mark and founded the Church of Alexandria. He died on May 8, 68 AD, in Alexandria, Egypt. That evening, as I read about this saint, I found it emotionally and spiritually supportive. St. Mark had arrived in Egypt also as a stranger, and his story of proclaiming the Good News of our Savior was quite interesting and inspiring. It was a call to action—I felt it was an honor and great blessing to be the heir of his faith and follow in the saint's footsteps in a different time and place.

St. Mark's First Mission

History tells us that when St. Mark first walked through the streets of Alexandria, his sandals were torn. While Ananias the cobbler was repairing his shoes, he cut his finger with the awl and cried out, "O, the one God." St. Mark healed the cobbler's finger and spoke to him about who the "one God" was. Ananias invited St. Mark to his home, where he and his household were baptized after having professed their belief in the Christian faith. Soon afterward, many others were baptized, and Ananias's house became the meeting place for the faithful. St. Mark ordained Ananias as a bishop before leaving Egypt to visit other believers in Pentapolis (eastern Libya today), thus fulfilling Isaiah's prophesy: "In that day there will be an Alter to the Lord in the midst of the Land of Egypt, and a pillar to the Lord at its border… Then the Lord will be known to Egypt, and the Egyptian will know the Lord in that day." (Isaiah 19:19–21)

Remember the Sabbath Day

There was no Coptic church service to attend in New York, but the city was full of magnificent churches. I could not stay confined in a hotel room on a Sunday, so I went out to attend the Mass at St. Jean Baptist Roman Catholic Church at the corner of Lexington Avenue and East Seventy-Sixth Street. After the Mass, the priest greeted a line of parishioners one by one. He welcomed me warmly with a smile and discerning look, sensing that I was a newcomer whose face he hadn't seen before. Afterward, the priest invited me to be his guest for a cup of coffee in his pastoral office.

After a cordial talk, he asked me straight out: "Why did you decide to leave your country?" I told him I just wanted to pursue graduate education and explore career opportunities, adding that such a path was neither probable nor possible in the country where I came from! Without further ado, he expressed admiration for the Coptic Church's history and tradition and knew all about the plight of the Christian people in Egypt. He had read much about the ongoing persecution of Christians by militant Islamists, then added he had never met an Egyptian before. Not wasting any time, he opened the drawer of his desk, grabbed a card, wrote a brief note on it, and handed it to me. The card belonged to Sophie Wojciechowski, Director of Social Work Division, ACSW (the Academy of Certified Social Workers). He then directed me, a first-time worshipper at his church, to the office of the American Council for Émigrés in the Professions (ACEP) at 345 East Forty-Sixth Street, Room 800. Within less than a week of my arrival, the good Lord had already opened a door. Amazing!

At the ACEP Office

The following day was a new beginning—visiting ACEP. I met with Ms. Wojciechowski, which included an extensive interview, an examination of my qualifications, and a thorough review of what I thought was my well-prepared CV. At ACEP, the well-trained staff assisted me every step of the way. The plan they devised would have me pursue graduate studies in my field of interest while simultaneously gaining "American experience."

ACEP was finally able to gain me admission at Fordham University. I was elated to receive an acceptance letter from the director of admission, Dr. Lucy K. Loughrey, and to start a special program that began in the fall of 1968, enabling me to finish that program in a year and move on to begin a career and earn a living. I also obtained the Jessie Smith Noyes Fellowship Award as well as a financial loan from ACEP to be paid back once I was employed.

Humbly, I beg the reader not to view the above description of my journey as anything other than the work of divine providence. The Lord has a much higher plan than what we often see or expect for ourselves. Once again, let me remind you that upon arrival in the States, I had no family, no friends, no place to live, and no one to call. There were no Coptic churches, priests, or even fellow Egyptians I could turn to for assistance or guidance. As His plan for me reveals itself in the following pages, please recognize what the Lord has done and is still doing for the expansion of His kingdom on earth. Just as I discovered as one of His children in a far-off land, I trust you too will come to know the deep meaning of "the Lord is my shepherd, I shall not want!" (Psalms 23:1)

Culture Shock

"Culture shock" is a term used in the field of behavioral science to denote the anxiety and stress that some people experience when they live in a different culture. Language barriers, significantly different customs, and other environmental challenges tend to isolate and prevent foreign nationals from interacting with others in their new home.

For a person who has never been in a Western country, American culture in particular can be hard to understand. Americans, for example, like to call most people by their first name, which is a far cry from the formality of Egyptian culture, where giving a title of rank or honor before and after the name is a must. Even today within the Coptic community, almost every child of second or third generation is taught to call adults, even those they meet for the first time, "Uncle" or "Aunt." Calling someone only by their first name would be considered offensive and disrespectful!

Visitors from other countries have noticed that when meeting someone, even a stranger, Americans usually smile. In Egyptian culture, facial expressions and other body language don't reveal their kindness and/or sentiment right away. Even affection between spouses or parents and children is only partially, even rarely, expressed.

Americans are disciplined when it comes to standing in line; they always wait their turn. They are also very time sensitive and extremely punctual, always arriving on time or apologizing if they are late. It is a wonderful cultural trait that is harder to find in other parts of the world.

It is normal for American women to have male friends who are just friends, and the same for American men. Egyptian culture does not encourage this type of friendship. American men try to share household responsibilities such as parenting and housework equally with their wives. Verbal, physical, and emotional abuse is considered domestic violence, and it is against the law in the United States, whereas some other cultures consider yelling, hitting, and beating as acceptable forms of discipline. With children, American culture encourages shaping behavior through time-outs and taking away privileges while ignoring mild misbehavior. The reward system is of significant importance, and logical and natural consequences are valuable tools.

These are just some admirable traits that deserve our deep understanding, appreciation, and application. Yet such cultural differences can significantly impact the life of a newcomer. Culture shock has caused serious negative reactions in many foreign families, including in the Coptic community. In fact, some of these differences are the direct cause of deep tension that can lead to damaged marriages and divided families as children leave home or apply to schools far away.

God... God... God!

At the Milburn Hotel, I met and befriended a young man. For the sake of anonymity, let's call him Jack. He appeared to have been living in the same hotel for some time. His room was across from mine, and we exchanged greetings once in a while. One day, Jack decided to ask what I did for a living. When I told him I was still looking for a job, he advised that what I needed was a strong recommendation or referral from a prestigious person in my field. Naturally, due to my status as a recently arrived foreign national, I knew no such person. Jack postulated that without knowing an honorary figure such as a congressman, it wouldn't be possible to get a job in my field or *any* field for that matter. Attempting to explain further, he added, "Do you know such a person?" The response came: "Yes, I know someone even higher."

Then he asked, "A senator?"

"Higher," I responded.

Appearing a bit surprised and incredulous, he asked, "And who would be that 'higher' someone?" Then mockingly he said, "You must know President Johnson!"

My answer shocked him when I responded "higher" for the third time! Looking me dead in the eye, he asked, "Who would that person be?" He never expected the answer: "He is God!" At that moment, he exploded with laughter, repeating the word three times. "God... God... God!" Then he excused himself and went into his room, slamming the door behind him.

The Unbelievable Happened!

That very afternoon, the phone in my own room rang for the first time. It was Jack. My first thought was that he was going to offer an apology for his impolite behavior that morning. Instead, he said that the director at the company where he was employed wanted to meet his neighbor at the hotel. Jack gave me the address and emphasized to be there as soon as possible before the end of the day. When I asked Jack about the purpose of this meeting, he said he didn't know, simply that it was the big boss's request...and then he hung up! Somewhat perplexed, this new green card holder tried to find his way to the address in Midtown Manhattan using the subway for the first time.

When I finally arrived at the reception desk, Jack was called and we walked together to the director's office. On our way there, he whispered that he didn't have the slightest idea what the director wanted exactly, but he had asked to meet me. The administrative assistant greeted us respectfully and ushered us into the main office of the "big boss." Inside the spacious fancy office of the director, an elegant man wearing a dark suit sat behind an oversize desk with decorative woodwork surrounded by leather chairs and other furniture. When we walked into his office, he stood up and welcomed both of us, then with a kind gesture asked me to sit down. Jack excused himself and returned to his own office.

The director initiated the conversation by saying he had heard interesting things about my talk with Jack that morning. He wanted to hear directly from me what had brought me to the United States and the circumstances that led me to embark upon such an adventure. He listened attentively as I gave him a brief account of my reasons for leaving Egypt and my expectations in the United States. He neither made comments nor interrupted at any point while I spoke. The entire time he remained cordial, smiling and nodding his head. At the conclusion of the meeting, he asked if I had documentation of my credentials that could help me find decent work! When I responded in the affirmative, he asked me to come back at an appointed time with the paperwork. That very week, the director gave me a job with decent pay.

If this was not the result of divine providence, what else could it have been? The proof came later when I learned the rest of the story. Jack, in his regular meeting with his director, wanted to lighten the mood with a "funny" story that day, so he shared his encounter with his "naive" hotel neighbor who was "fresh off the boat." He then recounted how I said I knew someone "higher" than even the president of the United States and that I meant God! When Jack started laughing, the director exclaimed that it wasn't a laughing matter and the person who said that probably meant it.

That first job was not in my field of choice, but it was decent work with assigned responsibility that required honesty, integrity, and fluency in the English language. When the time came to start graduate work at Fordham University, the director gladly changed his newest employee's schedule to evening hours. To maintain my regular weekly salary, I decided to extend my hours to work full days on Saturday and Sunday evenings with the corresponding increase in pay.

Jack became a good, caring friend. He was the same age as me, single, likable, and playful, with a wonderful sense of humor. He, however, did not share much about his life or his family. He made a good salary, but he was a permanent tenant at the hotel. Even after I relocated to a one-room rental property, Jack remained at the hotel, eating most of his meals out since there was no kitchenette in the room or any other cooking facility in the building.

One evening remains engraved in my memory. Jack appeared in my office at work looking pale, short of breath, and disturbed. He had come to say goodbye! We shook hands in a hurry, and he vanished in a flash while I stood there dumbfounded. Soon after, I received a call to go see the director in his office. Noticing my stunned reaction, he asked me to sit down and then explained that Jack was let go minutes before the arrival of the FBI to arrest him!

No further explanation was given. The director, however, gave me the rest of the evening off. He called in his chauffer to take me home in the company's limousine. Upon reaching home, my landlord stood at the door in awe of his tenant who arrived in a black limousine. After the driver stepped out to open the door and wish me well with, "Good night, sir!" the landlord followed me to my room with a suspicious look on his face, asking what happened and what I did for a living. It was an unforgettable day, but it left me sad all night. Losing the one friend that made life somewhat easier in this faraway land was more than difficult. I would never see Jack again, though he would never be forgotten. To this day, whenever the thought of him comes to mind, I say a prayer on his behalf.

Looking for a New Friend

Feeling alone, I searched my belongings for a good friend's name who had been in the States for a while. Makram Hemaya was not only a dedicated Sunday school servant back at St. Michael's Church in Shoubra, Cairo, he was like a family member to me. He was studying for his doctoral degree in another state. Regretfully, his telephone number was not listed and I could not reach him. Then I looked up another name and phone number that had been handed to me by HG Bishop Samuel, who was bishop of social and ecumenical services at that time. It was for Mr. Youssef and Mrs. Eva al Masri Sidhom. I called the Sidhom family that day, and the deep voice of a businesslike man came on the other end of the phone. When I introduced myself and explained who I was, the man's voice changed to a softer, more accommodating tone. He kindly offered to meet me, a fellow Copt, at their family home, and we set a time to get together.

Beneficial and Honorable Biographies

When I arrived at their home in Elmhurst, Queens, I was warmly welcomed by my hosts, Mr. and Mrs. Sidhom. Both of them were gracious and hospitable. They were thrilled to know their visitor matriculated in postgraduate studies at Fordham University and was already earning a living. That evening it became clear we took a liking to each other. Mrs. Sidhom was a bright, articulate, and soft-spoken woman who always wore a smile when she spoke or was spoken to. Mr. Sidhom was a dynamic, energetic person, confident and competent, with a wonderful sense of humor.

From what Eva and Youssef shared of their lives in America, I could readily see how it pointed to their dedication to serve. They felt they had embarked on a mission preplanned by divine order. Eventually, I would discover that both of them led others by example—they practiced what they preached. They knew that nothing could be accomplished unless people around them believed in the same mission and adjusted their lives to God's will.

The background of the al Masri Sidhom family was quite interesting. He was a reputable lawyer in Alexandria, and she was an educator and editor in chief of *al Misriyyah* (*The Egyptian Woman*), an Arabic biweekly magazine issued in Egypt back in the 1930s. She was the first admission as a coed at the American University in Cairo in 1928. In her senior year, she became an associate of Mrs. Hoda Charawi, leader of the Egyptian Feminist Union and founder of both *al Misriyyah* and *L'Égyptienne* magazines. In her capacity as such, she traveled to Europe twice to represent Egypt at the International Women's Conference.

Eva al Masri Sidhom

Eva's story of coming to the United States began in 1931, when she delivered the valedictory address at her college graduation ceremony in Egypt. Two years later, she traveled to America and earned her master's degree in one year from Smith College in Northampton, Massachusetts. Back in Egypt, Eva joined the Woman's Health Improvement Association. As a member of that group, she cared for malnourished children who were prone to suffer from tuberculosis. The association was responsible for giving children proper nutrition and placing them in a dry, healthy climate.

Eva came from a wealthy Christian family. They were charitable and faithful givers who recognized the plight of the poor and the destitute. As Eva engaged in charity work, she often left the security and luxury of her home to serve in Giza and as far as south as Luxor in Upper Egypt. She joined the Coptic Women's Benevolent Association and other Coptic charity organizations and shared the responsibility for an orphanage that housed young girls, teaching them to read and write as well as a trade. Eva supported the operation financially and volunteered her time to teach there.

Eva and her sister Iris never forgot the faith handed down to them by their parents, nor did they forget their love for the poor and taking care of their needs. When Eva and her husband came to America, they were on guard, knowing that the Western world was organized in the service of wealth. She not only had witnessed the life of the poor but also did something to alleviate it. She truly had followed His commandments: "Whoever gives to the poor will not want" (Proverbs 28:27) and "Whoever is generous to the poor lends the Lord, and will repay him for his deed." (Proverbs 19:17) They were not influenced by the Western culture of materialism, and neither did they ever find themselves in a state of want. They were surely paid for their good deeds.

I became good friends with the Sidhom family, and I was frequently invited to their home for CAA business and for leisure. One evening in the fall of 1968, Eva asked me if I ever thought about marriage. I responded that I had hoped to get married before leaving Egypt, but the father—who happened to be a family member—was not in favor of letting his precious just-graduated daughter immigrate to a foreign land.

At this point, Eva for the first time shared with me how she met her husband. They got engaged on June 20, 1948, and were married a month and a half later on August 5, 1948. Because her father was the head of a religious body called the General Coptic Community Council, the pope himself, three general bishops, and seven priests officiated what she called a "unique" wedding! The ceremony took place at St. Mark's Coptic Orthodox Cathedral. According to Eva, the church was packed full with dignitaries, distinguished guests, and family members.

CHAPTER 4

Discerning Insight

*By looking for the unexpected and discerning the surreptitious
features in the scenery within us, we apprehend our personality,
find out our identity, and learn how to cultivate it. Taking care
of our fingerprints will be an enduring endeavor.*

—Erik Pevernagie

I realize that many readers may not appreciate my drawing their
attention to the seemingly lavish lifestyle described at the end
of the previous chapter. The purpose, however, is to illustrate that
regardless of how wealthy one was or how prestigious the place one
occupied in one's homeland, he or she has to start life from scratch
in a foreign land. Immigration may or may not make the immigrant
better off. Eva and Youssef had to go through hardships to build their
lives in the United States, having to go through "hell," in the words
of Youssef, to reach their state of comfort.

Winston Churchill, prime minister of England during World
War II and again in the 1950s, once said, "If you are going through
hell, keep going." I have known difficult times as well. But again, we
have to remember that we are not in it for ourselves but for a higher
purpose and to submit humbly to His will.

Both Eva and Youssef came to the United States in June 1961
to study for a year at Texas Christian University (TCU) and return

home. According to Eva's personal memoirs, due to political upheaval back in Egypt, they were blacklisted and their property had been confiscated. Youssef's law office was closed, and for some reason, other measures were taken against them. Due to their circumstances, the INS allowed them to temporarily stay in the country, and they remained on temporary status until 1962. Later, Eva applied for admission at Hunter College in New York and was granted a student visa to remain in the States as long as she was attending school. Youssef was safe as well as long as she had permission to stay.

Finally, after applying to a variety of schools, she and Youssef were admitted to Rutgers University. There they studied to be professional librarians. He graduated in June 1965 and she graduated in January 1966, both with a degree in library science. They worked at New York University as librarians until retirement. Both were granted US citizenship on October 18, 1971.[5]

The Synaxarium (Lives of Saints)

The Coptic Synaxarium recognizes the lives of the saints as having an exceptional degree of holiness. The lives of the saints are presented as the standard operating model for human beings. It emphasizes the importance of the parental role to raise the child in fear of God and teach him or her true faith from early childhood. However, the term "sainthood" also retains its original Christian meaning. Any believer who is "in Christ," has been baptized, and in whom the Holy Spirit dwells ought to be a saint, whether in heaven or on earth. That is why the Apostles' Creed includes the "communion of saints." The Lord demands it: "Therefore you shall be perfect, just as your Father in heaven is perfect." (Matthew 5:48) The French poet Charles Péguy put it best: "Life holds only one tragedy, ultimately: not to have been a saint."

New Generations: Carry the Torch

The reason behind that introductory passage is to reflect on the struggle and forbearance of some of the first Coptic immigrants. They withheld neither service or money, nor did they lose hope in attaining their dream to live a righteous life in a permissive secular society. Their sacrificial love, prayers, and service, as well their patience and perseverance, were recognized by their friends, peers, and neighbors. Their kindness and their understanding of human frailty contributed to the establishment of the Coptic Orthodox Church in America. Regretfully, I can give only some examples of those who crossed my path over the years.

Concealed and Clothed with Humility

I know many humble Coptic Christians who have performed great deeds behind the scenes, always wanting to advance the cause of service without being recognized. They are still with us, but they just don't want to boast about what they do or who they are! However, their actions speak for their ideals and virtues. Some other names will be revealed only because the good Lord allowed it for our sake. He reveals some of their righteousness, accomplishments, and zeal so we may learn to emulate them, then praise and glorify His name. But there are also thousands of unknown soldiers of Coptic Christians who are not identified in these pages and who are known only to the Lord, and they will be richly rewarded. Their humility and wisdom taught them to guard their hidden treasures and the fruits of their work lest the evil one attack them.

This history has been revealed for the sake of the descendants of Coptic Christians everywhere. New generations may need to work harder to ensure that their faith is not forgotten and continues to grow stronger, especially in this increasingly materialistic world. Their aim should be to carry the torch of faith for the thousands who died and many others who are not recognized here or who wanted to remain unknown.

Eva's Parents

Eva's family was not only wealthy but also charitable, recognizing the plight of the poor and the destitute and faithfully working to address their needs. Eva's mother, Mrs. Slemah Mina (her maiden name), was an honorary president of the al-Salam Benevolent Society in Egypt. There, both Eva and her sister Iris Habib el Masri (the well-known Coptic Church historian) were in charge of organizing Christmas parties for the orphanage girls. According to Eva, "Their joy was beyond description and filled our hearts, too, with rejoicing."

Eva's father, Habib Pasha El-Masri (1885–1953), was a distinguished and highly educated lawyer, well published as a legal author and an impressive businessman. He loved his country and was a faithful son of the Coptic Church. This towering lawyer defended the Coptic Church's legal rights of ownership against the state policy of discrimination that led to the illegal seizure of the Anba Reweis Church's land on July 10, 1929. Because of his heroic defense, ownership of the land was restored to the Coptic Church on July 21, 1946, after seventeen years of litigation. On this recovered land in the Abbassia district of Cairo, St. Mark's Coptic Orthodox Cathedral was built. Today the seat of the Coptic Orthodox pope, the cathedral was built during the time of Pope Cyril VI of Alexandria, who consecrated the new building in 1969.

Habib El-Masri labored tirelessly in his field. He represented Egypt abroad and defended the rights of Egyptians living in other countries. His hard work, dedication, and loyalty earned him the highest rank in the Egyptian political and military system. King Farouk of Egypt conferred on him the title of "pasha," one of the highest titles in the twentieth-century kingdom of Egypt. Most importantly, he raised his children in fear of the Lord, teaching them not to live for themselves but to serve in humility, respecting the least and the needy. Early on they learned to be of service, to offer help to their neighbors and community without expectations of recognition or reward.[6]

Preserving National and Religious Identity

Preserving one's identity is of utmost importance to new immigrants yearning to establish themselves in a foreign land. A new settler faces a period of uncertainty in which their sense of identity becomes insecure, usually because they have suddenly become immersed in an unfamiliar culture. This is different than the term "identity crisis" coined by the developmental psychologist Erik Erikson. Although he believed that the formation of identity was an important part of the adolescent years, he did not believe that one's identity would cease to evolve. Instead, identity is something that shifts and grows throughout life as people confront new challenges and face different or difficult experiences.

The Sidhoms looked around and saw that various groups— American, Russian, Greek, Syrian—had their churches. Eva commented, "If we did not find our own church, we would be scattered and swallowed up by their churches." The Coptic American Association (CAA) was born out of this idea. According to the Sidhoms, they thought of incorporating the association not only as a means to fund a local Coptic church and preserve Coptic identity but also to develop a supporting national community. One way to do so was to formulate an association and contact Coptic Christians who were scattered around the United States, most likely pursuing postgraduate education for academic or professional degrees.

The Sidhoms established the association; then they started to contact potential members who would support the project. They set annual dues at ten dollars and collected it from Copts who lived anywhere in the United States. When Copts responded positively to the idea and paid their dues, Mr. Sidhom, as CAA treasurer, opened an account under the name Coptic Church Fund, which grew steadily. Apparently this was the very tool that facilitated interaction with other members, who used it to exchange information and develop contacts with other Copts across the country. Once the fund accumulated enough money, the Sidhoms wrote to Bishop Samuel, who was then the bishop of public relations and ecumenical services, expressing the mounting desire for a priest.

By year-end 1964, the association had registered more than two hundred members from different states. The Coptic American Association was officially registered as a nonprofit organization in the state of New York the same year. Mr. Nazeh Habashy was the organization's attorney who spearheaded this legal work.

The Fate of the First Priest Ordained to Serve in the United States

According to the organization's records, the CAA, at its inception, elected Dr. Michael Kamel its first president, Dr. Sami Boulos its vice president, Dr. Shawki Karas its secretary, and Mr. Youssef Sidhom treasurer. Dr. Saba Habashy was chosen to be the honorary president. The CAA struggled for the first two years of its existence, but its officers were able to heal differences and united in pursuing organizational goals. New branches of the organization were established in three states and Canada. The organization focused mainly on getting a priest to come to the States, and the church in Egypt responded favorably to their wishes. Mr. Wagdy Elias Abdel Messih, who taught in the Coptic Theological Seminary in Cairo and had a master's degree from an American university, was ordained on August 9, 1964, as ordered by HH Pope Cyril VI. He was given the name of Father Morcos.

Bishop Samuel facilitated financial support for the new priest with the CAA board. He urged members of the Coptic community to pledge their support in the amount of at least half of their tithes and send their pledge to the organization. In a letter dated August 18, 1964, the bishop included the wording of the pledge to be sent to members.

Unfortunately, Father Morcos was not able to come to America despite a letter from the office of the pope and the support of HG Bishop Samuel. Bishop Samuel next sought the support of the World Council of Churches to intervene on behalf of Father Morcos. The associate executive secretary of the council wrote in an effort to grant him an entry visa to the United States, but all efforts failed.[7] This was due to US immigration policies at that time. The Immigration and Nationality Act that was enacted June 30, 1968, was not yet in effect. Also known as the Hart-Celler Act, it changed the way quotas were allocated by ending the National Origins Formula that had been in place in the United States since the Emergency Quota Act of 1921.

On the other hand, Canada had adopted less discriminatory policies in the 1960s, resulting in the number of Coptic Christians in

Canada to significantly exceed the number of those in the United States before the Hart-Celler Act changed the way quotas were allocated.

Despite the growing number of Coptic Christians in Canada, they were not able to financially support a priest by themselves. The new priest was supposed to serve in both the United States and Canada. Father Morcos finally arrived in Montreal, Canada, on November 25, 1964. Before his arrival, Mr. Youssef Sidhom again filed a petition with the INS to allow Father Morcos to come to the States, but the CAA received an official denial on October 28, 1964. In the meantime, Bishop Samuel sent a letter to inform members of the CAA that Father Morcos had been approved as a permanent resident in Canada. At year-end, the CAA board of directors agreed with the Canadian branch of the organization to share in Father Morcos's expenses and financial support.[8]

New Church Council

For some reason, it was reported that HG Bishop Samuel had expressed his desire to create a new church council as a separate entity to independently handle all the church's affairs. The new council would be solely responsible for supporting and carrying out the responsibilities of the church. Thus, the CAA board of directors, on May 2, 1965, decided to consent to the formation of the council while continuing to pursue its mission of serving the Coptic community. The board expressed its support for the newly formed church council and encouraged members to donate to it at their discretion. Though Father Morcos welcomed the formation of a new council, he "vehemently" objected to the decision to separate the CAA from the Coptic Church. He wrote a letter, dated May 17, 1965, stipulating such a decision should be made only by Bishop Samuel, himself, or both as "representatives" of the Coptic Church.

CAA Response

The CAA board met and discussed Father Morcos's concerns. Mr. Youssef Sidhom, a lawyer by profession, responded to Father

Morcos's letters, informing him that "nobody can object to any decision made by the Board, which acts according to what it sees [as being] in the best interest of the Coptic Community, and in accordance to its goals as set forth in its By-Laws. Also, the decision to pursue [the] CAA mission separately from forming the new church council was originated with HG Bishop Samuel, and repeated by him several times and in the presence of Father Morcos. So, there is no point in objecting to it now."

Upon hearing of the CAA's decision to remain separate from the newly formed church council, HG Bishop Samuel acted to reconcile differences. He wrote to all concerned that Father Morcos would be sent to Canada "to avoid further conflicts and to serve the bigger Coptic community there. But his salary will be largely carried by the Copts in the U.S."[9]

CHAPTER 5

❖❖ ·❖· ◆ ·❖· ❖❖

The Domestic Church

Those of us who wish to gain understanding
must never stop examining ourselves,
and if, in the perception of your soul, you realize
that your neighbor is superior to
you in all aspects, then the mercy of God is surely near at hand.

—St. John Climacus

The Family

It is a well-known fact that the nuclear Christian family is considered the domestic church. The term dates all the way back to the first century AD. The Greek word *ecclesiola* refers to "little church." Our early church fathers understood that the home was fertile ground for discipleship, sanctifications, and holiness. Within the domestic church, parents are expected to cultivate a family life that is centered on Christ.

Since the era of HH Pope Cyril VI, the Coptic Church has witnessed a spiritual revival. Under HH Pope Shenouda III and currently HH Pope Tawadros II, all bishops and priests are quite conscious of the importance of family and the role of parents. All who care about the meaning and theology of the domestic church ought to expand the passion for the unique role that God has in mind for our lives and the lives of our family members.

One of the documents of the Second Vatican Council, *Lumen gentium* (Light of the Nations), illuminates the concept and the reality of the family's role as the domestic church. It is the secure place and protective environment where baptized children learn about their faith. The document states, "From the wedlock of Christians there comes the family, in which new citizens of human society are born, who by the grace of the Holy Spirit received in baptism are made children of God, thus perpetuating the people of God through the centuries."[10]

Just as our Lord Jesus Christ chose to be born and grow up in the Holy Family of Joseph and Mary, the church is nothing other than a family of God. The core of the church is comprised of believers who, along with their entire household, were baptized and desire that all should be saved. Yet in these troubling times, the world is quite hostile to faith and faithful people, and the family is burdened with huge responsibilities. As it has been said, raising children nowadays is a "mission impossible." Parents often find it very difficult to instruct their children in the faith while competing with destructive images of the digital world. It is quite a challenge to say the least.

Raising a faithful child is not the responsibility of the parochial school or even the Sunday school teacher, though both may affirm what the parents teach. Leading by their word and example, parents become the first preachers of the faith to their children. They should encourage them to build their lives in fear of the Lord as well as help them discover gifts that are endowed to them by their Creator that leads them to live spiritual and successful lives. Ultimately, it is the family, among other supportive family members, including the church family, that shapes the child spiritually from his or her earliest days. They are the provider of their first lessons in Christian living, and they help children enrich and sustain their gifts that lead them to live spiritual and successful lives.

True, it takes a village to raise a child, and but most importantly, it takes a firm marital commitment between the parents to remain faithful to each other. Through their love, support of one another, and active participation in the faith, as well as their commitment to raise their children with a love for Christ and His church, they can do it. The children will indeed become the salt of the earth and advocates of His radiating light, witnessing to all they meet along the path of life. By God's grace, the domestic church will remain forever the first place where young children experience the empowering unity, the bonding, and the shining light of living the faith in their own lives.

The Immigrating Family

Due to various circumstances, a Coptic family may have immigrated to a new country where no church services are available to them, but they may have an enduring desire to establish a branch of the Coptic Orthodox Church as an extension of their mother church. That was the dream of Coptic Christians who immigrated to the United States, Canada, Europe, and Australia. In America, their mission always has been to feed at the Lord's Table sooner rather than later. Celebrating the Lord's supper is what makes many one. As the apostle Paul teaches, the Lord's supper binds many into one. Yet Coptic families under these circumstances found themselves deprived from the church as the body of Christ when they first arrived in the United States.

Some attended the Syriac Orthodox Church of Antioch but yearned to have their own Coptic Orthodox Church. Thus, the Coptic family in the diaspora had one role: to seek the establishment of a church whenever it was possible but in God's due time. The responsibility and the obligation was and still is to pursue the life of what the domestic church is supposed to do, leaning only on God's grace and His promise, "For where two or three are gathered in My name, there am I in the midst of them." (Matthew 18:20) These families lived with the hope to again be part of the churchly life they once had in their motherland.

In the meantime, they faithfully lived the true life of the domestic church. Families came together, praying with each other and for one another. They met to read the Bible on Sundays and shared delicious home-cooked meals, thanks to the hospitable ladies of the Coptic community. Together they celebrated Christmas, Easter, and other holidays. They fasted over the forty days of Lent that precedes Palm Sunday and the rigorous seven days of the Holy Week, which precedes Easter. Many even insisted on fasting an additional seven days before the beginning of Great Lent.

Coptic Fasting and American Views

Many, if not most, Christian Copts fasted on Wednesdays and Fridays all year round. The Nativity Fast was observed in preparation for the Nativity of Jesus. They celebrated Christmas with the West on December 25 and also on January 7, according to the Julian calendar, which predates the Gregorian calendar and is commonly observed in the Coptic Church. They amazingly did all this fasting despite the lack of stores or restaurants that offered the kind of food the Coptic community habitually eats during these days. Many could not even prepare meals themselves, as it was hard to find the ingredients anywhere.

Even if it was possible to prepare some meals, it was difficult to invite fellow Americans to dine with you or even eat in their presence. They may enjoy the food, but inevitably they would ask, "Why do you fast most of the year?" or "What do you eat over the fifty-five days?" When hearing the answers, typical comments included, "Wow, that's rough. Glad we don't have your religion," or "Better you than me. I can't live without eating poultry, fish, or dairy products."

For many, it was a golden opportunity to speak about our faith, sharing with guests marvelous stories about the desert fathers and proclaiming the Good News. It was wonderful to speak about the virtues of our church fathers and their ascetic life dedicated to the pursuit of contemplative ideals and practicing self-denial and self-mortification. Those saintly fathers of Egypt's desert had learned to overcome desires of the flesh and lusting for the world's goods. Their austere life taught them not only to abstain from food; it empowered the spirit to control both the body and soul. Then the host may conclude—if a listener is attentive and interested—that fasting, prayer, and charity (or almsgiving) are pillars of our faith. They are commanded and observed as taught in the Bible. These pillars are the sure path to resisting the devil and his seductive temptations and deception to corrupt the souls of the believers.

The faithful life and experience as practiced by many immigrants and the miraculous work of their survival could be the subject of its own worthwhile book. Suffice to say here that many newcomers who gathered during holiday celebrations and on other occasions stated that their spiritual lives were much better than when they lived in their homeland—contrary to popular belief that to venture out of Egypt would surely lead to spiritual death. But this is true whether one lives in or out of Egypt. It depends entirely on the person and how he or she wants to lead their life. It has nothing to do with living in a land far from the mother church.

A friend who had served as a deacon and Sunday school servant while in Egypt once told me he thought that he had known God and was close to Him. It wasn't until he came to the United States that he discovered the amazing depths of God and His love.

The Coptic community in the United States became united in spirit and in truth. This included those who had established themselves in the country in the mid-1950s and early 1960s like the Sidhoms, Dr. and Mrs. Michael (Maher) Kamel, Dr. and Mrs. Saba Habashy, Dr. and Mrs. Sami Boulos, and Dr. Amal Boctor. The newcomers of the mid- to late 1960s included Mr. and Mrs. Ramses Awadalla, Mr. and Mrs. Nassif Banout, Mr. and Mrs. Iskander Saad, Mr. and Mrs. Nabil Bastawros, Mr. and Mrs. Samuel Saba, and Mr. and Mrs. Morris Demetrious, followed by many other wonderful people I had the pleasure of knowing who arrived in the 1970s and '80s. These were just some of the names of those who had shown loving care to new immigrants. All of these families were friendly, generous, and hospitable, serving substantial meals and showering their guests with warmth and moral and emotional support.

Dr. Saba Habashy is a fine example of someone who not only was a humble host but also a philanthropist who donated time, money, expertise, and talent to create a better world for Copts in the States and abroad. Among other things, Dr. Habashy established an educational fund to provide students of new immigrants with scholarships if they couldn't afford college tuition. He and many members of his family that I had the honor to meet were always friendly, kind, and gracious.

It was not all as easy as it may sound. The Coptic community overcame many obstacles and difficulties in their new home. American culture tended to emphasize traits such as self-centeredness, individualism, and permissiveness through its language, music, and liberal education that appeared alien to foreigners. Coptic parents feared these nontraditional cultural traits and how they might influence their children. They lived a churchly life as best they could and hoped for the day when they would have their own church where believers could gather as the body of Christ. As St. Paul describes, "There is one body and one Spirit, just as you were called in one hope of your calling; one Lord, one faith one baptism; one God and Father of all, who is above all, and through all, and in you all." (Ephesians 4:4–6).

Women's Role

One ought to give credit where credit is due. Thus, we acknowledge the pioneering work of women in establishing the first Coptic church and parish in the United States—St. Mark Coptic Orthodox Church in Jersey City, New Jersey. It would be a major injustice not to mention what Coptic women have done not only in their role in maintaining their domestic church at home but also in the wider Coptic community.

As mentioned, Eva al Masri Sidhom was one of these women who graciously opened her home to welcome immigrants, young and old. Eva felt strongly early on about preserving the spiritual life and identity of Copts in America. She, along with her husband, Youssef, was the one who conceived of establishing the Coptic American Association. She was a loving woman who lived a charitable life with her family long before she settled in the US. Bishop Samuel recognized this in her and Youssef and would give their names, address, and telephone number to those who were leaving Egypt for the States.

A Woman as a Leader-Servant

Eva didn't run for office in the newly formed CAA. Rather, she remained quite active behind the scenes. She started to contact Coptic Christians in every state and register them as members in the CAA, and she set the annual membership dues at ten dollars. Eventually, in 1968, she was elected president of the organization.

Ms. Suzie Habashy was another dynamic and gentle soul who played an important role in the early Coptic American community. Her presence, along with Eva's humble style of leader-servant, created a friendly and harmonious environment that made the business atmosphere informal. Each meeting was conducted in a relaxed manner and stuck to a previously prepared and agreed-upon agenda. Perhaps reflecting how we were assimilating to some of the positive aspects of American culture, meetings started and ended on time! A typical agenda looked like this:

1. Start each meeting with a prayer.
2. Distribute the printed agenda to members, with follow-up on any assigned tasks.
3. Deliver prepared remarks on various business items and other issues to the board.
4. Review the minutes from the previous meeting, followed by a formal motion to approve them before officially adding them to the records.
5. Review any pending tasks and incomplete or unfinished business.
6. Set the date and place for the next meeting that was mutually convenient to all members.
7. Address any remaining questions, concerns, or comments before making a motion to adjourn the meeting.

Passing the Torch

Mrs. Eva al Masri Sidhom carried the torch of establishing an American branch of the Coptic Church since the day she and Youssef established the CAA. For years, she and the rest of the board provided an invaluable service for the thousands of Coptic Christians who immigrated to the United States. Board members came and went, but she was a constant presence who was on hand to pass the torch when the CAA was dissolved and its funds transferred to the new church council of the Coptic Church of St. Mark.

The first board meeting of the church's new council met in St. Mark Coptic Orthodox Church in Jersey City on April 5, 1970. The attending members were Fr. Rofael Younan, Dr. Maher Kamel, Messrs. Nassif Banout, Ramses Awadalla, Albert Kamel, Iskander Saad, Khayri Wissa, Wassef Semaan, and Halim Habashy Awadalla, Mrs. Eva al Masri Sidhom, and myself.

In that meeting, Mrs. al Masri Sidhom spoke as the last president of the CAA and outlined a complete history of the organization's accomplishments over the years in service to the Lord and the Coptic community. She requested that this history be kept in the official records of the church council and announced that she had transferred the balance of funds in the CAA account, $3,800, to the new council. She also suggested that the council invite HH Pope Cyril VI to the dedication of the church. Members of the council unanimously agreed.

The council got to work preparing an official invitation to the pope. The missive would also vouch for the appointment of the Rev. Fr. Rofael Younan to be the permanent priest in the church. The board sent the letter on April 17, 1970, and on that historic day, Mrs. Eva al Masri Sidhom passed the torch to the second council. She truly was happy and might have repeated within her heart the words of St. Paul: "I have fought the good fight, I have finished the race, I have kept the faith." (2 Timothy 4:7)

Women and Community Service

As part of the social committee that included Mrs. Marie Fargallah and Mrs. Iskander Saad, Ms. Suzie Habashy and her sister Nena organized social activities and parties. The purpose of these gatherings was to celebrate special occasions and church festivities, promote socializing and conversation, provide news of interest, and welcome newcomers. It created a sense of belonging, support, guidance, and networking for the Coptic community at large.

The Coptic Woman: A Towering Figure

The women's rights movement in American culture fosters the idea that women must rid themselves of men's domination and claim their rightful place in the church. The Coptic Christian woman who truly knows her place before God as an equal to man would refrain from adopting such a combative ideology. A man and a woman both bear the image and likeness of God Himself. However, God calls upon both men and women to fulfill the roles and responsibilities specifically designed for them, a pattern that can be seen even in the Godhead (1 Corinthians 11:3). In Ephesians 5:21, the apostle Paul explains to men and women how to live the Christian life: "Submit to one another out of reverence for Christ."

Submission, however, does not mean blind obedience; it means that one voluntarily limits what one does naturally in a given relationship in order to benefit the other. So if a husband has a more dominant role in a marriage, instead of using that power to make his life easier, out of reverence for Christ, he will use it to serve his wife in order to benefit her. The same applies if the wife feels empowered; she may give this power in submission to her husband so that she may benefit him. In fulfilling the divinely given roles taught in the New Testament, women are able to realize their full potential because they are following God's plan.

As the saying goes in the twenty-first century, "From Adam's rib to Women's Lib, you've come a long way, baby." Indeed, some women have traveled a considerable distance from the Word of God! But not the majority of Coptic women (at least not yet), and one hopes new generations of Coptic girls will remain faithful to what the good Lord has prepared for them—to realize their full potential by following the path He has created and designated for them. Only in obedience to Him and His design will women truly be able, in the fullest sense, to give glory to God.

In Humility, Women Serve

When the Copts bought their first church, the building was not in good condition, to say the least. The property was located on West Side Avenue in Jersey City and had been closed for a number of years. It was the same inside and out—deterioration, dirt, and debris. The paint was pealing. The walls and floors were completely bare. There was only one toilet.

Undaunted, a group of dedicated ladies undertook the huge responsibility of cleaning it. They hauled out all kind of debris, swept the floors, cleaned every surface, and prepared it for the inaugural Sunday service on March 22, 1970. Although all of these women were familiar faces to me, I unfortunately am unable to recall all of their names, but well-known figures included the late Mrs. Leila Kamel, the wife of Dr. Maher Kamel, and Mrs. Pansy Awadalla, the wife of Mr. Ramses Awadalla. They all performed a magnificent job. Because of their tremendous efforts and the support of all the church members, no one who saw the church when it was bought and sees it today would recognize it. It was an amazing transformation.

Gigantic Women! A Word for the New Generations of Copts

When the feminist movement of the 1960s and '70s started, its purpose was to ensure equal rights and opportunities for men and women. Needless to say, this is what the Creator has intended from the beginning, for He created man and woman equal. Yet concerns about equality remain alive and well. When I speak to Christian communities, I have often been asked the question, "Why shouldn't a woman be a priest?" In our Coptic churches, the question is, "Why can't girls be ordained as deacons and serve inside and outside the altar?"

The answer always stems from scripture. There, we not only find women equal to men, but they are held in high regard as well. In the first chapter of the Gospel of St. Luke, the spotlight is directed toward two godly women: Elizabeth, the soon-to-be mother of John the Baptist, and Mary, the mother-to-be of the Messiah. Both were truly great and godly women. Both were humble women of no social or economic standing. Yet the worship of both of these women is such that they are models for all true disciples of our Lord and hopefully are models for all women of this world.

Two gigantic women, full of grace by whom and through whom salvation of the human race was accomplished. Emulating their model of humility, faith, hope, and love will elevate any woman to be a holy and prominent woman. And regardless of which gender occupies an office in the ecclesiastical structure of the church, a holy and prominent woman will always remain honored and respected.

CHAPTER 6

Evaporating Dream

*For the new religious consciousness the
declaration of the will of God
is together with this a declaration of the rights
of man, a revealing of
the Divine within mankind.*

—Nikolai Berdyaev

Surfacing Conflict

The Coptic community's dream to have a priest serving them suddenly evaporated when the decision was made that Father Morcos would have his permanent residency in Canada. His plan was to eventually extend his service to the US Coptic community, and Father Morcos indeed began his pastoral services in the States for about three weeks, from March 31, 1965, to April 20, 1965. As previously mentioned, during this visit, an apparent conflict of interest with the board arose regarding where his service ought to be in the States and where those services were most needed. To resolve this issue, the church decided to form its own organization to handle its own affairs. The resolution was brought up by HG Bishop Samuel and was met with approval by both the CAA and Father Morcos.

Bishop Samuel sent letters to all concerned, informing them that to avoid further conflicts, Father Morcos would primarily serve in Canada because it had the bigger community. However, his expenses and salary would largely be carried by the Coptic community in the United States. After consultation with the Canadian Copts, the CAA board in the States, and Father Morcos, it was decided that he would serve in Toronto two weeks, Montreal one week, and the US one week every month. Although the CAA had labored hard to create the legal body, draw up its bylaws, and reach out to Copts everywhere in the United States and Canada, it willingly accepted its separation from the organizational structure that Bishop Samuel implemented for the newly established church in Canada.

The CAA, however, maintained its relations with its established branches throughout the States and Canada. The organization continued to raise funds to financially support the newly ordained priest. Despite the CAA working very hard to get an entry visa for the priest to have him perform his services in the US, he ended up residing permanently in Canada. Members of the American Coptic community were disappointed, as they faced an unanticipated reality that the first ordained priest to serve abroad ended up not serving in the US.

Later, in December 1967, a consoling letter (in Arabic) was sent from Father Morcos in Canada to the Coptic community in the United States. He obviously wanted to restore unity and harmonious relations among all, thus healing a sense of alienation that some members of the Coptic American community felt.

In the letter, Father Morcos pointed to the role of the Coptic Church in evangelization. He wrote, "The Coptic Church had a history of evangelism proclaiming the mission of salvation in many nations including Ireland, Switzerland, Sudan, Ethiopia, and others." He urged us to have a similar mission in this country, which could only be accomplished if the faithful united around our beloved church and strengthened the bonds that bound us and deepened the spirit of love among us. The Coptic Church, he wrote, believed that all members of the congregation had "an important role" in serving the church. Their role was congruent to the role of the priest, and attaining church goals depended on every one of us doing their job in serving the church.[11]

Ordination of a Second Priest: Fr. Rofael Younan Nakhla

Fr. Rofael Younan Nakhla was ordained and appointed with the approval of HH Pope Cyril VI to serve and be based in Montreal, Canada. He would be the second priest after Father Morcos, who was based in Toronto. Father Rofael's designated services were to include the Copts in the States, and he arranged his time accordingly. I was honored to know this loving shepherd personally and serve with him. His presence blessed many homes of newly immigrated families across the United States. He loved the Coptic Church and was dedicated to ministering its teachings to others, including children.

Father Rofael was generous with his time and gifted with the ability to work well with others. Not only did he respect all members of the congregation, he also respected people in general. He was naturally friendly and open to different races, ethnic groups, and cultures. A soft-spoken gentleman, he refused to receive any compensation for his service beyond travel expenses. He was highly educated but also had the capacity and the desire to learn. He was indeed a loving, humble, and caring shepherd with an amazingly healthy self-image.

The Coptic American community was also blessed with the presence of Fr. Bishoy Kamel, who served in the States later on and was an exemplary priest. Father Bishoy was a disciple and admirer of Fr. Mikhail Ibrahim, the saintly priest of St. Mark Coptic Church in Shoubra, Cairo. Fr. Mikhail Ibrahim was the father of confession to Pope Shenouda III as well the spiritual father of generations of bishops, priests, monks, and laity.

Part-Time vs. Full-Time Priest

Though the Coptic community in the States was thrilled with Father Rofael's monthly visits, the hope continued to have a full-time priest to meet the enormous demand for priestly services. A meeting was called by the then CAA president, Mrs. Eva al Masri Sidhom, on March 15, 1969. In this meeting chaired by Dr. Sami Boulos, the qualifications of the priest were discussed. The members concluded that the ideal priest would meet certain requirements, as recorded in the meeting minutes:

> [The priest] must be of the highest caliber in the following areas: spirituality, character, personality, education, and English.
>
> He must be young in order to have empathy with the young men and women who are the future of the church.
>
> He must have a small family so he can devote most of his time to the services that he will be required to render.

Based on previous experience meeting the expenses of Father Morcos and his family and paying his salary, a financial goal was set. The association needed to raise between $10,000 and $15,000 before considering a request for a new priest.[12] In the meantime, Father Rofael's service continued by visiting the States once or twice a month mainly to celebrate the Holy Liturgy.

In April 1969, some dispirited community members secretly decided to act without the knowledge of the CAA and started collecting signatures for the purpose of acquiring the services of Fr. Mankarious Awadalla, a priest who was in the country visiting his son. They sent their signed petition directly to HH Pope Cyril VI, appealing to him to consider their request. According to CAA records, this act was considered an improper attempt to force a specific person on the community as a whole without calling for a general members' meeting to discuss the issue and collectively decide on a course of action. It also did not meet the criteria that had been agreed upon when the matter was discussed in a preceding general meeting on March 15, 1969.

The majority of the CAA agreed that members of the Coptic community had specific needs. Because they were now living in a different culture with a different language and societal norms, they desired a "young" priest. Most of the families appreciated Father Rofael not only for his dedicated service but also for his ability to understand Western culture and communicate with their youngsters. Parents were terrified of the culture of liberalism and permissiveness that might negatively influence their offspring and the family as a whole.

Immediately upon discovering the intention and unjustifiable act of the small group, CAA president Mrs. Eva al Masri Sidhom sent a letter to the pope on March 28, 1969, and a second was sent to Bishop Samuel on March 30, 1969, "to avert the consequences of such act." She pleaded with both the pope and the bishop to disregard the request made by the unknown group. She explained that the CAA had never heard from or dealt with them, nor had this group given them the courtesy of getting together to discuss issues of concern, if any, for the sake of all. Aware of the Coptic community's longing to fill the spiritual vacuum in their lives, the CAA asked HH Pope Cyril VI to consider the possibility of relocating Fr. Rofael Younan to the United States. The pope responded through HG Bishop Gregorios that he would consider their request and pray about it.

Concerns of Societal Issues: Lack of Transparency

This incident showed how a small group who wanted Fr. Mankarious Awadalla to stay apparently was not aware of the CAA's structured planning and financial concerns to bring in a new priest. It illustrated how the emotional reaction of some members of the Coptic community could override the worthwhile efforts of others. The group intended to address the issue directly and swiftly, dispatching their concern to the upper echelons of the church, despite the fact that direct communication with the pope was not a common practice of the Coptic laity.

The entire episode caused grave concern in the community. A small group rationalized issues from their point of view independently from the collective input and feedback of the majority, despite both parties having the same purpose and the same goal. Unfortunately, the minority group apparently was swayed by power-hungry individuals who wanted a position of leadership. Similarly, others were guided by bruised egos, disregarding the efforts of the majority out of a misguided sense of subordination and discrimination. The upper echelons of the Coptic Church clergy were not aware of such dynamics and maneuverings and rushed to calm the storm and try to make everyone happy.

In the biblical understanding of a loving, harmonious community, such an action may be considered improper, or at least an unfriendly way of communication. Such secretive actions and lack of communication usually causes disunity and division, and disunity and division in any church is a tragedy. Copts are supposedly descendants of one of the earliest civilized nations, and as such they should always strive to act in a civil manner. More importantly, as Christians, they must refrain from actions that divide the faithful and create disunity, not only by asking others not to behave in such manner but first asking of themselves not to behave similarly and to be more understanding than to be understood.

It is important for one to make his or her voice heard, not only to the pope but to God the Almighty Himself. However, etiquette is an unwritten code of conduct regarding the interactions among members of any community and their superiors. Learning to display proper etiquette in communication is a sign of polite prudence and learned experience. Keen understanding and consideration of others' time and priorities is a sign of emotional intelligence, which simply is the capacity to be aware of, control, and express one's emotion properly, as well as handle interpersonal relationships effectively and empathetically.

Whether an issue or complaint is sent to authorities in a hierarchy for urgent action, some tend to disregard the necessary transparency that leads to a fair decision about the matter. More significantly, engaging the highest level of authority by bypassing every level in between, whether in written form or otherwise, is an improper manner of communication. This practice intrudes upon the very busy schedule of the church leaders. Instead, proper steps should be taken. First, the immediate superior or whoever is in charge should be alerted, and the issue of concern should be brought to his or her attention. Second, transparency is a must; hence, the matter is raised only after being shared with whom it pertains. Third, it should be presented to ascending levels within the hierarchy without hidden agendas or conditions. In this way, the matter should contain all information necessary for making the right decision.

An Eyewitness's Input

I personally witnessed these events as they happened, and they were recorded and well documented at the time. As such, I consider myself in a position to give a firsthand description of what took place. In addition, these events were partially recorded in many publications, which I consulted while writing this book. I also was secretary of the CAA board in 1968[13] as well as a member of the newly formed committee that oversaw the establishment of St. Mark Coptic Orthodox Church in Jersey City, New Jersey. Incorporated on March 6, 1970, it was the first Coptic Orthodox Church parish and church building in North America, if not the Western Hemisphere.

Along with input and support from many wonderful colleagues, I undertook the task of writing this book for the sake of maintaining an important historical record of the Coptic Church in America and Canada. For the sake of future generations, it is a duty to explain the chain of events with the hope it will shed light on them and avoid future instances of secrecy and lack of transparency.

Writing about some of these events may raise embarrassing issues. However, embarrassment is one standard that historians use to gauge the accuracy of a recorded event. If an author chooses to include an embarrassing fact that may hurt his or her case, then it is unlikely that he is making up the story. Both proper and improper dealings among congregational members, boards, clergy, and laity need to be viewed from the scientific application of "standardized barriers to effective communication." Thus together, we contribute to efforts to avoid casual or unconstrained reports about other people or events in the future.

Acting in the shadow of secrecy and without mustering the courage to manage conflicts is neither healthy nor genuine. It typically involves details that are not confirmed as being true. In many cases, it might be based on mere perception or interpretations that cannot be adequately substantiated. Incidents and events need to be reported as they happened, although it unfortunately has not made a difference to those who want no part of its truthfulness.

This unwavering attitude not to be cognizant of others' perspectives resulted in confusion, conflicts, and disunity. Division ought to be avoided at any cost, especially in the land of emigration. I have done my best to report events as they were documented, leaving the reader to form his or her opinion and conclusion. The hope is to alleviate uncalled-for disagreements and divisions in the future.

CHAPTER 7

—◦••◦◦◦◦••◦—

St. Mark Emissaries in the United States

*It is the greatest mystery of life that satisfaction is felt not
by those who take, and make demands, but by those who
give and make sacrifices. In them alone the energy of life does
not fail, and this is precisely what is meant by creativeness...
If you want to receive, give, if you want to obtain
satisfaction, do not seek it, and forget the very word; if you
want to acquire strength, manifest it, give it to others.*

—Nikolai Berdyaev

Fr. Makary El-Soriany

Before he was ordained, Fr. Makary El-Soriany (December 8, 1920–October 6, 1981) was known as Saad Aziz Ibrahim. He was born to a very religious family that consisted of loving parents and eventually two younger brothers. A graduate of the college of law at Cairo University, early on he decided not to pursue his career in law and instead devoted his life to serve the Lord. He was a dynamic and dedicated individual who invigorated the Sunday school movement that revitalized Christian education in Egypt. He also was well known for loving the poorest of the poor, going wherever he needed to go, even the slums where they lived, to provide help and support.

Saad Aziz thus chose the monastic life of servitude, poverty, and celibacy. He was ordained a monk by Fr. Mina the Hermit, who later became Pope Cyril VI, and given the name Makary El-Soriany. I was blessed to know him while attending evening studies at the Coptic Theological Seminary in Abbassia, Egypt. He was a scholarly teacher and attentive listener who spoke with a soft voice, always wore a smile, and had a big heart. His unique views were practical and logical. He spearheaded the effort to establish the Institute of Coptic Studies along with Professor Aziz Suryal Atiya.

As a thoughtful and brilliant reformer, Father Makary enthusiastically occupied himself with relieving the plight of the Copts in Egypt. He wanted Christian graduates and professionals in every field to grow into leadership roles and achieve financial independence. His mission was to prepare and provide them with a vision to serve the needs of Christian Copts throughout the country. Discriminating educational policies made it difficult for Christians to obtain scholarships and further their education abroad, but he encouraged graduates in a variety of fields to study overseas and return to play a leading role in Egyptian society.

One of his urgent dreams was to build a state-of-the-art hospital that catered to Copts, and he took inspiration from America. In the mid- to late 1950s, the United States was expanding its training programs for young physicians not only from around the country but around the world. The purpose was to use incentives to attract and retain health professionals in rural areas in the States. The program was quite a success—it recruited a large number of applicants, and retention rates were nearly 100 percent. Besides its primary mission to fill the need for physicians in neglected parts of the country, it also aimed to improve relations with developing countries.[14]

Father Makary, who had spent time at Princeton University (1954–1955) majoring in social studies, saw a golden opportunity in the physician training program. He encouraged aspiring physicians to apply for training in the States with the goal to return to Egypt, practice medicine, and eventually take charge of Coptic hospitals. Unfortunately, many of the graduates never returned to Egypt, because the political scene had changed. Those who did return faced the same discriminating policies that were in place when they left, and they were never appointed to leadership positions in academia or the Ministry of Health. Thus, many of them again left Egypt to pursue their professional careers in the United States and Europe.

Father Makary, however, maintained contact with those who had left the country or who would leave after passage of the Immigration and Nationality Act in 1968. During his travels to Europe and the United States, he would pay visits to them and celebrate the Holy Liturgy in homes where the only Coptic church to be found was the domestic church. His structured and well-organized system consisted of interdependent entities, boards, councils, and active members. He compiled addresses and phone numbers and was instrumental in creating a fellowship between Copts in the States and throughout Europe.

Many early immigrants to the United States in the late 1950s and early 1960s were physicians who came to pursue medical studies and further their professional careers. From CAA records, they included Dr. Elhamy Khalil, Dr. Atef Moawad, Dr. Sami Boulos, Dr. Amal Boctor, Dr. and Mrs. Maher Kamel, Dr. Wadie F. Mikhail, Dr. Fouad George Zaki, Dr. Victor Bishara, Dr. Haroun Mahrous, and Mr. Youssef and Mrs. Eva al Masri Sidhom. Many of these people ended up settling in the United States after completing their education.[15] Fr. Makary El-Soriany's plans for their return to take a leadership role in their home country never materialized—the good Lord had other plans for these early comers. However, Father Makary maintained relationships with most of them.

When the door of US immigration opened in 1968, a second wave of doctors left Egypt. Among them were Dr. Khairy Malek and Mr. and Mrs. Ramses Awadalla, who decided to immigrate to the United States and start their lives anew. It was a difficult decision indeed and a daring adventure for well-established families to leave their friends, successful businesses, and livelihood behind. It is important to illuminate and reflect on the early work and daunting task of Father Makary in serving the early arrivals to the United States and Europe. He was a pioneer who encouraged Copts to build their communities abroad.

Father Makary (later ordained HG Bishop Samuel) encouraged Youssef and Eva al Masri Sidhom to be the central entity for contacts among Copts. Eventually, the Coptic American Association (CAA) was incorporated in the state of New York. Long before that, in the early 1950s, Pope Yousab II* chose Fr. Makary El-Soriany, Professor/ Dr. Aziz Sorial Atiya, and Fr. Salib Sorial to represent the Coptic Church in the World Council of Churches in New York after the WCC extended an invitation to the church for the first time. It was an opportunity for Father Makary to be one of the earliest priests to minister to Copts abroad, celebrating Holy Liturgy for them in Europe and United States.

Father Makary was not only consecrated by Pope Cyril VI as a monk but also was ordained as a bishop of the Bishopric of Public, Ecumenical, and Social Services. As such, Bishop Samuel continued his active service and representation at the World Council of Churches. Eventually, he was elected as a member of the central committee of the WCC and the secretary general of the African churches. In his new role as a bishop, he was instrumental in selecting and recommending priests for serving abroad.

Regretfully, his life was cut short. On October 6, 1981, he was killed while he sat behind President Anwar Sadat of Egypt on the day he was assassinated by members of the Egyptian Islamic Jihad. He is a martyr and a man of great conviction and immortal achievement. His services for the church and the country still attest to his devotion to serve across the globe. His indefatigable work and sacrificial love would always be a shining light in the global history of the Coptic Church.

* * * * *

In the previous chapters, we discussed the role of Fr. Rofael Younan Nakhla, the priest of St. Mark's Church in Montreal,

---

* Pope Yousab II (May 26, 1946–November 14, 1956) was the 115th pope. Previously, the Metropolitan of Girga, the Church Synod, and the General Congregation Council agreed to remove Pope Yousab II from office, stating that he was not fit for his duties, and he retired to one of the monasteries.

Canada. He came to the United States monthly to celebrate the Holy Liturgy and minister to members of the Coptic community as early as 1968. He continued his dedicated service until St. Mark Coptic Orthodox Church opened its doors for the first time to celebrate the Holy Liturgy on Sunday, March 22, 1970, in Jersey City, New Jersey. In these early years of the Coptic Orthodox Church in America, the following clergy and laity also blessed the Coptic community by their visits and service in the United States.

Fr. Mankarious Awadalla

As mentioned, Fr. Mankarious Awadalla came to New York in February 1969 on his way to visit his son, who was studying engineering in California. During his stay, he celebrated Holy Liturgy on February 16, 23, and March 2. After he had spent three weeks in New York, he left to visit for California. When he came back, he celebrated the Holy Liturgy on Palm Sunday, Good Friday, and Easter.

During these weeks, some members of the Coptic community enjoyed his presence and were very supportive of continued service in New York, but as discussed, the CAA abided by the majority decision to seek a priest with specific qualifications to deal with the first generation of immigrants—most importantly, to care for their offspring who only spoke English and were immersed in American culture more than their parents.

Fr. Mina Kamel Yanni

The Coptic community once again was looking forward to having Father Rofael relocated to the States. The good Lord, however, had a different plan. Fr. Mina Kamel Yanni was visiting the US in the summer of 1969 while his wife was earning a master's degree in Boston. He was known to be an energetic, dedicated young priest who had been ordained by HH Pope Cyril VI a few years earlier. Father Mina was serving at St. Mary Church in Omraneya, Giza, the third largest city in Egypt and the capital of the Giza Governorate. The CAA approached him to serve in New York with the support of Fr. Rofael Younan. He readily agreed and was kind enough to freely offer his time, spending four days each week from Thursday to Sunday, then returning to Boston to be with his wife the rest of the week. During those four days, he performed many spiritual activities, including Saturday evenings with vespers and Bible study and celebrating the Holy Liturgy on Sundays.

Father Mina also visited members of the community and performed other spiritual services. His first Mass was celebrated in one of the halls of Riverside Church in Morningside Heights at 120th Street near Columbia University. The service was continued thereafter at the Armenian church located at 630 Second Avenue. Father Mina's service lasted from the summer of 1969 to the first week in October, when he returned to Egypt. Dr. Hakeem A. Abdelsayed (ordained later as Father Gabriel) served as a deacon with Father Mina during this period.

On Sunday, August 31, 1969, approximately one month before Father Mina returned to Egypt, he made a surprising announcement after the celebration of the Holy Liturgy. A new organization had been formed, called St. Mark Coptic Church. The purpose of the organization was to build a church with that name in New York City. It was also claimed that the pope was interested in the project! Needless to say, attendees of the Mass that day were shocked to hear the announcement of a second organization for the first time. No one knew who organized it or when it was formed, whether it was incorporated and by whom, or even why it was formed in secrecy.

Following this announcement, in September 1969, I received a circular that consisted of two pages of announcements and brief news. The circular's masthead indicated it came from "Saint Marcus Coptic Orthodox Church," including as its address Post Office Box 1091, Wall Street Station, New York, NY 10005, and dated Monday, September 22, 1969. It was the first of several such circulars, and none of the issues contained the name or names of people responsible for issuing them. Later on, two issues dated March 2 and March 30, 1970, were full of unsubstantiated accusations against unnamed people. The March 30 issue included a report addressed to the Coptic people under the title "Demise of the St. Mark Church the Martyr and Evangelist in New York," accusing "subversive powers" who "fought against Father Morcos and Father Mankarious" and refused to submit to their will! It further stated that the "unnamed people" were the cause of the newly formed group, who had been overpowered and prevented from pursuing the goal of establishing a church in New York.

As a result of these conflicts, the office of the pope of Alexandria demanded that the CAA and the newly formed St. Mark Coptic Church be merged. A new election was to be announced, and only active registered members of the Coptic Church community would be allowed to vote for a new elected board. A letter from HH Pope Cyril VI was sent to Father Rofael, the CAA, and the St. Marcus committee, urging all to forget their differences, unite together, and pool all resources and efforts in service of the church, quoting St. Paul: "Now I plead with you, brethren, by the name of our Lord Jesus Christ, that you all speak the same thing, and that there be no division among you, but that you be perfectly joined together in the same mind and the same judgment." (1 Corinthians 1:10)

The CAA thus dissolved all assets and vested them in the new Coptic Orthodox Church of St. Mark in Jersey City. Both organizations appeared to reconcile their differences. A temporary council was formed, and Father Rofael was instrumental in uniting the groups. He was unanimously designated as the new president. Elected with him were Dr. Maher Kamel, vice president; Mr. Nassif Banout, treasurer; and Mr. Ramses Awadalla, secretary.

When the results were announced the day of the election, three people objected. Despite Father Rofael's efforts to persuade them to accept the results, they were not willing to do so. One of them insisted on sending an immediate letter of objection to the pope, and no one could persuade him otherwise. At this point, I need to remind the reader of what is meant by proper societal behavioral practices. Generally, it is inappropriate to engage the highest authority of the church with what by all accounts would be considered trivial matters. Such matters should be resolved peacefully and respectfully among members of the local Coptic community, especially when it relates to harmonious relations among members of the body of Christ.

St. Mark Coptic Orthodox Church Opened

The Holy Liturgy was celebrated for the first time in an independently owned Coptic church on Sunday, March 22, 1970. The celebrant was Fr. Rofael Younan Nakhla. It was a historic day engraved in the memory of all who attended. The congregation members were exuberant. That day, an alter to the Lord Almighty was consecrated in the heart of the state of New Jersey in the United States of America. That great day brought to mind Isaiah's prophecy: "In that day shall there be an alter to the Lord in the midst of the land of Egypt and a pillar to the Lord near the border." (Isaiah 19:19)

Today, Coptic American pilgrims to St. Mark Church who yearn to visit their first place of worship in the United States will be thrilled. Its current condition is a far cry from the deteriorating property that was abandoned for many years. The church is magnificently remodeled and decorated with wall-to-wall red carpeting. The altar is situated facing east, according to the Coptic Church tradition. An iconostasis—a wooden screen bearing icons—separates the sanctuary from the altar. The middle of the iconostasis is adorned with a luxurious red velvet curtain closing off the altar. At the top is a painting of the Lord Jesus Christ upon the cross flanked by His mother, St. Mary, and St. Mary Magdalene. Below the depiction of the crucifixion, covering the full width of the iconostasis, are portraits of the twelve apostles, a red votive light hung before each. At the top right of the main altar, there is a painting of the Lord Jesus Christ in majesty, or Christ Pantocrator, while at the top left is a painting of the Mother of God with Christ cradled in her arm. When the velvet curtain is pulled aside, the altar is revealed, covered in sacrificial red and fine white cloth laid on top as a reminder of Christ's purification of the world. Over the altar is an elegantly carved wooden dome supported by four pillars. Behind, an apse contains a stained-glass Christ Pantocrator. Large crystal chandeliers hanging from the ceiling shimmer above the congregation.

Rev. Fr. Hegomen Gabriel Abdelsayed: First Ordained Priest to Serve in the United States

Dr. Hakim Abdelsayed (April 3, 1927–December 2, 1993) came to the United States in 1969 under fellowship grants in Minnesota and Utah to further his education and research in history and theology. There he met and became a close friend of the late Dr. Aziz Atiya, and they worked together toward the establishment of the reputable Middle East Center at the University of Utah. He was a companion of Bishop Samuel, traveling with him and participating in activities of the World Council of Churches. He also was a member of the observational delegation led by HG Bishop Samuel to the Second Vatican Council of the Roman Catholic Church. The call to priesthood for Dr. Hakim Abdelsayed was actually presented and recommended to Pope Cyril VI by Metropolitan Athanasius and Bishop Samuel as a worthy candidate to serve the Coptic community in New York and New Jersey. Dr. Hakim, who was son to a priest, found it hard to decline such a worthy call.

On August 5, 1970, HH Pope Cyril VI ordained Rev. Fr. Gabriel Abdelsayed to be the first priest serving the first Coptic parish in the United States. Father Gabriel held a doctorate in history from Cairo University. Over the years, he taught at several institutions in Egypt and the United States, including St. John's University. He authored books about religion and history, including *Egyptian Monasticism and Cenobitism* (1963), *The Rise of the Second Mamluk Dynasty* (1967), and *St. Mark in Africa* (1968). He was instrumental in establishing many Coptic churches in the States. In his honor, Jersey City named one of its streets Fr. Gabriel Street. It was dedicated in a historic celebration attended by HG Bishop David, the mayor of the city and other local dignitaries, members of the congregation of St. Mark Church, and representatives of other Coptic churches and priests.

Worth Noting!

Father Gabriel was one of the architects, if not the main one, who planned Pope Shenouda III's first papal visit to the United States in April 1977. Speaking from the pulpit of his church, he urged every Copt to take the day off in honor of the pope's arrival and consider it a historic holiday. The pope indeed had a great reception when he arrived at Kennedy International Airport in New York; multitudes of fellow Copts, priests, and dignitaries were on hand for his arrival. It was indeed a joyous day with all its festivities and blessings. During the trip, the pope celebrated the Holy Liturgy, ordained the first Coptic priest and deacons in the United States, laid the foundation stones for several churches, and visited President Jimmy Carter in the White House. The president teasingly asked His Holiness what his thoughts were about Israel! Known for his sense of humor, the pope responded without missing a beat, "We all are the new Israel."

Father Gabriel had a distinct and wonderful relation with one of his deacons, Dr. Farid F. Shafik. According to this beloved son:

> His ministry was one of the "firsts" for so many endeavors, foundational for so many of the institutions and parishes that have come forth, the basis for different dioceses that have since formed, the establishment of the first Seminary in the United States, and so many people settled and ministered under his fatherhood.[16]

There was another touching story shared by Dr. Shafik regarding the last liturgy Father Gabriel attended at St. Mark Church. He recalled the event in September 1993:

> I had spent the night with him to ready him for the Liturgy the next day. I was not cognizant of the Gospel for the Liturgy that day, yet it is one that in remembrance, I hold dearly to my heart. As it was chanted, we were bringing him into the church and the fire-escape stairs from the outside did not allow for the original five to carry him in a chair up the stairs, but one had to release and only four were able to properly carry the chair

into the church. Upon entering the church we heard, and which led us to cry, the Story of the Four Friends lowering their friend before the Lord. Bishop Pisenti was in attendance and he also was touched by the scene and wept.[17]

CHAPTER 8

✦◦◦⟩◦⟨◦◦⟩✦

The Harvest Is Truly Plentiful

*We need today more than ever before, precisely
a "band of spiritual firebrands"
who can inflame minds and hearts with fire
of a loving knowledge of God and
Jesus Christ, the Redeemer.*

—Fr. Georges Florovsky

*A person is humble when he knows that his
very being is on loan to him.*

—St. Maximus the Confessor

Commissioned Priest: Fr. Bishoy Kamel

The small but growing Coptic community on the West Coast of the United States had no priest to serve it until the arrival of Fr. Bishoy Kamel (December 6, 1931–March 21, 1979). Pope Cyril VI commissioned Father Bishoy to serve in Los Angeles on November 9, 1969. That day was not a coincidence. By divine plan, the day was also the Feast of St. Mark the Evangelist and founder of the Coptic Orthodox Church in Egypt. Father Bishoy initially used a Syriac Orthodox Church building to accommodate Holy Liturgies and spiritual meetings and services. The congregation eventually purchased a building that was previously used by a Russian Orthodox Church congregation on Robertson Boulevard, near Hollywood. The congregation had $500 in its treasury, whereas the purchase price was $100,000. The congregation ended up purchasing the building by a miracle that will be recounted below.[18]

While actively serving in Los Angeles during his stay, Father Bishoy's ministry extended to cover a wide area of the United States. He visited Coptic communities, celebrated the Holy Liturgy, and ministered to their needs in San Francisco, California; Denver, Colorado; Houston, Texas; Portland, Oregon; and Seattle, Washington. Later, he visited Jersey City on May 15, 1974, where he spearheaded the purchasing of a temple on Bergen Avenue. The property was remodeled to become the current St. George and St. Shenouda Church. Father Bishoy ultimately helped found several other parishes and buildings throughout Egypt, the United States, Europe, and Australia.[19]

In 1995, the Coptic Orthodox Diocese of Los Angeles, Southern California, and Hawaii was founded. Pope Shenouda III enthroned HG Bishop Sarapion on December 23, 1995, at Holy Virgin Mary Church in Los Angeles as the bishop of the Diocese of Los Angeles, which includes St. Mark Church as well as several other churches. Pope Tawadros II elevated HG Bishop Sarapion to the episcopal dignity of metropolitan on Sunday, February 28, 2016, at the old cathedral of St. Mark (Clot Bey). His official title is the bishop of Los Angeles and metropolitan of Southern California and Hawaii. He was the first bishop of the Coptic Orthodox Diocese of Los Angeles and the first metropolitan in North America.[20]

A Church Miraculously Bought

According to the now well-known story, some congregation members discouraged Father Bishoy from buying the old church on Robertson Boulevard. They feared it would put them in debt. He, however, raised $23,000, some of the money from loans made by new immigrants who had little financial means to begin with. The "go-getter" priest, anxious to get the deal completed, took a cab to the bank to pay the down payment and sign the papers for a mortgage loan. Walking into the bank, he realized that he had left the money—$23,000 in cash!—in an unmarked envelope on the seat of the cab that took him to the bank. Not knowing what else to do, he went into the bank and told the loan officer he had misplaced the money and needed time to find it or replace it. He was crushed by the feeling that he had failed his congregation members. To top it off, he thought the congregation would think that Abouna was a thief. (Abouna is colloquial Arabic for "our father.")

After midnight, he heard a knock at his door. He asked Tasoni Angel, his wife, to open the door. He was surprised to see the cab driver standing before him. The driver admitted that after Father Bishoy had left, "I looked back and saw that envelope. I picked it up and found it full of cash and not marked. I thought about keeping it. I drove around and around. Then I said, 'This man must be a minister or a priest or something. But even if I wanted to give him the money back, how could I find him?' I then thought if I described the way you're dressed and the way you looked, somebody might be able to lead me to you. That is how I found that you must be Coptic [Egyptian] and the way to your apartment, which was the church address." The cab driver refused to accept the customary 10 percent reward and even gave a donation!

The Oneness of Soul and Spirit

Fr. Bishoy Kamel and Tasoni Angel Bassili were two souls who fully completed and complemented each other. They divinely met and were in agreement on the path they both had chosen to serve the Lord. As a theologian, Father Bishoy had invariably focused on soteriology, denoting the beliefs and doctrines concerning salvation, or the passion, death, and resurrection of Christ. However, both Father Bishoy and Tasoni Angel were gifted with a combined spirit that was larger than themselves, and both fully understood each other.

One dares to imagine that there was never any conflict about their destiny in life: "to seek and save" souls and to gather with the Lord. They both radiated the crystal-clear features of mental, verbal, and emotional harmony everywhere they went and wherever they served. Thus, they both were (and she still is) a true example of understanding, acceptance, and unconditional love.

Tasoni Angel is truly worthy of her title. ("Tasoni" is used to address an active nun or consecrated woman in service for the church.) She was consecrated for service in the church by HH Pope Cyril VI. After he gave her Holy Communion for the third and last time, he said, "Now you are a Tasoni—a Deaconess."[21] She continues to be active in serving St. George Church of Alexandria and beyond. She carries the torch of shared ministry that was passed to her and kindles the glorious role of women in the Coptic Church. Most importantly, both of these servants of the Lord had agreed to devoutly keep their marriage relationship within the spiritual realm. This continued a Coptic tradition associated with the well-known story of a second-century Coptic patriarch, Pope Demetrius I, who lived with his wife as a brother lives with a sister. Father Bishoy and Tasoni Angel renewed the old tradition.[22]

It was not a coincidence that Father Bishoy died on Wednesday, March 21, 1979 (12 Baramhat 1695). That very day, in the Coptic Orthodox calendar, is the feast day commemorating the revelation of the virginity of St. Demetrius the Vinedresser!

Father Bishoy's Spiritual Mentors

Fr. Bishoy Kamel was called to the priesthood and ordained by HH Pope Cyril VI. He was assigned to build St. George Church and its parish in Sporting, Alexandria, and to serve its community. However, his relationship with the pope started many years before his ordination as a priest. Sami Kamel, his name before ordination, used to visit the pope when he was a monk living a solitary life at the windmill in Old Cairo. Tasoni Angel related that Sami said, "When he was near the monk he felt that he was in the presence of holiness. This feeling never really left Sami. Pope Kyrillos [Cyril IV] was the great teacher of his life."[23]

Tasoni went on to say that because of his love for Pope Cyril VI, Abouna Bishoy would distribute the pope's picture in the church and to anyone he met while he was in the United States. He wanted to introduce the second generation of Coptic immigrants to the holy patriarch so they would be mindful of a model of fatherhood that reflected and spoke volumes about our traditions.

Father Bishoy's second spiritual mentor was Fr. Mikhail Ibrahim of St. Mark's Church in Shoubra, Cairo. Until his death on March 26, 1975, this saintly man was father-confessor to Abouna Bishoy and innumerable other clergy and laity, including Pope Shenouda III. He was an inspiring, righteous priest to emulate and be guided by his heavenly wisdom. Father Mikhail's humility, joyous presence, and modesty of words created an atmosphere of peace and inner tranquility wherever he went. He led sinners to repentance and the righteous to a life of sanctity by his heartfelt yet simple prayers. The altar was his heavenly place where he brought all complicated unresolved issues and countless petitions into the hands of the Lord, and miraculously, these also were resolved.

Father Mikhail was not only a model of saintly priesthood but also resembled the Good Shepherd in his deeds and love for all those who crossed his path. The Holy Spirit filled him with grace, compassion, kindness, and gentleness and clothed him with humility and modesty. Father Bishoy similarly was such an endearing icon of fatherly love that he was willing to lay down his life for his sheep.

I was truly fortunate to have known both wonderful priests well, and my life was truly blessed by them, as well as by HH Pope Cyril VI. This great shepherd and humble soul is one of the holiest giants and arguably one of the most influential servant-leaders of our times. My only hope for those who knew them and witnessed the lives of these spiritual giants is to continue tracing their footsteps, aided by God's grace.[24]

A Noteworthy Doctrine

The doctrine that Father Bishoy established and followed in his ministry is quite worthy of attention. The following are its significant points:

❖ The basic and main principle is that when Jesus calls someone for priesthood, the priest must be mindful and only focus on the Lord Jesus as the one primary example to emulate. The Lord is the source and the summit of the eternal power of our heavenly Father. Through this power, He redeems and exalts His children.

❖ Our heavenly Father gives worthy priests the authority to administer the ordinance of salvation. All of His children can qualify to receive ordination and access the power and blessings of the priesthood.

❖ Father Bishoy summarized his doctrine of love and service for the little flock with these words: "They are your children, Lord: some are good, others are evil, others are wasting themselves…they are all children… I am a servant and have no right to insult or despise any of them, because if I do, I would be insulting you or despising you… I only can serve them, love them, and assure them of your certain promise that you loved them all, because it is you who carries the sins of the whole world" (translated and paraphrased from Arabic).[25]

❖ Father Bishoy, a priest of unequivocal passion for the cross, always repeated the saying, "There is no saint without the cross." His authentic *theologia crucis*, or theology of the cross, has been reported as the key to his life (as reported by Fr. Tadros Malaty and explained by Dr. Rodolph Yanney).[26]

❖ The priest is like his Master. He renounces himself, follows in His footsteps, and carries daily his cross—the cross of service, of teaching, of perseverance with boundless love, and most importantly, of suffering. He carries them all patiently, silently, and courageously.

❖ The priest's personal life and deeds ought to be a living example for people to emulate. Father Bishoy said, "People don't need to hear about Christ anymore; they have heard enough. They rather need to see Christ in us" (as reported by Fr. Antonious Henein).[27]

❖ Father Bishoy's leadership role promoted harmonious relations with fellow priests, creating a loving and friendly atmosphere. This close-knit relationship motivated them in turn to work harder, cooperate, and be supportive of one another. Competition or inevitable differences of opinion were no match for the reciprocal love and understanding among fellow priests that Father Bishoy encouraged.

❖ The primary mission of the priest is his spiritual life and the edification of the church. Father Bishoy felt that a spiritual leader has the power to create leaders in all aspects of life. That statement was shared by Fr. Tadros Yacoub Malaty, who is credited with teaching past and present generations in America and around the world about the spiritual life and ministry of Fr. Bishoy Kamel. Father Tadros had enjoyed a close relationship with Father Bishoy from 1953 until his death.

❖ In the West, capitalism encourages people to invest in wealth and vast material possessions, but its inhabitants are often spiritually impoverished. Father Bishoy adopted a lifestyle characterized by asceticism. His purpose of pursuing a spiritual life, caring for children and the needy, and "seeking and saving souls" was vital to his ministry. Rather than being preoccupied by church politics and monetary affairs, these were his first priorities.

❖ Although Father Bishoy and Tasoni Angel's lengthy ministry took them across the globe and away from home, Egypt was their final destiny. Father Bishoy lived and died in the same small flat that he shared with Tasoni Angel in Alexandria—the same place that was also a shelter for the needy and for people with problems who stayed there until their problems were solved.

The life of Fr. Bishoy Kamel had many other glorious and illuminating aspects that deserve special notice. However, expounding on that is not within the scope of this book. I can only add that for decades, many Copts have considered Father Bishoy a contemporary though uncanonized saint. The Coptic Orthodox Church is expected to canonize him someday. Currently he is buried in the parish of St. George Church, for which he was called to build and ordained to serve by HH Pope Cyril VI. His shrine is at St. George Church in Sporting, Alexandria, where his relics are kept inside a tomb and visited daily by the congregation and many more of the faithful from other churches in Alexandria and beyond.

CHAPTER 9

<figure>❖</figure>

Christ Ambassadors and Laborers to His Harvest

Therefore Pray the Lord of the harvest to send out
Laborers into His harvest.

—Matthew 9:38

Professor Aziz Suryal Atiya

In the first few chapters of this book, we spoke about some of the newly immigrated families to the United States. Some were considered to be of the elite class while living in their homeland, Egypt. I have revealed a little about their heritage, their upbringing, their educational background, and their charitable contributions and services to the Coptic Church and Egyptians in general while in Egypt. However, as they settled in their new land, they had to struggle and build their lives from scratch. They were cognizant of their Coptic heritage, held to their faith, and thus were instrumental in creating an organizational body to serve the Coptic community at large.

Now we turn to the present. Professor Aziz Suryal Atiya (July 5, 1898–September 24, 1988) was a humble man who started out in life with no social or economic standing. He was of a modest beginning, yet one wishes that every Copt would learn of his path in life, be encouraged by his determination to reach the pinnacle of success, and emulate his character and his virtues. I had the pleasure of meeting him in early 1987 while he attended the Holy Liturgy at St. Mark Church in Jersey City. Needless to say that his reputation preceded him as one of the most admired scholars in the field of history and among the Coptic societies of learning.

He spoke in the church that Sunday after a long introduction by Fr. Gabriel Abdelsayed, and his speech was impressive. He had the ability to deliver a complex subject in a way that made it easy for all to understand. He reminded members of the congregation of their spiritual heritage of scholarly Copts such as Origen, who was the first to establish a systematic Christian theology. St. Anthony, the founder of monasticism in the world, was another giant spiritual figure. A third one was St. Pakhomious, whose rules governing monastic life were carried to Europe by missionary monks and adopted by the great monastic orders that arose there. He then spoke of Alexandria, which attained supremacy in ecclesiastical affairs during the fourth century and the first half of the fifth.

After the Holy Liturgy, the congregation had the opportunity to meet Dr. Atiya, where he delighted them with further talk about the history of the church, including another giant figure, Dioscorus I (August 8, 444–September 17, 454), the twenty-fifth pope of Alexandria, patriarch of the See of St. Mark, and the champion of orthodoxy. He related that the Church of Rome and the emperors of the Byzantine Empire in Constantinople decried what Dr. Atiya granted were the "high-handed actions" of Dioscorus I. In 451, he was summoned by Emperor Marcian (450–457) to a council in Asia Minor. What followed was a disaster for Coptic Christians and a rupture in the unity of Christendom. The Copts and the churches of Ethiopia, Syria, and Armenia were declared heretical by the Roman Catholic and Eastern Orthodox Churches when they rejected a reference by the council to Christ's having two natures: human and divine. To the Coptic Monophysites (a person who holds that in the person of Jesus Christ there is only one nature, not two), such a claim was a denial of Christ's divine nature, whereas the orthodox churches insisted that Monophysites were denying the full humanity of Christ. When the Copts refused to accept the council's decisions, the Byzantine rulers, determined to impose church unity, carried out a bitter repression of the Coptic Church. In 639, the Arabs invaded Egypt, and the Copts thought it would end the repressive regime of the Byzantine Empire. Little did they know that the Arabs would impose their own repression.

While Dr. Atiya spoke, sharing and reflecting on aspects of church history, his spirituality, faith, and elegance shined through his body language and his words. That was no surprise; his life and achievements had been the talk of many speakers and the subject of extensive writings by many authors around the world. Dr. Atiya was among the top of his class in high school and was admitted to the college of medicine at Cairo University. As an Egyptian patriot, he demonstrated against British occupation and was terminated from the university in 1919. He was imprisoned twice and ended up without a college degree or even a job to earn a living. When he was asked then about his future plans, he would respond simply that "the Lord is my shepherd."[28]

The young Aziz did not give up. He educated himself at home and retook the baccalaureate exam, scoring the second highest grade among his peers. He then joined the school of law at Cairo University, though once again he left the school to support his family after his father lost his business. While working two clerical jobs to financially support his family, he continued his education at night, graduating in 1927 at the top of his class. He continued his studies at the University of Liverpool in England as was granted a scholarship by the Egyptian government in 1929. He earned a BA with first-class honors in medieval and modern history in 1931 and an MA in medieval and modern history with honors. He then enrolled in the University of London and earned his PhD in 1933. Never done with learning, he continued his graduate education back at the University of Liverpool, where he received his doctor of letters in 1938.[29] He also was awarded an honorary doctor of laws degree (LLD) from Brigham Young University in 1967.

In Egypt, his career advanced considerably from a high school history teacher in 1940 to associate professor of medieval history at Cairo University. Then he left the university to join Dr. Taha Hussein—the then minister of education—in founding the University of Alexandria. In recognition of his scholarly effort and dedication, Dr. Atiya was promoted to the rank of professor there. He then held a foundation chair in medieval history until 1954. He also served as vice dean of faculty of arts (1949–1950) and chairman of the History Department (1952–1954).[30] Dr. Atiya published more than forty volumes in four languages: English, French, German, and Arabic. Fluent in these languages, he mastered the art of research skills and was a world-renowned speaker in diverse institutions and many countries across the globe. In the United States, he founded the Middle East Center at the University of Utah.

Professor Aziz Suryal Atiya accomplished three major tasks for the Coptic Orthodox Church. First was the establishment of the Institute of Coptic Studies in Cairo in 1954. Second was his extensive research that culminated in the publication of his book *History of Eastern Christianity* in 1968. Third, he served as editor of the *Coptic Encyclopedia*, an eight-volume work covering the history, theology, art, architecture, archeology, and hagiography of Coptic Egypt. The encyclopedia entries were written by over 250 Western and Egyptian experts in their respective fields of Coptology. The encyclopedia is the crown jewel of Professor Atiya's work, who regretfully did not live to see it carried into print.

According to Claremont Graduate University (CGU), the Coptic community in diaspora was very supportive of the idea of producing an English-Coptic encyclopedia. This project would have never materialized without their support. The production of this encyclopedia is therefore strongly linked to the growth of the Coptic migrant community in the West.[31] As a result, we see that Coptic immigration not only played a significant role in the spread of Coptic churches around the world but also was a direct cause in the spreading of Coptic civilization across the globe.

These accomplishments build on the tradition of the Catechetical School of Alexandria, the oldest catechetical school in the world, by extending its roots into the West. This great school of learning was for Christian theologians, clergy, and educators from around the world. According to St. Jerome (347–420), the Alexandrian school was founded by St. Mark the Apostle.[32] The modern-day work of Professor Aziz Suryal Atiya and countless others was guided by divine providence to deploy minds, hands, indefatigable work, and sacrificial love in support of Coptic Christians living in the West. As one can imagine, the aim is to revive the spiritual life, Christian theology, and writings of the church fathers.

This brief summary of Dr. Atiya's work does not pretend to say all that can be said about his many accomplishments, but it is an attempt to note the highlights of his career. Despite his modest beginning and harsh early years, he was able to overcome all and reached the pinnacle of academic life. Most importantly, his humility, faith, kindness, and perseverance are all wonderful virtues attributed to his deep love, dedication, and service to the Coptic Orthodox Church and humanity at large. He is truly an exemplary Copt to emulate.

Rev. Fr. Antonious Baky

St. Mary and St. Antonious Church was established in the borough of Queens in New York City. Members of the congregation of St. Mark Church who lived in that area had grown tired of traveling back and forth to Jersey City. A group of Copts spearheaded by Mr. Nassif Banout, Mr. Nabil Bastawros, and others formed and incorporated the new church. At first, the newly formed congregation conducted their spiritual service in a nearby rental space in a Protestant church. They were in dire need of a priest to shepherd the flock and to have their own church closer to where they lived, so they communicated their desire to HH Pope Shenouda III.

In March 1972, the pope delegated Fr. Antonious Baky for the service of this church. This righteous priest worked around the clock to establish the church. He was close to each family, knowing their needs and concerns as new immigrants in Queens. It was a heavy burden, and the demands apparently were overwhelming. Though he was a vibrant young priest, the Lord called him within two months to join the Triumphant Church. Father Antonious suffered a heart attack and departed joyfully to heaven on May 2, 1972.

Hegomen Fr. Tadros Yacoub Malaty

Immediately, Pope Shenouda III delegated Fr. Tadros Yacoub Malaty to Queens, who was serving at the time at St. Mark Church in Los Angeles. He served at St. Mary and St. Antonious Church until a replacement could be found. Fr. Tadros Malaty (ordained November 25, 1962) is a scholarly Coptic theologian and published author. However, he mastered the art of mediation and proved to be an adept crisis intervention strategist. He is well known for his tireless traveling and amazing capacity for handling a myriad of crisis situations. His careful strategy and heavenly wisdom in solving complicated issues within the church and among members of congregations cannot be matched.

The last two popes of Alexandria and the current one have called on Father Tadros to manage difficult situations involving specific churches and clergy as well as situational crises, including large-scale traumatic events in Egypt and around the world. Father Tadros is one of the pioneers who came to the United States in the late 1960s, commissioned to serve in the land of diaspora. During his stay in New York, he encouraged the congregation to find a property or purchase a vacant church as a perpetual place for worship, even a small one, rather than renting a space. He prefers to have a small church in every borough rather than a large one that forces worshippers to travel long distances to attend services. The Queens congregation was looking to do just that for their families, and Father Tadros found a Baptist church for sale in the neighboring borough of Brooklyn on Sixty-Seventh Street and Eleventh Avenue. The modest offer made by the small Coptic community was not accepted by the seller at that time.

Hegomen Fr. Mina Kamel Yanni

Father Mina once again returned to the United States, delegated by HH Pope Shenouda III to serve in St. Mary and St. Antonious Church in Queens. He served with Fr. Tadros Yacoub Malaty for a brief period. Father Mina arrived in New York on Thursday,

September 14, 1972. Vespers and the Holy Liturgy were offered the following Saturday night and on Sunday. Father Tadros soon after traveled back to Egypt, beginning his ministry at St. George Church in Sporting, Alexandria.

Upon Fr. Mina Kamel's arrival, he and the board of St. Mary and St. Antonious Church made a better offer to buy the vacant Baptist church and negotiated good terms to satisfy the loan. The deal was approved by the board and accepted by the seller. The opening celebration of St. George Church occurred on Sunday, December 31, 1972, and the first Holy Liturgy was celebrated on Monday, January 1, 1973. Father Mina began serving at both St. George in Brooklyn and St. Mary and St. Antonious Church in Queens. He celebrated the Holy Liturgy on Sundays at St. George and on Saturdays at St. Mary and St. Antonious Church.

Fr. Mina Yanni's service extended to other communities in other states as well. He and the other early priests carried the responsibility of meeting the spiritual needs of several communities until they were large enough to financially support a permanent priest. St. George Church's congregation in Brooklyn experienced such growth. The church building was expanded in 1984 and again in 1996, increasing its capacity to five hundred people. St. George Church is noteworthy for nurturing a score of dedicated new priests to serve in other churches across the United States. I was invited as a speaker to conferences addressing the challenges of marital relations and family issues. Mr. Nassif Banout related narratives of St. George's history of expansion.

Hegomen Fr. Youhanna Tadros Guirgis

HH Pope Shenouda III decided to find a permanent priest for St. Mary and St. Antonious Church in place of the late Fr. Antonious Baky. In January 1973, he ordained Fr. Youhanna Tadros, who already lived with his family and worked in the United States before ordination. Father Tadros came to New York in March 1973 to serve the congregation in Queens and surrounding areas. He was well known in the Coptic community as Abouna Hanna, and his church is one of the most well-organized Coptic churches in the country. Father Hanna was famous for his strict expectations from both young and old worshippers. He demanded absolute respect and understandably considered the angels and Almighty God Himself to be invisibly present during the Holy Liturgy. During the liturgy, praying and listening to the voice of God was of utmost importance, and all had to be quiet, standing in awe while the Bible was being read. For him, once you entered the sanctuary, it was not the time or place to speak with those around you.

To Father Hanna (departed May 22, 2018), the church was more than a building; it was a sacred place set apart for the worship of God. It's God's house, a house of prayer, where the saints and angels dwell. This was one of his unwavering messages to the congregation and all who attended the service. Children were quite welcome, but parents had to be mindful of their behavior. His stern face silently reprimanded those who dared to forget or happened to be attending service for the first time. His sternness, though, was matched by his broad smiles and warm hugs. His joy and love were always affectionate and genuine.

Pope Cyril VI in the Life of Father Youhanna

Father Youhanna loved and admired Pope Cyril VI and fondly wrote about him in the church's monthly magazine, *Path of Life* (*Tarik El-Hayah* in Arabic). He spoke of the pope as a spiritual giant and considered him a saint long before he was canonized as one. Father Youhanna was a strong supporter of Pope Kyrillos Publications, which was formed to import spiritual and religious books for the new generation of Copts who were born in or immigrated with their parents to America.

True enough, Father Hanna's prophecy of Pope Cyril VI's early sainthood was fulfilled, a first in the history of the popes of Alexandria. Pope Cyril VI, just forty-two years after his death, was canonized as a saint by the Holy Synod of the Coptic Orthodox Church headed by HH Pope Tawadros II. On June 20, 2013, in Cairo, the Holy Synod declared the official recognition of Pope Cyril VI (Kyrillos VI) and Archdeacon Habib Girgis as saints. Their names are included in the Coptic Synaxarium and mentioned in the Mass among the saints of the church. As saints, Coptic churches may be built in honor of their names.

Father Hanna once wrote that the number of documented miracles performed by Pope Cyril VI and his patron saint, St. Mena, are immense. These well-documented miracles have been known for decades, and he predicted that they may never stop as long as there is life on earth.

Father Hanna was a humble priest, and like Pope Cyril VI, he was a man of prayer. He was laser-focused on developing a life of prayer and always exhorted people to pray with the holy hours (*Agpeya*) and, if possible, all seven hours in the Coptic Book of the Canonical Hours. Many who heeded his advice discovered the wonders of memorizing and reciting the psalms and praising the Lord for His love through these daily prayers.

The life of our beloved Father Youhanna was complemented by his wife, Tasoni Samia. She was a loving wife, a dedicated mother, and a leader-servant who, through her sacrificial love, served discreetly. She opened her heart and home for members of the congregation, visitors, and newcomers to the US. She and Father Youhanna offered room and board from the heart, and many people have spoken highly of their love, warmth, and generosity.

Incredible Annual Retreats

Since the mid-1980s, St. Mary and St. Antonious Church has been offering family retreats. It started as long weekends organized by Father Youhanna and myself as an invited speaker. Due to its success, it became an annual event, opening to other churches in the early 1990s. The retreats were held every Memorial Day weekend in major cities outside New York, including Philadelphia, East Brunswick, Cherry Hill, and Boston. They were offered at little cost to allow as many families as possible from every church to join. The retreats were well structured, all-inclusive, and were centered on preplanned themes that were carefully selected for personal growth, emotional healing, and spiritual enrichment.

The retreats focused on creating trusted relationships through intellectual stimulation and challenges based on applicable research. New scientific findings were shared to encourage healthy family relations. Workshops incorporated hands-on techniques in problem solving (e.g., role-play) to give participants skills to handle problematic social and family interactions. Spiritual and emotional support for each member of the family via designated spiritual meetings and recreational activities were an integral part of the retreat. Leisure time and taking fun breaks were also built into the weekend.

All these topics and activities were specifically designed to deliver a powerful life transformation. Planners and speakers made sure to offer topics that were age appropriate for children. Special sessions were conducted for couples, teens, and parents with special challenges dealing with children.

The retreats and conferences were spearheaded by the very kind, loving, and humble priest Hegomen Fr. Antonios Makaryus (an engineer by profession who pursued a postgraduate degree in counseling). He was assisted by many dedicated servants, all of who were well organized and detail oriented, but most of all by Emad Fahmy, a successful CPA and doctor in counseling candidate, and his wife, Suzy, who was an articulate professional in corporate America. They were supported by an army of servants and soldiers who the Lord knows by name (such as Wedad Dimyan). These motivated people worked every year behind the scenes with open minds and hearts and without a single complaint to meet the needs of the flock. They all belong in the "Hall of Fame" of our Coptic community, and their contributions should be treasured for generations to come.

The Summit of Success

Archangel Raphael and St. John Chrysostom's Eleventh Annual Family Conference at the Marriott Philadelphia West Hotel on May 29–31, 2010, was a smashing success. Its planning, organization, and agenda provided a wonderful model for future conferences. The family-selected, age-appropriate topics were well received according to participant feedback. For the first time, a new generation of leaders who were once young participants in these family retreats led youth meetings and discussions.

Mr. Sherif and Mrs. Dalal Samaan led a youth group on the topic "My Truth, Your Truth, Who's Truth." Mr. Randy and Mrs. Mary Wikris led the teens in a discussion on how modern media and social networks encourage promiscuity and careless sexual encounters. The presentation "What Do You Do and Who Do You Listen To?" included a powerful movie that featured life situations out of today's headlines.

Most importantly, Father Antonious spoke on the theme, "The Need for Change and How to Make the Actual Inner Transformation Before Disaster Strikes." I was an invited speaker at the retreat who was privileged to speak about several topics: "Obstacles to Mental and Personal Growth," "Oneness Yet Diversity within Marital and Family Unity," and "The Connection between Acquired Emotional Intelligence and Inner Transformation."

CHAPTER 10

◄•••)◆(•••►

History Is Made: Coptic Mass Celebrated in Philadelphia

Yesterday is history, tomorrow is a mystery, today is a gift of God, which is why we call it the present.

—William Keane

Philadelphia: Home of American Independence

Philadelphia is well known as the birthplace of independence in the United States and the nation's cradle of liberty. It began back in 1776, when the thirteen American colonies announced their independence from the British Empire with the Declaration of Independence. Philadelphians, along with other Americans, still mark this day of freedom every July 4. The Liberty Bell was rung on July 8, 1776, to celebrate the first public reading of the Declaration of Independence. It bears the legend, "Proclaim liberty throughout all the land unto all the inhabitants. It shall be a Jubilee for you." (Leviticus 25:10)

The Angel of the Church of Philadelphia

The following biblical message is addressed to the angel of the church in Philadelphia:

"These things says He who is holy, He who is true, 'He who has the key of David, He who opens and no one shuts, and shuts and no one opens. I know your works. See, I have set before you an open door, and no one can shut it; for you have a little strength, have kept My word, and have not denied My name.'" (Revelation 3:7–8)

As a member of the Coptic American Association of New York, I had the good fortune to visit Philadelphia, the great city of brotherly love, in September 1969 on a temporary assignment. Eventually I would be appointed to work at Thomas Jefferson Medical College of Thomas Jefferson University. While in New York, I would join Father Rofael on home visitations with Copts who were newly arrived in the area. Father Rofael, upon finding out about my intended move to another state, was very supportive and promised to come and visit. He gladly did, and during that visit, he met with a few families who had recently immigrated and lived in Philadelphia. Father Rofael encouraged them to join other members in New Jersey and New York for the monthly Mass he conducted there.

A couple of these families continued to attend the service every time Father Rofael celebrated the Holy Liturgy in New York. Many new Coptic settlers were not able to make the trip to New York but yearned for him to celebrate Mass with them in Philadelphia. He planned the visit and celebrated the Holy Liturgy at the Central Presbyterian Church on Broad Street near city hall in October 1969. There were no more than six Coptic families present, three of whom were of other denominations. They were joined by many members and friends from the New York area, and it was a joyous day. This gathering planted the seed that paved the way to establishing St. George Coptic Orthodox Church in Philadelphia. The following day, the Sunday edition of the *Philadelphia Inquirer* announced, "History Is Made: Coptic Mass Celebrated in Philadelphia."

After Father Rofael's visit to Philadelphia, a few families started to make the weekly trip to St. Mark Church in Jersey City, New Jersey, joining others at the celebration of the first Holy Liturgy on Sunday, March 22, 1970, and beyond. The celebrant was Fr. Rofael Younan Nakhla. These trips continued for almost a year and a half. Meanwhile, spiritual activities continued to take place within the domestic church of several families in the Philadelphia area, satisfying a persistent need to preserve a Coptic identity and form important community bonds.

The Amish: An Ideal Culture

Coptic families admired the local Amish people and their view of the church. For them, the word "church" doesn't refer to a building but to the congregation. Their services are held in individual homes on a rotating basis. These practices reminded the Coptic community of the importance of the domestic church in their own lives. The Amish's actual service is approximately three hours, followed by lunch and Sunday school service for children and young adults—a familiar lengthy practice in the Coptic Church. Many Copts enjoyed visiting the Amish community in Lancaster, Pennsylvania, admiring how they lived a simple life and were reluctant to adopt the conveniences of the modern world. As fellow Christians and hospitable by nature, they welcomed many Coptic families into their homes. Their simplicity, generosity, and warm reception fascinated our new arrivals to Pennsylvania, and their fellowship and practice had a big influence on more than a few families of the Coptic community. In the 1960s, one rarely encountered anyone who even knew what the word "Copt" meant, let alone where they came from. The Amish did not ask, nor did they wish to make anyone uncomfortable. As such, many families from both communities enjoyed genuinely close relations.

Copts needed all the support they could find in their new land. Coptic families, small in number as they were, became supportive of one another, spending at least Sundays together. A few families understandably felt uncomfortable and insecure within the sometimes overwhelming American culture, and some suffered tremendously from homesickness and even wished to return to Egypt.

Cultivating Awareness: Who Are the Copts?

In a new environment and culture, Coptic community members were not always aware of how they came across to others. The Copts were and are proud of their heritage. Some might have inadvertently appeared pompous when they spoke about themselves, and it became obvious to others that the rhetoric needed to be toned down. Looking for a way to solve the issue without offending anyone, the approach was to rely on the feedback of peers, friends, and mentors. Individual Copts would seek candid, critical, and objective perspectives on how they were presenting themselves. In the interest of positive assimilation, they also asked to be called out if anyone noticed behavior that seemed odd or not in tune with acceptable norms of communication. A modest view of one's own importance, especially among simple, kind, and humble people like the Amish, certainly helped to open doors among other cultures.

Therefore, some people thought it would be a good idea to prepare a pamphlet explaining who the Copts were. It was written in simple terms and without excessive jargon. The writers believed it would be a powerful way to explain the complex history, background, and beliefs of Coptic Christians, as well as their love for their church. The title of the pamphlet was *Who Are the Copts?* It was professionally printed and shared with guests or anyone who wanted to know about the small Coptic community. Later, it was revised and reprinted by St. George Church after it was incorporated in 1973. The original pamphlet, though, has been preserved in the archive of St. George Coptic Church of greater Philadelphia.

Al-Karma Magazine

In 1971, *Al-Karma* (*Vineyard*), the first Coptic magazine written especially for Copts, debuted. The name of the magazine was not randomly chosen—it was meant to commemorate Archdeacon Habib Girgis's famous magazine, *Al-Karma*. He was the dean of the renowned Coptic Theological Seminary in Cairo, Egypt. His original *Al-Karma*, first issued in 1907, was very popular.[33] The new edition of the magazine was published monthly with a mission to serve Coptic Christians throughout the United States.

The revived *Al-Karma* was spearheaded by Drs. Nabil and Norma El-Shammaa. They were assisted by Mr. Rafik Maurice Khalifa, and I contributed articles in the early days. The magazine was designed to explore spiritual living in more depth for church members. It also covered pressing issues that members were facing in their daily lives as newly settled immigrants. It was written in both English and Arabic, with a special section for children and a news corner.

Many of the articles talked about how to become happier and healthier living in the here and now. They encouraged readers to maintain their spiritual life in a materialistic society that did not yet have an established Coptic Church. By sharing community news and welcoming newcomers in a new land, it encouraged those who were homesick for their mother church in Egypt. It presented ways to become grounded in ourselves, our Coptic community, and the world we lived in. Special sections were devoted to "Where to Go for Help," the healthy upbringing of children, and making better choices for schooling at home and in public schools.

The magazine also listed the names and telephone numbers of Coptic priests all over the United States, though there were only a few of them at that time. This allowed readers to reach out for confession, spiritual guidance, and needed spiritual services such as baptisms, prayers, and visitation of the sick. *Al-Karma* served the community by allowing people to link together, exchange information, and develop new contacts. The magazine was offered free of charge and contained no commercial advertisements, nor did the names of the editorial and production team appear in its pages.

The publication of *Al-Karma* lasted for at least a couple of decades. When Dr. El-Shammaa's family moved to Washington, DC, he established *St. George* magazine to serve the Coptic community nationwide. This unique publication remains a pillar of the Coptic community and is currently overseen by HG Bishop Michael. Most importantly, the practice of not carrying the names of those who prepare, write for, edit, and distribute the magazine speaks volumes about the humble precedent of the late Dr. Nabil El-Shammaa and his family.

Forming a Planning Committee

The hope that had been lurking in the hearts of the Copts of Philadelphia began to draw near. They greatly desired to live a spiritual life and to have a church of their own where they could gather as members of the body of Christ. The small Coptic community yearned to pursue a life they had lived within the bosom of their mother church in Egypt.

Although the establishment of a church was an important goal, the general impression was that it would take a few years for this dream to come true. The small Coptic community simply could not raise enough money to buy or even rent a property for a church as well as meet ongoing financial obligations for a full-time priest as mandated by the mother church in Egypt. In the face of these difficulties, a committee was created to plan for such a project and work on its costs and funding resources.

Initial thoughts and input from members of the Coptic community were gathered, and many didn't consider the project possible at the time. The role of the committee was simplified, and its members focused their efforts on summarizing the estimated costs. That would give the community the basic information they needed to determine their funding requirements.

However, another serious project took priority, and that was to teach children their faith in Sunday school. It was the responsibility of the parents to teach their children the traditions and dogma of the Coptic Church, as well as principles such as justice, fear of God, and other virtues that safeguarded them from a liberal and permissive society.

Forming the Pope Kyrillos Committee

A committee was formed consisting of a group of dedicated individuals known for their long history of service. Their mission was to outline practical steps to achieve the following goals:

- Raising the second generation of Christian Copts in complete accordance with the faith and doctrine of the Coptic Orthodox Church of Alexandria.
- Designing an age-appropriate curriculum with a clear list of learning goals.

- Identifying constraints that would impact curriculum design due to culture differences, language barriers, and limited time during weekly Sunday meetings.
- Importing and distributing religious, educational, and spiritual books, including books that reflected on the lives of the saints and early church fathers such as St. Basil the Great, who defended the orthodox faith against Arian heresy.
- Distributing material on the lives of contemporary saints, including St. Abraam, Bishop of Faiyum; Abdel Messih El-Makari; and Pope Cyril VI.
- Translating select religious books for children who spoke and communicated in English, being sure to retain the original tone and intent of the biblical message and tradition of the church.

It is worth noting that most of the committee members sponsored these activities and distributed these imported books free of charge to whoever requested them anywhere in the country.

Within a few years, the committee asked some of its members to officially incorporate these structured activities to facilitate the importation and distribution of these educational and religious books across the nation. Articles of incorporation were filed for the purpose of carrying on its perpetual mission with a vision to reach every Coptic family and community in the United States and Canada. The entity was finally incorporated in Pennsylvania on June 6, 1975, as a nonprofit organization pursuant to law approved November 15, 1972 (see Appendix I: Pope Kyrillos Certificate of Corporation).

The new organization received unlimited support from the late Mr. Sabry Abdalla, author and publisher of the history and miracles of Pope Cyril VI for decades, and Ms. Soad Messiha and Mr. Mina Sabry Esq., proprietors of the St. Mina Bookstore in Cairo. Without their tireless support, dedication, and sacrificial love, the Copts in Pennsylvania and other states would not have the wealth of books they do for their education and service, and the history and treasures of Coptic Church theology, soteriology, faith, and tradition would never have reached the faithful.

Incorporating St. George Coptic Orthodox Church

The families in Philadelphia yearned to have a church of their own. Some members decided to go from passionate thoughts about creating a nonprofit entity to making it a reality. To begin the process of incorporating the church, both the state and federal government required the bylaws of the corporation specifying how it would conduct business, the duties of its directors, and the responsibilities of its officers and employees.

The first step was to present a final draft of the church bylaws to the office of HH Pope Cyril VI for review and approval. The first ever Coptic Orthodox Church bylaws for a US church was finally approved by Pope Cyril VI and was received on December 3, 1969. The new bylaws satisfied the required documentation for filing with the state of Pennsylvania, other states, and the federal government to ensure tax-exempt status. The original historic copy of the bylaws was presented to HH Pope Tawadros II on October 6, 2018, during the golden jubilee celebration honoring the first immigrants to the United States. (A copy is still preserved at the library of St. George Church of greater Philadelphia.)

The second step was to choose a business name. The name needed to be unique—it couldn't be confused with any other existing entity. The process started by contacting the Department of State, Commonwealth of Pennsylvania, in Harrisburg on April 1972. On November 17, 1972, the authorization to select a name for the church was finally approved. The preliminary letter of approval stated the following:

> The Name "Coptic Orthodox Church of St. George" (Non-Profit) appears presently available for Corporate use and has been reserved in this office for a period of sixty days from November 17, 1972 to January 15, 1973, inclusive. On submitting papers to the Department of State, please refer to this letter.

The letter was signed by James G. Krause, State Corporation Bureau Director.

The third step required the incorporators to advertise that they had formed a corporation with the Pennsylvania Department of State in two newspapers of general circulation, one being a legal newspaper. On December 15, 1972, notice of publication was advertised in the *Philadelphia Inquirer* and the *Legal Intelligencer*, stating the following:

> NOTICE IS HEREBY GIVEN THAT Articles of Incorporation will be filed with the Department of State of the Commonwealth of Pennsylvania, at Harrisburg, Pa. On Monday, the 15th day of January, 1973, for the purpose of obtaining a Certificate of Incorporation of proposed business corporation to be organized under the Business Corporation Law of the Commonwealth of Pennsylvania, approved May 5, 1933. The name of the proposed corporation is Coptic Orthodox Church of St. George.
>
> The purpose for which it is to be organized: Administering the liturgy and the sacraments in Philadelphia, Pa.

The fourth step was to file the articles of incorporation, which was done on May 3, 1973, and carried the official number 3-1-73-22-303,304. The articles of incorporation of the Coptic Orthodox Church of St. George were approved and filed under, and pursuant to, the provisions of the nonprofit law approved November 15, 1972, by Act 271. The Pennsylvania Department of State issued an official certification of approval on May 31, 1973. The certificate had the seal of the state of Pennsylvania and was signed by the secretary of the commonwealth, C. Delores Tucker (see Appendix II).

The fifth step was to submit an application to the Pennsylvania Department of Revenue to obtain a Certificate of Sales and Tax Certificate of Exemption. The correspondence application exemption number was 32204150; the Department of Revenue then issued exemption number 75-29475-4. The certificate was issued to St. George Coptic Church.

The sixth step was to apply to the Internal Revenue Service, Department of the Treasury, in Philadelphia seeking tax-exempt status under section 501(c)(3) of the Internal Revenue Code as of May 1973.

The seventh step was to request an official copy of the tax-exempt certificate for display. The certificate, which included the employer identification number 23-7447 806, testified that St. George Coptic Church was not a private foundation within the meaning of section 509(a) of the tax code.

CHAPTER 11

The Law of Supply and Demand

In our own lives the voice of God speaks slowly,
a syllable at a time. Reaching the peak of years,
dispelling some of our intimate illusions and learning how
to spell the meaning of life-experiences backwards, some of us
discover how the scattered syllables form a single phrase.
—Abraham Joshua Heschel

St. George Church

St. George Coptic Orthodox Church in Philadelphia started as a sprout that would take four years to grow into a small tree. Economic theory dictates that there is a relationship between supply and demand. Generally speaking, the demand for something underlies the forces behind the allocation of resources. Applying this theory, the case for appointing a priest to serve the few Coptic families in Philadelphia was not viable. Even though celebrating the Holy Liturgy started there as early as October 1969 by the Rev. Fr. Rofael Younan, Pope Shenouda III, the new pope, whose papacy began on November 14, 1971, would not allow a permanent priest to serve in Philadelphia until the number of families had reached at least thirty. The reasoning, understandably, was for the small community to be financially able to support a priest. The Holy Liturgy, however, was occasionally celebrated by visiting priests from Egypt who happened to be in the area.

It would take until late 1972 to reach the numbers of families required to send a priest. The pope delegated Fr. Tadros Yacoub Malaty to oversee family registration and to report the census accordingly. Also, a map had to be drawn of the location of these families in Philadelphia and the surrounding area to show exactly where the majority of them resided. This was the direct reason why a couple of churches in New York were delegated priests before Philadelphia. Most newly immigrated families resided in New York and New Jersey, and the Coptic population was concentrated there. In fact, that was the same reason why Fr. Morcos Elias Abdel Messih, the first priest ordained for America, ended up residing permanently in Canada. Despite all, arrangements were eventually made to have him serve in the United States.

Canada had opened its door to immigration in 1964, and the Coptic community there had been sizable even before the United States enacted its new immigration laws in 1968. It became clear then that starting a church in any part of the world other than Africa would depend on the density of the Coptic population in the area so the necessary financial means to support a priest would be in place. Having said that, the hierarchy of the Coptic Church never abandoned any group anywhere in the world (as far as we know) who needed service, regardless of their financial situation. That in turn placed more burdens on many priests by adding responsibilities beyond their role to serve only their congregations. Priests had to fly from one place to another to meet the needs of those without a permanent priest. They flew far and wide, caring for the needs of the Copts scattered all over the US and Canada.

Responding to a question crediting him with building churches worldwide, Pope Shenouda III said with all humility, "I did not build churches; the people did!"

The records of the early church illustrate that very point. They reflect that a general meeting of the Coptic Orthodox Church's priests was held in the Holy Trinity Monastery for the Russian Orthodox in Gordonville, New York, on November 13 and 14, 1970. The meeting was held based on HH Pope Cyril VI's instructions to call a general meeting for the only four priests that were in North America at that time. Also in attendance were the secretaries of the boards of their perspective churches, thus representing their congregations. Fr. Morcos Abdel Messih was chosen to chair the meeting and Fr. Gabriel Abdelsayed to act as secretary.

Two important subjects were discussed. First, the distribution of services and activities among the four priests and prospective churches in different states was established. Second, each of the four dioceses would set up a special fund for serving their regions. In addition, each diocese would contribute fifty dollars monthly to a general fund starting January 1, 1971, for expenses devoted to social and general services in all of North America, including publishing activities, quick financial support for the needy, and seminars and general meetings. The regions of the priests' services were as follows:

- Fr. Tadros Yacoub Malaty: California, Colorado, Oregon, Texas, Utah, and Washington.
- Fr. Marcos Elias Abdel Messih: Ontario, Illinois, Iowa, Michigan, Minnesota, Ohio, Wisconsin, Alberta, British Columbia, Saskatchewan, Manitoba.
- Fr. Rofael Younan Nakhla: Quebec, Indiana, Kansas, Kentucky, Maine, Massachusetts, Missouri, Pittsburgh, Rhode Island, Tennessee, Newfoundland, New Brunswick, Nova Scotia.
- Fr. Gabriel Ameen Abdelsayed: New York, New Jersey, Alabama, Connecticut, Florida, Georgia, Louisiana, Maryland, North Carolina, Philadelphia, South Carolina, West Virginia, Washington, DC.[34]

St. George Church's First Priest: The Very Rev. Fr. Mankarious Awadalla

Upon hearing the news that the pope had assigned Father Mankarious to serve in St. George Church in Philadelphia, many people were elated. I knew Father Mankarious when he celebrated the Holy Liturgy in New York in February and March of 1969. He resumed his service after returning from visiting his son on the

West Coast and celebrated the Holy Liturgy on Palm Sunday, Good Friday, and Easter of the same year. Many congregation members saw an opportunity to have their own shepherd and gathered signatures to petition the pope to continue his service in New York.

The CAA board called a meeting to discuss the issue and concluded that Father Mankarious might not be the perfect choice as their priest. The given reasons were "age, language barrier, and having a big family" as well as a lack of financial resources to support him. The CAA communicated their objection to both Bishop Samuel and Bishop Gregorios and sent a separate letter to HH Pope Cyril VI.

New York's Loss Was Philadelphia's Gain: A Brief Biography of Rev. Fr. Mankarious Awadalla

Father Awadalla was born in Cairo, Egypt, on December 15, 1913. He enrolled in secondary education in 1928 and finished his baccalaureate degree among the top graduates in all of Egypt. His parents wanted him to join the faculty of medicine. Against their wishes, he instead joined the Coptic Orthodox Seminary to fulfill a childhood dream to serve the Lord. He received his bachelor's degree in 1936 and ranked first in his graduating class. He was taught by distinguished professors, including the renowned late Archdeacon Habib Girgis, Hegomen Ibrahim Atiya, and Mr. Yassa Abdel-Massih, to name a few. Before he was delegated to serve in Philadelphia, he served in Cairo at the church of St. Virgin Mary in Shoubra, the church of St. George in Heliopolis, and the church of St. Virgin Mary in Zamalek.

Fr. Mankarious Awadalla had been a grateful disciple of Archdeacon Habib Girgis (1876–1951). He taught at the Coptic Theological Seminary in Cairo and authored five books on Coptic Church dogma. In these books, he elaborated on the principles, canon, and seven sacraments that were instituted by Jesus and entrusted to the church. He specialized in divine revelation, i.e., the Word of God (Bible and tradition), the Word of God incarnate (Jesus), and the truths connected to divine revelation. In his books, Father Mankarious guided his seminarians to understand that the sacraments, divinely instituted, were dogma and part of the Holy Liturgy.

This brief reflection barely covers all he had written regarding Christian dogma as taught and practiced in the Coptic Church. The aim here is only to highlight the crux of his writings for the reader to get a flavor for what dogma meant and still means in the Coptic Christian faith.

Father Mankarious was a reputable teacher who taught orthodox liturgical studies, canonical tradition, and the Old Testament. For almost two decades, he was the editor of *The Church Teaching* magazine. Father Mankarious served in the United States and eventually settled in Canada after serving St. George Church in Philadelphia (1973–1974).[35] After moving to Canada, he became the third priest to serve the newly immigrated Coptic community. He ministered in the Ottawa and Mississauga areas, and for over twenty years he undertook the monthly service for the congregation of Kingston, Ontario. By the grace of God, he founded the Church of Ti Agia Maria and St. Demiana the Martyr in 1990 in Etobicoke, Canada, where he served until his departure in December 2009.

Father Mankarious's Mentor

Father Mankarious presented his published books in gratitude and recognition of his renowned mentor, Archdeacon Habib Girgis. He had been an influential professor who taught Father Mankarious during his undergraduate studies. He eventually became a contemporary saint when he was canonized by the Holy Synod of the Coptic Church on June 20, 2013. At the turn of the twentieth century, Archdeacon Habib established Sunday schools to fight against the radical influence of Western Christian missionaries who aimed to encourage Copts to adopt their brand of faith. The archdeacon occupied a prominent place in the hearts of the Copts as a devout educator and author. He remains a pioneer of Coptic religious and theological education.

Among Professor Habib Girgis's books are the three-volume *Summary of Faith Fundamentals* in 1909 and *Orthodox Christian*

Principles published in three volumes in 1937. His famous magazine, *Al-Karma*, was first issued in 1907, and he was a contributor to many other books. He was the dean of the renowned Coptic Theological Seminary in Cairo, and both HH Pope Shenouda III and Father Mankarious were among his disciples. Archdeacon Habib Girgis was well known as a gifted and zealous saint whose vision and legacy continue to enlighten and guide the Coptic faithful all over the world.

The Joyous News

When it was officially announced that Pope Shenouda III delegated Father Mankarious to St. George Coptic Orthodox Church, the congregation was overjoyed. As an accomplished teacher and highly virtuous priest, he truly was an unexpected and amazing gift. He at first was assigned to serve on a temporary basis since he was en route to visit his son, who was studying engineering in California and was a superb deacon who served with his father occasionally in Philadelphia. HG Bishop Gregorios regarded Father Mankarious as a high-caliber priest and author. Regarding Father Mankarious, he wrote to Eva al Masri Sidhom, president of the CAA, "I testify that he is one of our best priests, especially his knowledge, his character, and his spirituality."

Serving St. George in Philadelphia

Father Mankarious started his service praying the Holy Week preceding Resurrection Sunday in April 1973. The service took place in a rented section of the Tabernacle Baptist Church located at 3700 Chestnut Street in downtown Philadelphia. On Sunday, May 20, a general meeting was called for election of the board of deacons. Nominations were made from the floor, and the voting was carried out by secret ballot. Since Father Mankarious was designated unanimously as the president, the group decided to elect a vice president, a secretary, and a treasurer. When the ballots were tabulated, the results were as follows: Dr. Lewis Khella, vice president, Esmat M. Gabriel, secretary, and Dr. Nabih Abdou, treasurer. Members of the board who were elected were Mr. Raafat S. Mishriky, Dr. Nabil A. El-Shammaa, Dr. Rodolph M. Yanney, Mr. Sidrak F. Wasef, and Dr. Morris F. Guirguis. The election's results were submitted to the Pennsylvania Department of State in Harrisburg as a final step to remain in compliance with the state regulating body. A letter was drawn and signed by each member and elected officer of the board of deacons and sent to the state on May 22, 1973 (see Appendix III).

The structure of incorporating and electing the governing body of the church was completed. However, the church was still in its infancy; deacons or qualified subdeacons were either not available or not well trained to help with Pascha, Good Friday, and other highly specialized services of the Holy Week. Father Mankarious, most of the time, was a one-man show. He would call on his son Makary, a well-qualified, well-trained, and gifted young man, to lend a helping hand. When he had the opportunity to serve, he would fly back from his school in California to be of help. He had a beautiful voice and masterly filled his role as a deacon.

The church at that time had only two ordained deacons. There were no tunics (*tunia*) or stoles (*patrachil*) for others to wear. There was no Coptic altar per se, no liturgy prayer books or hymn books available for members, and no consecrated items to officiate services like baptism.

Despite all, Father Mankarious was a peaceful, loving, and caring man who almost always wore a smile. He was the right person for the congregation, a seasoned priest and educator who patiently carried out his responsibilities despite his relatively advanced age.

Father Mankarious was quite unfamiliar with the city of Philadelphia and could not drive on its busy highways, so he mostly depended on his son or someone else to drive him around. However, he swiftly mastered the use of the public transportation system. Members of the congregation were happy with his presence among them and wrote a petition signed by the church board and most members of the congregation requesting to have him continue his service on a permanent basis. The pope agreed, and the spiritual service continued unceasing for fifteen months.

Eventually, Father Mankarious could not continue living a solitary life in Philadelphia without his wife and children for so long. His son Mark, who was in his early teens, would visit to help him, but he still needed the support, care, and love of his family. Regretfully, at the end of April 1974, Father Mankarious officially requested to be transferred to Canada, where his family had settled. The pope hesitantly approved the transfer, and it took place in July 1974. The church of St. George sadly had to respect his wish, but he remained in their hearts and minds. The congregation was grateful for the time he spent serving and blessing the flock with his presence.

Noteworthy Chronicles: Father's Prophecy

One of Fr. Mankarious Awadalla's hopes and dreams during the Yom Kippur War was that the United States would free itself from dependency on Arab oil. During the war, the oil-producing Arab states of OPEC imposed an embargo on nations supporting Israel in the war. The embargo had immediate and long-lasting effects. One had to get up as early as four o'clock in the morning to get gas. Cars waited in long lines during the gas shortage. Father Mankarious actually prophesied that the day would come when the United States would no longer be dependent on Arab oil. That seemed hard to believe at that time. Lo and behold, his prayers and prophecy have been fulfilled. According to oilprice.com on May 2, 2018, the United States is not only independent from importing foreign oil but also exported a record 8.3 million barrels per day. May the good Lord bless his soul.

Historical Perspectives: The Church First Financial Report

The first financial report prepared by the treasurer of St. George Church, Dr. Nabih Ibrahim Abdu, and dated from August 1972 (when the church was in the process of being incorporated) to September 9, 1973, showed an income of $5,969.50, expenses of $4,437.83, and an ending balance of $1,531,67. That balance included $360 credited to a newly formed Washington church. The average monthly salary of the priest serving approximately thirty families then was $600 plus expenses for transportation, telephone, and insurance.

In 1973, $100 was the equivalent of $580.06 in 2018. An average monthly salary of $700 back then would be equivalent to $4,060.42 a month today.

Miraculously Healed

In 1982, Father Mankarious suffered a mild heart attack at the age of sixty-nine, and by the grace of God, he fully recovered from it and continued to serve his flock with vigor, passion, and dedication until he departed. To ensure that the good Lord had healed him completely, he went for a swim and kept swimming to the point of exhaustion. He did not suffer any debilitating symptoms, such as shortness of breath, dizziness, or chest pain. He stated it was a miracle and felt that the Lord extended his life to allow him to continue serving Him.

Pope Shenouda III's Congratulatory Message

On December 13, 2009, the Church of Ti Agia Maria and St. Demiana the Martyr celebrated the sixty-fifth anniversary of her beloved Father Mankarious's ordination. The ceremony was attended by HG Bishop David of the United States, distinguished guests, and a large number of priests in the region. HG Bishop David, representing HH Pope Shenouda III, delivered a special message from His Holiness, congratulating Father Mankarious for his lengthy, loyal, and dedicated service to the Coptic Orthodox Church in many countries.

The following is an excerpt from HG Bishop David's speech in celebration of Father Mankarious's earthly life:

> We always say to the priest may the Lord keep
> your priesthood in purity and righteousness. And
> truly the Lord has kept the priesthood of Father

Mankarious in purity and righteousness, and he has departed this world in the Orthodox Faith which he has always kept in his life.

I am talking about Orthodoxy because Abouna Mankarious represents a truly Orthodox Priest. Any new invention does not belong to the Orthodox teaching, but if we want to reach the Promised Land we have to make sure that we follow in the footsteps of the flock that preceded us.

This is a good example to follow, his love for Orthodoxy, his love for learning, his love for teaching, and he wrote books in a time when there weren't many people who wrote scholarly works, which means not just to write anything but to go and research and produce scholarly books, and he wrote "Manaret El-Aqdas" in five volumes, which I read as a young man and I learned a lot from them.

Many of his students became priests, many became bishops, and also as you heard, Pope Shenouda when he was learning, Father Mankarious was one of the teachers at that time.

CHAPTER 12

One Body with Many Members...
Why Divided?

When faith is completely replaced by creed,
worship by discipline, love by habit;
when the crisis of today is ignored because of
the splendor of the past; when faith
becomes an heirloom rather than a living fountain;
when religion speaks only in the
name of authority rather than with the voice
of compassion—its message becomes
meaningless.

—Abraham Joshua Heschel

As new Coptic arrivals settled in the Philadelphia area, a change in the composition of St. George Church's population gradually took place. Understanding the composition of the congregation will help the reader understand conflicts that eventually arose. Though homogeneous members of one religion and ethnicity, there were still significant differences of opinion on various matters. That in turn hindered cooperation among members. The congregation at the time consisted of clusters, some based in Philadelphia, others in Delaware, and a third in South Jersey. Each group yearned to someday have their own little church, and as such they preferred to ask the priest to travel to their respective locations rather than drive the significant distance to attend the Holy Liturgy in downtown Philadelphia.

Fr. Angelos Boghdadi: The Church's Second Priest

HH Pope Shenouda III, who knew that Father Mankarious would be leaving the area in a few months, had already planned to ordain a priest specifically for St. George Church in Philadelphia. Though technically the second priest, Fr. Angelos Boghdadi was considered the first priest to be ordained by the pope to serve abroad. Father Angelos was a lawyer by profession and a student of the pope during his postgraduate studies at the Coptic Theological Seminary. Apparently, Father Angelos was admired by his peers because of his bold defense of the faith while in Egypt, and he suffered discrimination and threats at his workplace. Obviously, Father Angelos was a brave man, speaking up when he saw something or someone being treated unfairly. As such, he had been subjected to embarrassment, physical danger, and the possibility of losing his job by the Egyptian authorities.

In July 1974, the pope sent this newly ordained priest to replace Father Mankarious and to serve at St. George Church. Unlike the preceding priest, Father Angelos was new to priesthood and had no hands-on experience except for a brief time as a priest in Egypt before he was assigned to serve abroad. He, however, was willing and ready to learn as a humble, energetic, and dedicated priest.

When he arrived at his assignment in Philadelphia, he was faced with a new reality. Members of the congregation were busy establishing their lives and careers and adjusting to life in a new land. It was difficult for everyone to gather on Sundays because they were scattered over many parts of the Delaware Valley, consisting of southeastern Pennsylvania, central and southern New Jersey, and the state of Delaware. In addition, there was a growing Coptic Protestant population in Philadelphia that competed with the Christian Orthodox community for members. They were friendly to newcomers, offering professional help, support, and home visitations, as well as planning social gatherings, trips, and Bible studies.

St. George was still in its early stages in a rental space at the Baptist Tabernacle Church at 3700 Chestnut Street. Not happy with the location, many members preferred relocating to South Philadelphia, so the church moved to a new rental space. It was a small, single-story, vacant Syrian church located at the corner of Tenth and Federal Streets. Despite its size, it was the favored choice of members of the congregation who lived in South Philadelphia and South Jersey. The seating capacity didn't exceed thirty people. The layout didn't resemble a small Coptic Church; it was transformed slightly to accommodate a small altar, but there was no room for deacons to sit in front of it, and no room for baptizing children. There was no air conditioner, and the windows were inoperable and couldn't be opened on hot summer days.

Despite its flaws, the rental price was reasonable, and it was considered a temporary arrangement until the congregation could grow and build or buy their own church. One upside was that it was located next to a Lebanese grocery and bakery where members could buy their supply of Middle Eastern groceries. One might dare to say the store was an attractive draw for many to come to church on a weekly basis!

Father Angelos and his family rented a two-room apartment in the northeast of Philadelphia where many Copts lived. The priest, his wife, his two young daughters, and younger son were a tight-net family, warm, kind, and thrilled to welcome guests at their small apartment.

The priest's wife, Tasoni Yvonne, was a cheerful and tranquil lady. She was very supportive of her husband and very concerned about her children and their future in a liberal society and permissive culture. However, her faith was strong, and she trusted that the Lord who had chosen them to relocate and serve in a new country would shield them from any harm.

The first few months were a breeze, filling the hearts of many with sweet anticipation of fruitful years to come. However, the new priest began to emphasize the orthodox teaching of faith in the Coptic Church in his weekly homily. He boldly addressed the issue of curbing migration of his flock to other denominations. He pit-ted orthodoxy and Protestantism against each other regarding key issues in Christian faith. He emphasized the presence of Christ in the Eucharist.

Whenever the occasion permitted, he would explain additional sacraments in the Coptic Church, including baptism, confirmation, repentance and confession, unction of the sick, matrimony, and holy priesthood. He would strongly declare that the Lord Jesus Christ instituted all these sacraments. He would insist on confession before receiving communion. He was willing to take confession anytime a member wished, either in or outside the church, unless you had a different father in confession. Baptized members had to have been baptized by an ordained priest by the laying on of the apostolic hand.

Some of the members started to feel offended on behalf of members of other denominations. Spouses who were married to non-orthodox members rejected his teachings. They constantly argued with Father Angelos regarding these issues at meetings in the church and in homes, both in his presence and in his absence. Those who defended Father Angelos's strong positions on orthodox belief were avoided or shunned completely. Conflict started to ensue, and the honeymoon was over.

A point of contention emerged in board meetings and in general regarding the nature of the relationship between a priest and his congregation. To many people, it appeared the relationship was more like an employer and employee rather than a shepherd and his flock or a father and his children interacting with mutual respect.

The dynamic in the church continued to become contentious. Some members attempted to "gag" Father Angelos from speaking boldly and truthfully about orthodoxy and defending its beliefs and traditions. I witnessed an incident where the board treasurer demanded the priest visit members' homes if he wanted to receive his monthly salary. He claimed Father Angelos needed to restore peace with some "offended" members and convince them to fill a monthly pledge form committing to active membership. In another incident, a senior priest in the Coptic Church who had been with the congregation for years became quite annoyed at what appeared to be similar treatment from the church board. Rather than receive his monthly salary in person from the board treasurer, he requested that each month his check be placed on the altar where he would pick it up!

All of this tension was exacerbated by the behind-the-scenes politics at the inception of the Coptic Church in New York. As discussed earlier, conflict arose there because of hidden agendas, competing motives, and displays of power. People acted in secrecy and were not interested in resolution. When the source of conflict and those behind it were identified, sincere efforts to smooth things over by the peace-loving majority were not welcomed. Voices of reason and calls for unity went unheeded or were flatly ignored.

Protocol for Grievance Procedures

There has to be a written protocol in the church to deal with a grievance initiated by an individual or group. For the sake of the spiritual mission and salvation of souls, people ought to work their way up the chain of command, beginning as local as possible starting with the priest and then moving on to the bishop, the metropolitan, and then the pope. Most members of St. George Church would have preferred a disputing party to discuss matters of concern openly and frankly. Every effort would have been made to examine the problem carefully and try to find a solution. But in the case of Father Angelos, the disputing party was well aware that the priest was not only adamant in defending the faith and tradition of the Coptic Church but also would not budge. Obviously some members of the church became uncomfortable and unhappy with him because of his stance.

Behind-the-scenes petitions were signed and dispatched to the office of the pope of Alexandria, followed by international telephone calls, telegrams, and even travel to Egypt to present their point of view. Preparing for such a meeting takes advanced planning with the pope's administrative staff. It would take quite some time for the pope to take action, because he usually delegates his representatives to travel abroad and meet with most, if not all, members of a church congregation to verify the nature and source of complaints and the motive behind them.

Direct complaints to the office of the pope are a strange phenomenon of the Coptic laity in the diaspora. Most complaints focus on a priest's performance or lack thereof. One dares to say these "tactics" have been of grave concern to many. A small group rationalizes issues from their point of view and acts on their own rather than transparently sharing their concern. They prefer secrecy and working behind the scenes instead of soliciting collective rational input and sincere feedback from others whose goal is peace and tranquility in their place of worship.

HG Bishop Youhannes: The Late Bishop of Tanta, Egypt

HG Bishop Youhannes was delegated by HH Pope Shenouda III to look into the situation with Father Angelos and gather information. In the spring of 1976, His Grace the bishop, accompanied by Deacon Hani Bebawy (the Very Rev. Fr. David Bebawy), visited my family at our home in Levittown, Pennsylvania. The bishop, well known for his humility and kindness, addressed his concern about the church in Philadelphia. He concluded the meeting by saying he adopted a charitable approach and "the authority of love" in running the affairs of his diocese.

On Sunday, His Grace celebrated the Holy Liturgy at St. George Church. After the Holy Communion, he met with members of the congregation and listened to their concerns and hopes for their church. He sympathized with their concerns, alleviated their tension, and asked probing questions. The members felt good to be heard and supported, although the faces of some looked pinched and anxious even while they were nodding and saying, "Everything's fine." Finally, the bishop conveyed the pope's support and looked forward to resolving the issues of concern, concluding with words of affirmation and kindness.

One Body… Undivided

If there is hope for Christians to move forward together as one body with many members, it lies in the promise that Christianity can bring those of different viewpoints to the same table. They can work collaboratively based on a larger shared faith and the greater common good. Much of what Christians know or think they know could improve if they are transparent about their intentions and wishes and acknowledge the complexity of how other people actually feel. Admittedly, conflict within the one body is here to stay in our earthly life. Congregations will always find themselves dealing with inflated egos, self-promotion, power plays, ploys, and envy. These are "acts of the sinful nature." (Galatians 5:19–21)

Congregation members with disputes are, first and foremost, Christians. As such, they ought to respect the role of the faithful majority along with their spiritual leaders and heed their input rather than object to or ignore their wise intervention. The aim is to facilitate understanding, manage conflict, and restore unity, which requires discussing matters of concern openly and frankly. They must trust that the Holy Spirit dwells inside every believer. All must battle against sinful desires to enjoy the fruit of the Holy Spirit.

Christians know that the Holy Spirit gives them the power they need to reject disunity and disharmony and remain one body in Christ. They must heed St. Paul's wisdom in his letter to the Ephesians:

> I then, a prisoner for the Lord, urge you to live
> in a manner worthy of the call you have received,
> with all humility and gentleness, with patience,
> bearing with one another through love, striving
> to preserve the unity of spirit through the bond
> of peace: one body and one spirit, as you were
> also called to one hope of your call; one Lord,
> one faith, one baptism. (Ephesians 4:1–5)

We may never attain the unity described by St. Paul's inspired words. Eventually one realizes that some disruptive individuals or groups just do not want to engage in solving whatever issue is at hand. It is not crucial, then, to keep trying to engage and reason with them when they clearly do not want to reciprocate. Some individuals hold grudges, which gives them a degree of moral superiority. Others adopt a combative stance against anything and everything, no matter how rational, beneficial, or worthy it may be.

Another unfortunate pattern of behavior is when people who one wouldn't normally think of as controlling insist on a particular action or viewpoint regardless of different or even better viewpoints. The same goes for those in leadership positions: they have goals, ideas, and expectations for how others should act and think in the "right" way. There's nothing wrong with declaring what is biblically correct; it is another thing to dictate, demand, and reprimand in the absence of a charitable attitude and humbly serving in the leader-servant role.

Seeking and Saving Our Souls

In the final analysis, we all need to be diligent in maintaining peace and inner tranquility. During the inevitable times when things become less than peaceful and harmonious, all should do their best to maintain charity as members of the one body, staying calm and not slipping into inappropriate or sinful behavior such as anger, gossip, frustration, and resentment. The best advice is to take to heart St. Thomas Aquinas's inspiring wisdom: "To know whom to avoid is a great means of saving our souls."

CHAPTER 13

The Bicentennial Celebration:
Historical Perspectives

A people without the knowledge of their past
history, origin, and culture is
like a tree without roots.

—Marcus Garvey

Bicentennial Celebrations (1976)

On Sunday, July 4, 1976, America celebrated the two hundredth anniversary of the adoption of the Declaration of Independence. President Gerald Ford stated that one of the greatest moments of his life was serving as president during the country's Bicentennial celebrations. He joined millions across the United States in celebrating freedom and democracy, traveling throughout the country and participating in numerous events. In his opening remarks at one such event at Independence Hall in Philadelphia, the president stated:

> The American adventure began here with a firm reliance on the protection of Divine Providence. It continues in a common conviction that the source of our blessings is a loving God, in whom

we trust. Therefore, I ask all the members of the American family, our guests and friends, to join me now in a moment of silent prayer and meditation in gratitude for all that we have received and to ask continued safety and happiness for each of us and for the United States of America.[36]

Egyptomania: The 1976 Treasures of Tutankhamun Tour

The Treasures of Tutankhamun tour was planned to coincide with America's Bicentennial celebration. The show opened at the National Gallery of Art in Washington, DC, on November 17, 1976. President Ford had signed the Arts and Artifacts Indemnity Act in 1975, overcoming a major hurdle to the Tutankhamen exhibition involving concern over insuring priceless treasures from damage and loss. The American and Egyptian curators selected fifty-five artifacts for the journey.

The Treasures of Tutankhamun tour owed its inception to two other presidents: Richard Nixon and Anwar Sadat of Egypt. President Nixon, on his journey of peace in the Middle East in June 1974, made Egypt his first stop and met with President Sadat for negotiations. The pact they discussed included a provision for an American tour of artifacts from the tomb of the pharaoh Tutankhamun (ca. 1341 BC–ca. 1323 BC). Eleanor Boba, writing for the online encyclopedia of Washington state history at HistoryLink.org, reports:

> It is impossible to overstate the phenomenon that was Tut during the run of the exhibition. As Egyptomania goes, perhaps it can only be compared to the excitement that greeted the discovery and unveiling of the young pharaoh's tomb in 1922.[37]

Rev. Fr. Angelos H. Boghdadi: A Distinguished Representative

During the Bicentennial celebrations in July of 1976, the 484-foot Egyptian yacht *El Horria* (Arabic for "freedom") visited

Washington, DC, to deliver an ancient Egyptian stela—a carved stone pillar signifying dedication and commemoration. The stela, which would be installed in the Smithsonian Institution, was Egypt's bicentennial gift to the United States. First Lady Betty Ford went aboard and toured the yacht, making note of the fact that the queen's stateroom was bigger than the king's.

On July 20, 1976, a reception was held on the *El Horria* docked on the Delaware River at the foot of Chestnut Street. The Rev. Fr. Angelos Boghdadi was among the distinguished guests representing St. George Coptic Orthodox Church in greater Philadelphia. He chatted warmly with former brigadier general and US ambassador to Belgium John Eisenhower and his wife, Barbara. The *Philadelphia Inquirer* has the one and only picture of the three of them conversing and smiling on the deck of the Egyptian yacht.[38]

History of El Horria Yacht

The senior Egyptian officer aboard the yacht was Adm. Mohammed Aly Mohammed—a gracious host, friendly, confident, personable, and well spoken. According to the *Philadelphia Inquirer*, a tour of the yacht revealed magnificent inlaid woodwork and furnishings: "The Empress Eugenie of France was aboard the Egyptian yacht when it sailed through the Suez Canal in 1869—the first ship to pass through the canal. As a thank-you gift, the Empress gave the vessel a magnificent piano."[39]

The guests marveled that almost all the original furniture was still in the reception rooms and salons and the original artwork depicting Egyptian antiquity was still on the walls. The original name of the yacht was *El Mahrousa* (Arabic: "the protected") from the time of Khedive Ismail Pasha of Egypt and Sudan (1830–1895). He was known as "Ismail the Magnificent," and his philosophy can be glimpsed in a statement he made in 1879: "My country is no longer in Africa; we are now part of Europe. It is therefore natural for us to adopt a new system adapted to our social conditions."[40]

The yacht carried three Egyptian rulers to their exile abroad: Khedive Ismail, Khedive Abbas II, and King Farouk I, along with the latter's recently born son, Fuad II, the last ruling members of the Muhammad Ali dynasty. This marked the end of monarchy in Egypt following the 1952 revolution and the founding of the Republic of Egypt, after which the yacht joined the Egyptian navy and was renamed *El Horria*. It was renamed back to *El Mahrousa* in 2000 and recently became the first ship to cross the New Suez Canal extension in 2015.[41]

1976 Census of Clergy in North America

During the tenure of Fr. Angelos Boghdadi, *Al-Karma* (*Vineyard*) magazine published a special directory listing the name and telephone numbers of all the churches and priests in North America at that time. There was tremendous demand for priests' services. They performed not only spiritual ministries but also provided physical and emotional support to families and children and even financial help whenever they could. The Coptic community was scattered across America and Canada, and every priest had to travel far and wide to meet these needs.

The listing appeared in the February 1976 issue of *Al-Karma* (volume VI, number 66).[42] There were only twelve churches and twelve priests in the US and Canada at the time.

Coptic Orthodox Patriarchate
Diocese of North America
*"I am the good shepherd. The good shepherd
lays down his life for the sheep."*

Need Help? Call Us.

1. Church: St. George Church, P.O. Box 2766, Philadelphia, PA 19120; Pastor: Fr. Angelos Boghdadi. Telephone: (215) 289-8648

2. Church: St. George & St. Shenouda Church, 835 Bergen Avenue, Jersey City, New Jersey 07306; Pastor: Hegomen Fr. Antonious Younan. Telephone: (201) 434-9594

3. Church: St. Mark Church, 1600 S. Robertson Blvd. Los Angelos, CA. 90035; Pastor: Hegomen Fr. Flimon Mahrous, Church Tel. (213) 275-3050, Res. Tel. (213) 267-4059

4. Church: St. Mark Church, 437 West Side Avenue, Jersey City, New Jersey, 07304; Pastor: Hegomen Gabriel Abdelsayed, Church Telephone: (201) 333-0004, Res. (212) 592-1564

5. Church: St. Mark Church, 4900 Cleland Avenue, Los Angeles, CA. 90042; Pastor: Hegomen Fr. Ibrahim Aziz, Telephone: (213) 257-2776

6. Church: St. Mark Church, 122 S. Park Street, Roselle, Ill. 60172, Pastor: Hegomen Morcos Beshay, Telephone: (312) 386-3974

7. Church: St. Mark Church, 22 Innes Avenue, Toronto, Ontario, Canada; Pastor: Hegomen Fr. Morcos Elias, Church Tel. (461) 651-6334, Res. (461) 651-2295

8. Church: St. George Church, 1105 67th Street, Brooklyn, N.Y. Pastor: Fr. Mina Kamel Telephone: (212) 259-1564

9. Church: St. Mark Church, 901 Bellwood Drive, Highland Hgts., Ohio, 44143; Pastor: Fr. Mikhail E. Mikhail, Telephone: (216) 268-2829

10. Church: St. Mark Church, P.O. Box 643, Houston, TX. 77401, Pastor: Fr. Mousa Mina Telephone: (713) 661-5244

11. Church: St. Mark Church, 7005 Blvd Maisonneuve, Montreal, P. Q. Canada; Pastor: Hegomen Fr. Rofael Younan, Telephone: Res. (514) 336-2010

12. Church: St. Mary & St. Antonious, P.O. Box 127 Elmhurst, Sta. A, Elmhurst, New York; Pastor: Fr. Youhanna Tadros, Telephone: (212) 779-2440

HH Pope Shenouda III's Plan

During his visit in the spring of 1976, HG Bishop Youhannes reported that HH Pope Shenouda III was planning to make his first visit to the United States early in 1977. The pope, however, and the Holy Synod were engaged in matters regarding the status of the church in Ethiopia. At that time, Pope Shenouda had severed relations with a sister church in Ethiopia after the Marxist regime arrested and executed the orthodox patriarch Abune Tewophilos. Although the government of Ethiopia denied this had occurred, the Coptic Orthodox Church of Alexandria refused to recognize the enthronement of any other patriarch as long as Abune Tewophilos's death remained unresolved.[43]

Formal relations between the two churches resumed on July 13, 2007.[44] The Ethiopian Orthodox Tewahedo Church was administratively part of the Coptic Orthodox Church of Alexandria from the first half of the fourth century until 1959, when it was granted its own patriarch by Pope Cyril VI on June 28, 1959.[45]

Historical and Prominent Spiritual Leaders

The Coptic Church will be forever grateful to three distinguished spiritual leaders of modern times. They are Pope Cyril VI (Kyrillos VI), Pope Shenouda III, and Hegomen Fr. Mikhail Ibrahim. I have written extensively on both of these popes in my book *Contemporary Leadership Styles Analysis: The Exemplary Leadership of Pope Kyrillos VI & Pope Shenouda III*. Copts cannot speak about these two popes without mentioning Fr. Mikhail Ibrahim, another spiritual giant. He had a unique spiritual life that intertwined with the lives of both popes, creating great camaraderie and a powerful relationship between them. Their formidable talents, though different in style— and supported by the Lord's gracious gifts—had the most influential effect on the history of the Coptic Church in modern times.

Whenever Father Mikhail was in the presence of Pope Cyril VI and a priest would walk in to meet with the pope or seek his blessings, the pope would immediately direct his visitor to greet and ask for the blessings of Father Mikhail first. They had been very close since the time when the pope was still a monk by the name of Fr. Mina el-Metawahed (Mina the Hermit). They frequently celebrated the 5:00 a.m. Holy Liturgies. Both were saintly priests who loved people, cared for them, and attended to their needs, and thousands of believers sought their blessings, enlightenment, guidance, and consolation. They were gifted confessors who heard innumerable confessions and gave absolutions and spiritual counsel to countless people any time of the day or night.

The long relationship between Father Mikhail Ibrahim and Pope Shenouda III was of a paternal nature. Father Mikhail was father of confession for the pope while he was still a monk (Fr. Antonious El-Syriani) and later as a bishop of Christian education and dean of the Coptic Theological Seminary.

Their relationship lasted until the departure of Fr. Mikhail Ibrahim on March 26, 1975.[46] HH Pope Shenouda III, eulogizing Father Mikhail on the day of his departure, said the following:

Fr. Mikhail Ibrahim: A Heavenly Guest

He was a guest from heaven, and heaven delegated him to live among us for a while, to offer to humanity a righteous sample and a shining example of the true spiritual life... He is now our heavenly representative who knows what we go through and could ask God on our behalf in all what he knows about us... I never saw him except with a smiling face, cheerful, kind, offers more than he receives, filling everyone he meets with peace and tranquility.

A Man of Prayers

He was a man of prayers. All the problems that confronted his children, he would solve it all with prayers. At times he did not give advice or guidance, not even talk about a solution. But simply he says "we pray" and his prayers were mighty.

He was also a man that surrendered everything to God: I recall when his wife died, and after [funeral] prayers, he stood inside the church,

lifted up his hand, and said in a very heart touching voice, "Thank You, Lord."

An Exemplary Priest

> He is a wonderful human being [who] gave us
> an example that priesthood is not just science
> but Spirit...we all felt [he]—as layperson—[was]
> deeper than those who are in priesthood. When
> he became a priest, God gave him a profound
> gift.

Burial in St. Mark Cathedral

> When I requested from St. Mark Church in
> Shoubra to have him buried here in the Cathedral
> [St. Mark Coptic Orthodox Cathedral, Abbassia,
> Cairo] beneath the main altar behind the shrine
> of St. Mark...the reason I said to them was the
> following:
>
> I said that Hegomen Mikhail is a fabled
> man and belongs to no one church. His children
> [are] everyplace, [in every] neighborhood and
> every town, and it is not right to limit [his burial]
> to a specific place. It is preferable to bury him
> here in a public place.
>
> But the real inner and deep reason that I
> wanted to have the body of this righteous man to
> be of a support for us in this place to receive his
> blessings...

Here the pope cried. HG Bishop Youhannes, bishop of the
western region, continued the eulogy.[47]

CHAPTER 14

◆—◇◆◇—◆

Historical Glimpses of the
Leadership of HH Pope Cyril VI

*History may record that his greatest act of healing was effected
when he healed the fracture between the sister churches of Egypt
and Ethiopia. It has been one of the tragedies of more recent history,
possibly one that present Holy Synod in Cairo will overcome, that
festering wound has been left open for some years where Kyrillos the
healer brought only blame, but the present tragic divisions (1994)
merely emphasize his ministry of agape and Reconciliation.*

—Father John Watson

Pope Cyril VI's Surmounting Challenges

Pope Cyril VI, born on August 8, 1902, was the 116th pope of
Alexandria and patriarch of the See of St. Mark from May 10,
1959, until his death on March 9, 1971. This great pope's life was
most influenced by the writings of his spiritual mentor, St. Isaac of
Syria, the bishop of Nineveh and seventh-century ascetic. Pope Cyril
VI wrote extensively about St. Isaac's writings and spirituality. This
influence was most evident when the pope became the leader of the
church. He was faced with bureaucratic and administrative challenges from the old guard who seemed unwilling to accept change.

The Coptic Church as an institution was difficult to reform to meet the needs of twentieth-century demands. Although rigid thinking lingered, change seemed possible with a new spiritual pope in place.

In addition, Egypt was immersed in a revolution and coup d'état after the winds of popular anger had blown King Farouk off his throne. Describing the political scene, *Time* magazine wrote:

> In six weeks, Egypt's new regime has sent Farouk I into exile, legally abolished aristocracy; declared war on corruption, promised land reform to break up the great estates, raised the rich man's taxes…lowered the poor man's prices for sugar and cotton cloth, abolished censorship, relaxed restrictions on foreign investments. It was a revolution of the middle class, engineered by soldiers but broadened by the support of businessmen, professional men, office workers and students who believed that they had found their leader.[48]

Regarding the change that took place in daily life and abolishment of corruption, *Time* wrote in the same article:

> Reform in Egypt (or anywhere else in the Middle East) is not simply a matter of passing laws against sin. Corruption is not only the result of the greediness among the rich; to millions, it is almost a way of life, prompted by insecurity, hopelessness, and fear of what tomorrow may bring—or take away.

As for the state of the Coptic Church, it suffered from an impoverished spiritual life and agonized over the absence of a good shepherd to lead the church on the right path.

Glimpses of hope appeared with the enthronement of Pope Cyril VI, although his arrival was accompanied by complicated relations between clergy and the laity. The challenges were due to long-lasting problems involving two nonclerical bodies that took care of church affairs. The first was the popularly elected Coptic Lay Council (*El-Magles El-Mili*), which appeared on the stage in 1883–1884 to act as a liaison between the church and government.[49] The second was a joint clerical committee known as the Coptic Community Council (*Waqfs*) that appeared in 1928 to oversee the Coptic Church's endowments and monitor its management in accordance with Egyptian law.[50]

Another issue was the desire of Haile Selassie, emperor of Ethiopia (1930–1974), to split from the Coptic Church of Alexandria and transfer the pope's throne from Alexandria to Ethiopia. Along with the chronic problem of the Coptic endowments, the Ethiopian situation added to the complexity of the state of the Coptic Church at that time.

All these challenges occurred amid the military rule of the Egyptian revolutionary officers that began in 1952. The nation was facing devastating economic challenges. The new rulers were striving to reevaluate the country's internal and external policies that impacted the lives of the Egyptian people and reinstate or repair relations with foreign countries. The nation hadn't yet recovered from the invasion of its territory in October 1956 by Israel, England, and France during the Suez Crisis.

Pope Cyril VI and His Spirituality

His Holiness Pope Cyril VI, as the guardian of the Coptic Church, was filled with extreme paternal love and tenderness. His fatherhood was characterized by humility and self-denial. His life was of love, care, and service for people regardless of their faith, and anyone who had physical or spiritual needs was welcome in St. Mark's Cathedral. He fasted and celebrated the Holy Liturgy daily, appealing for God's mercy on all. The way he dressed, ate, and lived reflected amazing simplicity, as though he were still a monk rather than the leader of the church and pope of Alexandria.

Behind the large, well-furnished reception salon in St. Mark's Cathedral, Pope Cyril VI lived in a monastic cell similar to what we had read about in the lives of the desert fathers. I was privileged to see this tiny devotional space—it had no furniture except a small metal four-poster bed, a wooden chair, and a small table and lamp. In a corner of the room behind the bed was a tiny lavatory.[51] When people became concerned about the humble status of his cell and asked permission to renovate and refurnish it, the pope would smile, thank them, and say, "The room in its current state is still much better than the manger where the Christ was born."

Pope Cyril VI the Miracle Worker

The pope's long ascetic life practicing self-discipline and abstention from all forms of indulgence gave birth to a gentle and humble soul. His thoughts, deeds, and decisions were clothed with heavenly wisdom, spiritual wealth, and deep knowledge of regional and global affairs, including modern ecumenical movements. Thousands of people from everywhere and from all walks of life would come daily to pray with him and visit with him. His door was wide open to anyone who wanted to see him or seek his help and be blessed. He was a prophet, a powerful exorcist, a healer, and a true clairvoyant.

The pope was credited with being an instrument for healing cancer, paralysis, diabetes, and deafness by anointing the sick with holy oil. Fr. John Watson had personally experienced the miracle of healing by the pope. In his book *Abba Kyrillos: Patriarch and Solitary* about the life of Pope Cyril VI, Father John stated the following about his miracles:

> Thaumaturge is the word. Kyrillos was by every account a healer and wonder worker. Entire volumes are devoted to this aspect of his life and to reports of healing associated with his tomb, pictures, icons, and after-death appearances. Many of the miracles have been subject to professional medical scrutiny, and there is every reason to believe that they are genuine. Many hundreds of miracles have been reported.[52]

This diligent and good shepherd loved his sheep with unconditional love, resembling the Lord's boundless love. His tears during
his consecration acclaimed his sacrificial love. He did not want to
be chosen to the high office of the pope, nor had he sought it at any
time. It was the Holy Spirit that guided others to his selection and
chose him for the office of the papacy. He announced his genuine
feelings in his first letter to his people:

> Oh how I have wished to open my heart to all of
> you to see the deep love I have for all. It is a love
> sprouting from the heart of our savior who loved
> us and redeemed us with his blood.[53]

Pope Cyril VI and His Leadership Style

Pope Cyril VI's unique leadership was characterized by paternalism that manifested the fruit of the Holy Spirit. His servant-lead-
ership style was distinctly Christlike. As a result, he favored compassion above all else to solve unresolved issues in the church. This
empathetic approach did not have a title at that time, but today it
would be described as compassionate "transactional leadership."

Along with this style of paternalism, he adopted what became
known as "delegative leadership." In this approach, the leader does
not make every decision; instead, he steps into a situation and shares
his vision for a better solution and better future. The leader then
trusts others to execute the plan and see its fruition. Thus the leader
mentors those below him to develop the traits and skills to become
successful leaders as well.

This type of pragmatic leadership allowed him to deal sensi-
bly and realistically with the here-and-now objective reality of a vast
religious institution. Pope Cyril VI was not only a visionary but a
pragmatic thinker led by the spirit to figure out how things should
be done. His coaching approach allowed for gradual transformation
while maintaining the normal flow of daily operation of the church.
By setting himself as an example, he motivated others to perform at
their best. He was not only making sure that everything within the

See of St. Mark flowed smoothly, he was also planning for a church revival and spiritual awakening. Before his enthronement as the 116th pope of Alexandria, the church was in a state of stagnation that engulfed the life of the faithful and lasted for decades.[54]

Pope Cyril VI found himself surrounded by highly traditional and conservative ideologues who were unwilling to budge. At the same time, he felt strongly that the line of communication with the Ethiopian Church ought to be open and the relationship with the twin church restored. Against the counseling of many in the hierarchy of the Coptic Orthodox Church, he decided to take action.

For a long time, Haile Selassie, emperor of Ethiopia, clashed with Bishop Cyril, a Coptic metropolitan who was consecrated by Pope John (Youhannes) XIX on June 2, 1929. The emperor repeatedly caused him trouble, forcing Aba Cyril to keep returning to Egypt, where he ended up staying for good. One of the emperor's supporters asked for his dismissal from his position. Once the emperor returned to Ethiopia from exile in 1941, he sought to modernize the country over the following decades; he then tried to sever relations with the Coptic Church and form an independent Ethiopian church.[55]

A few days after His Holiness Pope Cyril VI was enthroned, he acted to achieve reconciliation with the twin Ethiopian church. The pope sent his second letter dated May 16, 1959, to Emperor Haile Selassie, in which he said in part:

> The increasing spiritual and social needs of the people of God these days and the responsibilities of the church towards them are doubled day after day. This requires care about organizing the shepherding and management tasks in a way which enables the church to perform its message, and to perform its responsibilities in the best way possible so as to appease our conscience before God in facing such huge commitment of those we serve. (2 Cor. 8:20)
>
> This structuring will include with God's grace, all the regions of the See of St. Mark where

> God's work is expanding in a remarkable way...
> we would have the pleasure to elevate the position
> of the head of St. Mark Church in Ethiopia, thus
> rendering our very special concern; we should
> organize his authorities in ordaining according to
> the guidance of the Holy Spirit.

This matter was put to rest when HH Pope Cyril VI conse-crated Abuna Basilios as Patriarch Catholicos for Ethiopia on June 28, 1959, based on a treaty and protocol that had been already prepared and signed on June 25, 1959.[56] In gratitude, His Holiness the pope was awarded the Grand Cordon of the Star of Solomon by Emperor Haile Selassie.

Currently the relationship between the Coptic Orthodox Church and the Ethiopian Tawahedo Church can be summed up in the words of the late Abuna Paulos, patriarch of the Ethiopian Church who passed away in 2012. He visited the Coptic Orthodox Church and met HH Pope Shenouda III on July 13, 2007. This visit was intended to further solidify the relationship between the Ethiopian Church and the Coptic Church after their time of separation. At this occasion, Abuna Paulos stated:

> A little girl does not stay forever in her mother's
> arms. She grows and becomes an independent
> woman in her own right. This does not mean she
> does away her mother; she still needs her advice,
> guidance, and comfort. But she has become
> independent.

St. Mena: The Pope's Patron Saint

As soon as he became pope and patriarch on St. Mark's throne in 1959, Pope Cyril VI laid the foundation stone of the new monastery of his beloved St. Mena in the Western Desert near Alexandria, Egypt. Countless miracles have happened through the intercessions of St. Mena the Martyr and the twenty-first-century Coptic saint

Pope Cyril VI. Some people wonder how long these supernatural miracles will continue. The answer is they are still happening (the latest on March 9, 2019) and have been for almost five decades. Pope Kyrillos Publications in America and the St. Mina Bookstore in Cairo jointly investigate, research, and record genuine miracles of both saints before publishing an annual listing. ("Mina" is a common variant spelling of the saint's name.)

To this day, thousands of pilgrims from all over the world continue to flock to St. Mina Monastery, which has become known as "Lourdes of the East," to receive spiritual and physical healing. Pope Cyril VI stated in his will his desire to be buried at the monastery of his beloved saint and patron. After the pope's death, his body was transferred to the monastery on Thursday, November 23, 1972, and prepared for enshrinement. The late Abba Mina Ava-Mina, the abbot of the monastery, and his monks were amazed to find that the body of Pope Cyril VI had not decomposed. Incorruptibility is a Coptic Orthodox Church belief that divine intervention prevents the normal process of decomposition of some human bodies (specifically those of saints) after death as a sign of holiness.

Under the direction of his spiritual director, Abouna Abdel-Messih el-Habashi, the pope developed his exceptional asceticism. As well, his years in the windmill and many years of ministry in Old Cairo as Father Mina were very important in shaping the life of the monk who became a pope yet continued to live as a monk.

According to HH Pope Shenouda III, during his life Pope Cyril VI celebrated the Eucharist daily. It is calculated that he celebrated the Divine Liturgy at least 12,500 times. On the occasion of the inauguration of the cathedral of the great martyr St. Mena at Mariout on November 24, 1976, and according to the publication *Abba Kyrillos: Pope Kyrillos VI and the Spiritual Leadership*, Pope Shenouda stated:

> Today, Saint Mina is happy because of the foundation of this great cathedral in his monastery. Today, the spirit of Pope Kyrillos VI also rejoices as he sets the foundation of this church. No

doubt, he is happy now for this accomplishment of the construction of the church. No doubt he prays with you today and blesses you all.

CHAPTER 15

❖···》◆《···❖

Global Evangelization upon the Return of St. Mary to Egypt

The most significant event in the patriarchate of Abba Kyrillos was an act of grace. It was a miracle for which no natural explanation is possible. From 2ed April 1968 until 29th May 1971 apparitions of Blessed Virgin Mary were witnessed by nightly crowds of up to quarter of a million Christians, Muslims, and Jews... The appearances of Our Lady of Zeitoun in Egypt are widely regarded as a seal of approval upon the ministry of Abba Kyrillos.

—Father John Watson

Evangelization In and Outside Egypt

Pope Cyril VI, after he settled the dispute between the Coptic Orthodox Church and the Ethiopian Church, then focused his concern on evangelization in Africa, the Middle East, Europe, the United States, Canada, and Australia. He sent evangelists to spread the Christian religion and founded an institution to prepare African youths for ministry. Then he established a division for African studies at the Institute of Coptic Studies in Cairo.[57]

It is worth noting that when Copts started to immigrate in the mid- to late 1960s to the United States, Canada, and Australia, most, if not all, Coptic clergy were against immigration. It was considered fleeing from persecution in Egypt as St. Peter did. Outside Rome, along the Via Appia (Appian Way), one of the most ancient roads, there is a church called the Church of St. Mary in Palmis (Chiesa del Domine Quo Vadis). The chapel was built in the seventeenth century in memory of a story that goes back to the times of Jesus. While St. Peter was fleeing from persecution in Rome, he bumped into Christ and was surprised to come upon his Master. So he asked Jesus, "Lord, where are you going?" And the Lord replied, "I am going to Rome to be crucified again."

The only person who was supportive of immigration was HH Pope Cyril VI. As we found out later, His Holiness had the revelation that it was God's plan for the Coptic Orthodox Church to expand abroad. True enough, in a few short decades, the Coptic Church grew to be a global institution and is still growing in every part of the world.

His Holiness also directed his attention to the internal affairs of the church. He visited churches in different governorates all over Egypt to strengthen and consolidate the faith and create a more effective and coherent church. The multitudes warmly welcomed him and eagerly planned huge celebrations wherever he went. People of all ages waited hours in anticipation of Pope Cyril VI's arrival. Churches were packed with exuberant Christian and Muslim worshippers. He prayed with them, blessed them, and miraculously healed some who suffered from a variety of ailments. No pope ever had done what Pope Cyril VI did to revive people's faith, restore their moral consciousness, and unite them with a spirit of togetherness and sense of belonging. All over Egypt, Copts were once again filled with joy as proud members of an apostolic tradition and historical Coptic Church. His Holiness was a saintly model; people learned from his humility, paternal love, patience, and gentleness of soul. He was a man of prayers, mindful of God's presence at all times, who led the movement to revive Coptic Church heritage, dogma, and rituals in daily celebration of the Holy Liturgy. Most importantly, he traveled far and wide to mend hurt due to internal problems of the church, whether among members of committees or among the people and the clergy. Many of these problems were complicated, difficult, and long lasting, yet with his paternal affection, gentle soul, and prayers, he restored a sense of tranquility and peace among people who rejoiced and praised the Lord for his peacemaking efforts.

Rev. Dr. John Watson of Kent, England, wrote in this regard:

> Pope Thumaturgos (miracle worker) was perhaps at his best when applying a solution to the wounded body of his own Church at home in Egypt. There was much need for a curative ministry… Kyrillos lived fully for the Coptic present by constantly referring to the Coptic past, just as the contemporary Christian existence confirmed in the daily Eucharist.[58]

As a result, harmonious relations between the shepherds and their flock finally were achieved. Coptic people were thrilled with his prayers, fatherly love, and dedication to revive their spiritual life and attain a sense of peace. This became evident when the pope maintained an "open door" policy throughout his reign. That meant anyone could meet with the pope and communicate his or her concern or even simply seek his blessings and counseling. The aim of this direct communication was to raise the bar of intimacy and cultivate understanding and harmony. Such meetings with individuals or groups had no human barriers or system in place that might stand between or prevent direct contact with His Holiness.

When the pope was questioned by an American journalist about the future of the Copts, he replied in the third person:

> His great ambition is to see the church in a spiritual revival that resemble the early days of the Apostolic Fathers. As a Hermit, he has had deep experience with prayer and great faith that prayer will lead the church to this great revival. He is trying to encourage all Coptic congregations to develop this experience with prayer.[59]

This vision, as well the open door phenomenon, was historic papal policy that had never happened before and possibly would never happen again. Similarly, an event that never occurred in the history of all the Coptic Orthodox popes or in the history of any other pope worldwide was the apparition of St. Mary on the dome of St. Mary Coptic Orthodox Church.

The Apparitions of the Holy Virgin St. Mary: St. Mary Returns to Egypt

As mentioned earlier in the book, from Tuesday, April 2, 1968, until May 29, 1971, during the reign of Pope Cyril VI, the blessed Holy Virgin Mary Mother of God appeared on the dome of St. Mary Coptic Orthodox Church in Zeitoun, Cairo. The apparitions occurred for several hours at sunset, during the night, and at dawn. They were sometimes accompanied by luminous heavenly bodies shaped like doves moving at relatively fast speeds. The apparitions were seen by millions of Egyptians and people from around the world. Miracles occurred as many chronically sick people were cured and others gained their sight and shouted with joy as they saw her. Paralytics in wheelchairs stood up and walked, praising the Lord, while onlookers could not believe what they were seeing right in front of their eyes.

His Holiness Pope Cyril VI entrusted a committee of bishops and priests to investigate the apparitions. On May 4, 1968 (Coptic calendar Baramuda 6, 1684), the Coptic Orthodox Church officially confirmed the apparitions after a thorough investigation.[60] The pope officially assigned the responsibility of documenting the event and all the miracles associated with it to a special committee headed by HG Bishop Gregorios, bishop of postgraduate studies, Coptic culture, and scientific research.

The apparitions were also witnessed by Catholic priests from the local Coptic Catholic Church and nuns from the Sacré-Coeur order. Based on their testimony, an envoy from the Vatican arrived on the evening of Sunday, April 28, 1968, saw the apparition, and sent their report to His Holiness Pope Paul VI in Rome. Also, the

late Rev. Dr. Ibrahim Saied, head of the Protestant church at Kasr
Eldobara, Cairo, affirmed that the apparitions were true.

Eyewitnesses to the Apparitions

One of the witnesses was HG Bishop Athanasius of Beni
Soueiff. He was appointed personally by HH Pope Cyril VI to visit
the church of the apparitions and to make a detailed report after a
thorough investigation. The following is an excerpt from his official
report:

> I first heard about the apparitions on April 2, but
> we needed some time to be sure about the story. I
> came with a number of friends from Beni Soueiff
> on the evening of April 6, and went directly to
> the church. We prayed all the way from Beni
> Soueiff, about two and a half hours. All agreed to
> spend the time in private prayers. The first thing
> we saw when we got to Zeitoun—about 11 P.M.
> There was a very large gathering of people and
> we stood among them until 3:45 in the morning.
> At dawn some of those who had come with me
> came running from the northern street along the
> church and said: "The Lady is over the middle
> dome." I was told that some clouds covered the
> dome; when something like fluorescent lamps
> began to illumine the sky. Suddenly there she was
> standing in full figure.
>
> The crowd was tremendous. It was too dif-
> ficult to move among the people. But I tried and
> worked my way in front of the figure. There she
> was, five or six meters above the dome, high in
> the sky, full of figure, like a phosphorous statue,
> but not so stiff as a statue. There was movement
> of the body and of the clothing. It was very diffi-
> cult for me to stand all the time before the figure,

as human waves were pushing me from all sides. One would estimate the crowd at 100,000. In an hour or so I think I stood before the figure eight or nine times. I began to tire and thought it was sufficient for me.

After I left the crowd I again heard cries from the people. It seemed very unfair for me to leave while the blessed Mother was there. The fence around the courtyard had broken down, so I returned to the little office building south of the church. I stood inside for one hour, from four to five o'clock, looking at the figure. It never disappeared. Our lady looked to the north; she waved her hand; she blessed the people, sometimes in the direction where we stood. Her garments swayed in the wind. She was very quiet, full of glory. It was something really supernatural, very, very heavenly.

I saw a large strange pigeon. It came from behind us—I don't know where—proceeded to the church and returned. Several brighter spotlights moved quickly over us. Greeks were praying Greek; others were singing Coptic hymns. It was something really above human experience. It attracted and captivated us.

I stood there and tried to distinguish the face and features. I can say there was something about the eyes and mouth I could see, but I could not make out the features. That continued until about five minutes before five. The apparition began to grow fainter, little by little. The light gave way to a cloud, bright at first then less and less bright until it disappeared. I went there many times later, but that was the appearance that left the greatest impression upon me.

On another night I visited the church. I took the door keys and entered, locking the door from the inside. As I stood on the ladder that led from the second floor to the top, my eyes turned to the ceiling or inner dome. No one could see me. I was shaking all over. I took hold of the ladder. I felt there was something unusual there. I prayed: "If you are there, Holy Mary, let me see you. I just want to give witness to you."

Then I heard people shouting. I hurried outside and saw the Virgin standing one meter from where I had been. There was no message. One cannot say what message heaven may intend, but definitely faith in God, in the supernatural has been strengthened. Christians and non-Christians reported that what they saw in Zeitoun brought them back to faith in God. Hundreds of missions could not do what the apparitions have done. People are beginning to think of Christianity in a new way, especially those who were antagonistic. The communion of saints and other traditional views of Christianity are emphasized. Non-Catholic Christians are coming to think of the place of the blessed Virgin in our religion.[61]

A second testimony was provided by HG Bishop Samuel, bishop of public, ecumenical, and social services. He was a permanent member of the Central Committee of the World Council of Churches and a founding member and vice president of the All Africa Conference of Churches. A famous figure in and outside Egypt, in the words of Hassanein Heikal, editor in chief of the Cairo newspaper *Al-Ahram*, Bishop Samuel was "in effect the Coptic Orthodox Minister of Foreign Affairs." As mentioned earlier, His Grace spearheaded the efforts to establish the Coptic Orthodox Church abroad.

With regard to the apparitions, he stated the following in his own words:

> At 2:45 in the morning the Blessed Virgin appeared in a complete luminous body as a radiant phosphorescent statue. After a short while the apparition vanished. It reappeared at four o'clock and remained until five o'clock—dawn. The scene was overwhelming and magnificent. The apparition walked toward the west, sometimes moving its hands in blessing, and sometimes bowing repeatedly. A halo of light surrounded its head. I saw some glittering beings around the apparition. They looked like stars, rather blue in color...[62]

A third testimony was given by HG Bishop Gregorios, prelate for higher studies, Coptic culture, and scientific research. He was a scholar and was considered one of the most, if not the most, knowledgeable theologians in the Coptic Orthodox Church. He obtained his divinity BA from Cairo University and a diploma in Egyptian archaeology. He earned his PhD from the prestigious Department of Biblical Studies at the University of Manchester, England. He was delegated by Pope Cyril VI to form the medical and scientific committee to investigate cases of miracle cures that resulted during the apparitions of the Holy Virgin St. Mary in Zeitoun. The following is his statement regarding the apparitions in his own words:

> The events have no equal in the past, neither in the East nor in the West. St. Mary has appeared in many different forms since April 2, 1968. She is still appearing from time to time (January 1969). The most glorious apparitions took place between April 27 and May 15.
> Before the apparitions took place some birds that look like pigeons—I don't know

what they are—appear in different formations. Sometimes two appear on the dome just as they had come out of it. However, the dome is closed; the windows do not open. Everyone watches to see where they come from. They might be seen flying eastward, then wheeling about and flying to the west, and while one watches them, they suddenly disappear.

I remember particularly on June 9, the birthday of Our Lady (in Coptic calendars) I was in Zeitoun when I saw two pigeons very white, very bright, luminous, radiating light. I was determined to watch them. They became tiny flakes of the cloud and seemed to enter heaven. They do not flap their wings; they glide. In a flash they appeared; and disappeared in the same way. They do not fly away but above and around the center dome. They stay quite near and close to the church when they vanish. Whatever formation they take, they keep. Sometimes as many as seven of them fly in the formation. They appear and disappear in this formation. They fly very swiftly. They are not light on one side only, but are completely lighted. One does not see feathers at all—just something bright. They are radiating creatures, larger in size than a dove or a pigeon. Sometimes as one of them flies lower, it gets larger and larger. People realize these are not pigeons. They are there to honor St. Mary, and usually appear some time before an apparition.

I have myself seen not less than ten forms of the apparition. Once I saw an opening in the sky, like the opening in the sanctuary in the Coptic Church. St. Mary appeared in this opening. She appeared larger than natural size, young, beautiful, all light. It was the color of the sky in Egypt.

She wore something on her head like a veil. She looked like the sorrowful Mother. She did not look happy. She stood for as much as two or three hours in the same spot.

People who went to Zeitoun on Saturday, May 4 at 9 p.m. saw her in radiance until 5 a.m. on Sunday, May 5. For eight hours she was visible to thousands and thousands of people. I was there myself that night. Many went home to get their families and friends, Most of those present were Moslems.

Sometimes Our Lady has appeared aside or in the palm tree in the churchyard. Our Lord has also been seen as an Infant. She holds Him to identify herself. Jesus is always on her left arm. According to Eastern custom, the queen should always be on the right side of the King. Sometimes He is wearing a crown, sometimes not. The same is true of St. Mary. She may appear several times in the same night, once with the crown and again without it. But she is always like a queen, very beautiful, very healthy, standing upright. She moves about, enabling all to see her. She moves very slowly. At times she has the olives branch in her right hand. Sometimes she lifts both hands in blessing.

The most wonderful scene I experienced was one under the northeast dome, above the icon of our Lady. It occurred on the feast of the Flight of the Holy Family, June 1st. About nine or nine-thirty at night a light appeared in the center of the opening beneath the small dome. The light took the shape of a sphere, moving up and down. Then very slowly it moved out through the supporting archway and took the form of St. Mary. It lasted two or three minutes, and as usual

the people shouted to her. She usually acknowledges their greetings with both hands, with
one, if she should be holding the olive branch
or Christ Child. She looks somewhat happy and
smiling, but somewhat sad, always kindly. She
then returned to the dome and the figure became
again round ball of light and gradually faded into
darkness.

After 10 minutes the cycle started again. I
saw it several times between 10 p.m. and 3:30
a.m., at about ten-minute intervals. As she would
disappear under one dome and darkness had
come, she would appear under another of the
domes, or over the entrance into the courtyard.
It was St. Mary in complete form that I saw, head
to foot, very bright, not bluish, yet not hurting
the eyes. It actually seemed to soothe the eyes.
No features were visible. No features could be
distinguished, but her outline was that of a very
beautiful figure. This scene I saw countless times.

There is also the phenomenon of the incense.
The smoke of incense, very bright, comes out of
the large dome in unbelievable quantities. The
cloud goes up to ten or twenty meters or more. It
is dark red. There is no other cloud in the sky but
the one over the dome. It then takes the form of
St. Mary, as stars appear and disappear over the
church.[63]

CHAPTER 16

—◆••◖••◖◗◗◆••◗••◆—

Historical Glimpses of the Leadership of HH Pope Shenouda III

Remember your Leaders who spoke the word of God to you.
Consider the outcome of their way of life and imitate their faith.

—Hebrews 13:7

Blessed are the people whose shepherd is Pope Shenouda III.

—Mar Ignatius Jacob III, Syrian Orthodox
Patriarch of Antioch and all the East

HG Bishop Shenouda

On September 30, 1962, Pope Cyril VI ordained Fr. Antonious El Syriani as Bishop Shenouda. He was the first bishop to be devoted to Christian education in the history of the Coptic Church. He also became dean of the Coptic Theological Seminary in Egypt. Due to his leadership style and popularity as an eloquent speaker and gifted teacher, enrollment of full-time and part-time students increased considerably. Women were motivated and encouraged to pursue theological studies and were admitted to the seminary. New faculty members were appointed to meet the significant increase in students, including professionals who sought to enrich their lives with the depth of religious studies. Bishop Shenouda's reputation for erudition and teaching was recognized by the educational establishment, including the Association of Middle East Theological Colleges. He was overwhelmingly elected as president of the association in 1969.

Enthronement of Pope Shenouda III

When His Holiness Pope Cyril VI departed in peace on March 9, 1971, the Holy Synod met on March 22 for the purpose of electing the new patriarch. On October 31, 1971, Bishop Shenouda was among the top three candidates who received the highest number of votes by the Coptic Christians registered to vote. The three names were then placed on the altar during the Holy Liturgy celebrated for the purpose. At the end of the Divine Liturgy, His Eminence Metropolitan Antonious laid his hand on a young boy who was then blindfolded, and in the presence of the entire Coptic community, the boy was given the task of extracting one of the three cards that contained the three names. They were Bishop Samuel, a monk by the name of Timothy al Maqari, and Bishop Shenouda.

As the congregation prayed the Lord's Prayer and chanted "Lord have mercy," the boy picked one of the folded cards and gave it to Metropolitan Antonious, who opened it and then happily declared that the Lord had chosen a shepherd for His church—His Grace Shenouda, bishop of education. On November 14, 1971, at the Cathedral of St. Mark in Cairo, His Holiness Pope Shenouda III was enthroned as the 117th pope of Alexandria and patriarch of the See of St. Mark.

Pope Shenouda III continued his educational role and became the first patriarch of Alexandria since the fifth century to have been the dean of the Coptic Theological Seminary. He expanded the ministry of Christian education by establishing several seminaries in Egypt and abroad. On November 29, 1993, he officially opened the Institute of Pastoral Care. His Holiness was a gifted writer, the author of hundreds of books and countless sermons.[64] He visited more than thirty foreign countries, including becoming the first Coptic pope to visit the United States in 1977.[65] He had also been the chief editor of the Coptic journal *El Keraza* since 1965 and remained so throughout his papacy.[66]

Pope Shenouda III in Philadelphia

On April 18 and 19, 1977, the city of Philadelphia welcomed HH Pope Shenouda III. The reception was held in the historic Cathedral of St. George Greek Orthodox Church in downtown Philadelphia. His Holiness started the reception with prayers of praise and thanksgiving, then delivered a brief speech about the purpose of his trip to shepherd the Coptic community and look after their spiritual needs. Bishop Samuel then spoke in English about the role of the Coptic Church in ecumenical relations that emphasized the desire of the church for attaining Christian unity.

During this visit, His Holiness was accompanied by HG Bishop Youannes, HG Bishop Tadros, HG Bishop Antonious Markos, and HE Metropolitan Pakhomious (El-Behera). The clergy of St. George Greek Orthodox Church spoke next, welcoming His Holiness and the bishops, priests, and deacons of the Coptic Orthodox churches. Then a representative of the primate of the Greek Orthodox Church gave a brief history of the role of the church during the Bicentennial Clergy-Laity Congress of 1976 that was held in Philadelphia, with its headquarters at St. George, and attended by hundreds of priests and thousands of faithful.

After the celebration concluded, guests had the opportunity to hear about the role of St. George Greek Orthodox Church's involvement in the life of the Greek community, particularly its recent attention to the growing population of the elderly, especially widows. In 1977, the very year the pope visited, the Greek community saw the opening of Athenagoras Manor, a ninety-four-unit apartment complex for low-income elderly. This was the first and largest such senior housing established by a single parish in partnership with the Department of Housing and Urban Development. At the end of the reception, the pope blessed the attendees and gave each of them an autographed photo of His Holiness marked with the memorable date of his first visit to the United States and the city of Philadelphia.

Pope Shenouda III's Ecumenical Visit

While HH Pope Shenouda III was in the States, he received an invitation from His Eminence John Cardinal Krol, archbishop of the See of Philadelphia, to visit St. Charles Borromeo Seminary of the Roman Catholic Archdiocese of Philadelphia in Lower Marion Township. There he was greeted cordially by the archbishop and was kindly asked to speak and share his wisdom with the seminarians. It was amazing how His Holiness was in tune with the universal call to holiness as a teaching of the Roman Catholic Church based on the scripture of St. Matthew: "Be you therefore perfect, as also your heavenly Father is perfect." (Matthew 5:48)

At the conclusion of the visit, the pope and bishops, accompanied by Cardinal Krol, were taken on a tour of the seminary and its facilities, including its remarkable library. On this solemn occasion, His Holiness gave Cardinal Krol a gift of St. Mark's picture beautifully engraved on a silver plate as well as souvenir medals commemorating this historic visit. The cardinal gave HH Pope Shenouda III a commemorative Bible honoring the blessed visit along with a book on the history of the archdiocese and the monastery of St. Charles Borromeo.

Meeting with the Coptic Community

El-Papa Shenouda met with members of St. George's congregation the following day at the place of his lodging. St. George Church at that time was in a small rental space in South Philadelphia. The pope did not want to meet there with all members of the congregation, though he wanted to address their concerns about Father Angelos, a bold defendant of the orthodoxy and traditions of the Coptic Church, as described in detail in a previous chapter. HG Bishop Youhannes had been delegated by His Holiness to evaluate issues of concern in May of 1976. The pope had already received HG

Bishop Youhannes's assessments and was aware of the root cause of the conflict.

Time for Decision-Making

The kind, loving, and careful Pope Shenouda III sat attentively, listening to all points of view. The members who were upset with Father Angelos outlined their issues. They were armed with facts about the absence of religious education in schools, the permissive American culture, and their attempts to use logic to sway the opposing members. They thought that by piling on knowledge and using reason to explain their side of the situation, they could win the anointed and chosen leader to their side. However, they were doomed to fail, because decision-making was based not only on logical presentation and good reasoning but also on equanimity and balanced emotion. When the meeting with the pope concluded, the faultfinders had every reason to hope for a change. They walked away with a sense they had won the argument.

A second meeting took place with Father Angelos and his family. They were happy to see the pope and welcomed meeting with them. His Holiness tenderly asked each of the children about their lives in the new land, how they were getting along in school and their social life, and whether they missed anything or hoped for better things. He listened to their responses with tender love and care. The two daughters were in their senior years of high school and had already applied to colleges, waiting for letters of acceptance. Both were looking forward to continuing their education in the States.

Then the priest's wife had a turn to share her feelings and hopes for her future life with her husband and children in the new land. As she started to speak, suddenly her peaceful demeanor changed and she broke down in tears, begging the pope to let her family return to Egypt! They had traveled thousands of miles and thought they would be part of a larger family, the Coptic congregation of St. George. Obviously the pope was touched, possibly even surprised by the request. With a fatherly demeanor and soothing words, he consoled her, assuring her of his support and concern for her and her family's well-being.

HH Pope Shenouda III took everything he had heard into account, including Tasoni's request and the future of both daughters' education. By the end of his trip, he made a final decision that was aimed at taking care of the entire family. His Holiness's decision was as follows:

- ❖ Father Angelos, Tasoni, and the youngest son were to return to Egypt by the end of the school year.
- ❖ Father Angelos was to serve with His Holiness at St. Mark Cathedral in Egypt upon his return by July 1977.
- ❖ Both daughters would stay in Philadelphia to continue their undergraduate education.
- ❖ Both daughters would remain under Esmat Gabriel and his family's care and guardianship. (See Appendix IV for the official letter signed by HH Pope Shenouda for this very purpose.)
- ❖ Upon the departure of Fr. Angelos Boghdadi, liturgical and spiritual services would cease until further notice.
- ❖ These decisions would be partially known but would not be announced in their entirety until the departure of His Holiness.

In July 1977, the church board was in charge of vacating the priest's rental apartment and storing the furniture at the homes of various church members. There was no record of where these items were stored, including the priest's car. From July 1977 to mid-1980, St. George Church remained a preserved title but without the possibility to continue either by renting or purchasing another property. The congregation faced the threat of discontinued spiritual services due to lack of a physical space. However, Holy Liturgy was ministered occasionally by Fr. Bishoy Demetrious, priest of St. Mary Coptic Orthodox Church in East Brunswick, New Jersey. Other times liturgical services were provided by visiting priests.

St. George Congregation Declines the Offer

Dr. Youssef Banoud, an occasional visiting member, learned of the situation and offered to buy the rental property when it was put up for sale. This move would have expedited the arrival of a priest to serve St. George Church once again. The negotiated price of the property was $19,700. An initial intent for purchase was signed by the seller and prospective buyer—the church. Mr. George Morcos of Roslyn, Pennsylvania, mailed a questionnaire to members of the church. Unfortunately, no interest was expressed verbally or in writing to buy the property. Even though finances were available and at hand by the cheerful donor, many members of the congregation failed to take advantage of such a generous gift and the sale never materialized. This was the end of an era in the history of St. George Church in Philadelphia.

St. George Church's Holy Myron

Before leaving the States to return to Egypt, Father Angelos delivered the Holy Myron to a trustworthy member of the church. The Holy Myron is the oil with supreme power of sanctification in the Coptic Orthodox Church. The purpose of the Holy Myron is to sanctify and consecrate to God by anointing. The instruction that was given along with the Holy Myron would be handed to the future priest who would be assigned to resume ministerial service at St. George Church. By the end of 1977, a message came from Egypt to the one who was entrusted with the Holy Myron to contact Rev. Fr. Youhanna Tadros of St. Mary and St. Antonious Church in Queens, New York.

Many graciously recall how Father Youhanna had labored extensively on behalf of the St. George congregation. He continued to referee relations between the faultfinders and the shepherd of the church. In fact, he traveled back and forth from New York to Philadelphia before and during the pope's first visit to the States. He encouraged members of the congregation to restore peace and be in full accord and one mind. He requested all to earnestly pray and do their utmost to stand in support of the priest and his family.

In 1978, a precise message was received to take the Holy Myron to St. Mary and St. Antonious Church in Queens and deliver it into the hand of Father Youhanna. It became quite clear that St. George Church would be without an assigned priest for months or even years. The writing was on the wall, and admittedly, it was a sad time. Fr. Bishoy Demetrious occasionally celebrated the Holy Liturgy for some members of the congregation, but there was no full and regular ministerial and spiritual service. Most Coptic families were disappointed, and efforts to restore service had been seriously considered. Regretfully, some members acted as if the concern was not their priority, or at least they were indifferent.

Finally, in the spring of 1979 a conference call was initiated with HH Pope Shenouda III to reopen the church and continue the liturgical service in Philadelphia. The call was placed by Dr. Nabil El-Shammaa, Mr. Maurice Demetrious of Delaware, and myself. At the conclusion of the call, His Holiness blessed the efforts to resume the search for a new church and start anew. The pope promised to assign a new priest once the callers were ready. In the meantime, the concerned members asked His Holiness's permission to invite Fr. Bishoy Demitri of St. Mary Church in East Brunswick, New Jersey, to temporarily serve the spiritual needs of families in Philadelphia and to carry on a monthly celebration of Holy Liturgy on a Saturday. His Holiness graciously agreed.

Incorporating St. Mena Church in Northeast Philadelphia

Based on HH Pope Shenouda's directions during the conference call, the message was related to Fr. Bishoy Demitri, and he began monthly service in Philadelphia. However, efforts began, supported by Father Bishoy, to start a new church. Therefore, articles of incorporation were filed with the Commonwealth of Pennsylvania on March 26, 1980. Proof of publication appeared in both the *Philadelphia Inquirer* on April 25, 1980, and the *Legal Intelligencer* on April 28, 1980. Articles of incorporation were also approved (#80-20 343).

CHAPTER 17

❖❖❖

A New Start: St. Mena Coptic
Orthodox Church

*I stand in awe of the many "coincidences," "chance" meetings,
synchronicities, and fateful detours that have impelled and guided
me on my life's journey.*

—Peter Levine

In the absence of a permanent priest, Fr. Bishoy Demitri was called
upon, and he kindly provided liturgical service for St. George
Coptic Orthodox Church starting in May of 1979. However, a physical space was needed to resume liturgical service at the newly established church—St. Mena Coptic Orthodox Church.

Fr. Bishoy Demitri

His Holiness Pope Shenouda III ordained the deacon Hanna
Demitri to be Fr. Bishoy Demitri on May 22, 1977. The ordination took place during His Holiness Pope Shenouda's III visit to
the United States in 1977. He also laid the cornerstone of St. Mary
Coptic Orthodox Church in East Brunswick, New Jersey, on April
17, 1977. On November 20, 1982, Pope Shenouda III delegated
Bishop Antonious Markos, general bishop of African affairs, to rep-

174

resent His Holiness at the opening of the church. Father Bishoy was the priest who spearheaded the effort to build St. Mary Church, and it was completed due to this shepherd's true love and dedication, the sincere care and enthusiasm of the board, and most importantly, the fellowship and generosity of the parishioners.

On Wednesday, November 19, 1980, the Very Rev. Fr. Demitri Girgis and his two sons, Fr. Shenouda Ava Bishoy and Fr. Bishoy Demitri, prayed thanksgiving, raised incense, and officiated a Holy Liturgy on a temporary altar located in an old house on the purchased land where the church was set to be built. Together they prayed to the Lord to complete the building of His new house of prayer. In this old house Father Bishoy also performed the first baptismal event by baptizing a baby girl named Amy Minna on Thursday, November 23, 1978, preceding the celebration of St. Mena Feast on November 24, 1978.

Though the church started as a little seed planted by a few families, by the grace of God, the seed-bearing plant grew and multiplied. The first priests to visit and bless the land upon which the church was built were the beloved Fr. Bishoy Kamel with his wife, Tasoni Angel, and the beloved Fr. Rofael Younan. The latter was the priest who prayed the first Holy Liturgy in the Church of St. Mark in Jersey City. Father Bishoy Kamel, during his visit on October 4, 1977, ate from the fruit of the apple trees on the church property and prophesied (according to Father Bishoy Demitri) "the Virgin Mary will produce spiritual apples to nourish the souls hungry for the word of God." The Lord blessed St. Mary Church, and as the prophet Ezekiel said, "It was planted in good soil by many waters, to bring forth branches, bear fruit, and become a majestic vine." (Ezekiel 17:8)

As we look back, we give thanks to the Lord who called Fr. Bishoy Demitri, recalling the words of the prophet Jeremiah: "Blessed is the man who trusts in the Lord and his hope is in the Lord. For he shall be like a tree planted by the waters, which spreads out its roots by the river. And will not fear when heat comes; but her leaf will be green, and will not be anxious in the year of drought, nor will cease from yielding fruit." (Jeremiah 17:8)

Father Bishoy, despite his long suffering, was an example of patience, persistence, and gentleness of soul. Through many ailments, he continued to praise the Lord, and faithful everywhere had seen and heard of his steadfastness and how the Lord was compassionate and merciful. Many of the early settlers in the United States knew how this blessed shepherd began his life in New Jersey as a devout deacon. He was honest in the small matters, and he gave his best. The Lord richly rewarded him with a great helper and confident wife, Tasoni Sonia, a dedicated and loving servant. He also blessed both of them with two beautiful, faithful daughters and an abundance of fruitful ministry.

St. Mena Church: A New Beginning

As Father Bishoy started his ministry for the St. Mena congregation, a physical space was needed. Miraculously, a place was found in the northeast of Philadelphia: the chapel situated on the grounds of Eden Hall at 4800 Grant Avenue. It was discovered by a pious family who lived in the same part of town, Mr. and Mrs. Sedrak Watson. The chapel was part of a Society of the Sacred Heart convent situated in a large park. The property was originally a private estate and was purchased by the sisters in 1847. One can barely describe the beauty of this chapel. The stained-glass windows were magnificently designed, and the detail and craftsmanship in such a compact space was exquisite. Yet the Eden Hall Chapel had deteriorated considerably and required a major renovation and repairs.

Professional contractors and an army of volunteers from the congregation were responsible for providing the materials, equipment, and labor to complete the project at a considerable cost. However, the completed work was magnificent. Credit should be given where credit is due, including to Dr. Nabil El-Shammaa, Mr. Raouf Gobran and his family, Mr. Sidrak Wassef and his family, Mr. Ghobrial Gerges and his son Mr. Nabil Gerges, Dr. Ikram Abdou, Dr. Youssef Banout, Dr. Raef Marcus, and Dr. and Mrs. Esmat Gabriel. Fr. Bishoy Demetrious, by the nature of his ecclesiastical status, was unanimously elected president of the founding board and the interim shepherd of the new St. Mena Church.

History of Eden Hall Chapel

According to Fairmount Park Commission records, Frank Wills, a noted English ecclesiological revival architect, designed the building in 1845. Prominent people have been linked to the site over the years, including St. John Neumann, two aunts of Jacqueline Kennedy Onassis, and St. Katharine Drexel, whose parents were entombed in a crypt adjacent to the chapel. Negotiations were held with the Fairmount Park Commission, under whose jurisdiction the chapel fell. In appreciation of the magnificent restoration work done by the St. Mena congregation, a lease was drawn for an annual rent of one dollar, including all utilities. Once again, the beloved and Very Rev. Fr. Mankarious Awadalla returned from Canada to celebrate the first Holy Liturgy at St. Mena Coptic Orthodox Church. The opening day was a joyous and historic day. All attendees thanked God and praised His holy name.

Other priests followed, starting with Fr. Bishoy Demitri, who celebrated the Holy Liturgy. Then a schedule was established, and the congregation was blessed by several reverend fathers who regularly came to celebrate the Holy Liturgy, including Fr. Shenouda El-Baramousy (HG Bishop Michael), Fr. Salib Ava Mina, and Fr. Rafail Gurguis, who served at the time at St. George and St. Shenouda Church in Jersey City and currently serves at St. Antony Church in Medford, New Jersey. Other visiting priests from Egypt and elsewhere delighted the congregation with their ministry and blessings. In honor of St. Mena, the patron saint who the church was named after, a candle stall in the sanctuary of the church was erected with a colorful picture of the saint.

St. Mena the Miracle Worker

According to the Coptic Synaxarium, St. Mena (AD 285–309) was a martyr and wonder worker. He was the patron saint and spiritual companion of the late Pope Cyril VI. He was born in the city of Niceous, Egypt, to righteous Christian parents. His mother was a barren woman and his father, Audexios, was a prominent figure in the Roman Empire. The mother, heartbroken because she had no children, was praying in front of St. Mary's icon, asking to be blessed with a child, and she heard an "amen." When she gave birth to a son, she named him Mena.

When Mena grew up, he joined the army, ultimately achieving high rank in part due to his father's prominent status in the military. He was sent to Algeria to serve his country. After a few years, he resigned from the army to devote his life to worshiping the Lord. Later on he was tortured and martyred because he refused to renounce his Christian faith.[67]

St. Mena is a famous Coptic saint well known in the East and West due to the many miracles attributed to his intercession and prayers. That is the reason why the monastery of St. Mena is a popular pilgrimage site and as mentioned before is considered the "Lourdes of the East." Today, thousands of pilgrims from all over the world continue to flock to it to receive spiritual and physical healing.

Pilgrims who visit St. Bernadette of Lourdes can get small bottles of miracle water shaped like the Virgin Mary as souvenirs. But St. Mena's jars of miracle water were in existence centuries before the St. Bernadette bottles at Lourdes. The little jars were made of clay and bore the likeness of St. Mena the Martyr, and they held either healing water or holy oil. Pilgrims to the monastery of St. Mena in the fourth century would bring jars home to their families, friends, and sick relatives. Archaeologists have unearthed them in Germany, France, Italy, and Croatia. Some have been found in Sudan and Jerusalem as well. These jars bear the likeness not only of St. Mena the martyr and miracle worker but also two camels at his side.[68]

The Coptic Orthodox Church of St. Mena continued to serve members who mostly resided in northeast Philadelphia and South Jersey. However, a segment of the Coptic community did not want to join the new church and appeared indifferent. They were the ones who were directly responsible for the service at St. George Church to stop for more than two years.

St. George Church's First Property

On June 26, 1980, a two-story, 120-year-old building located at 100 West Third Avenue in Conshohocken, Pennsylvania, was purchased for $61,500. It was used as a gymnasium but originally was built and occupied by an evangelical church. The building's top floor was remodeled as a sanctuary and prepared for service. After a sizable down payment was collected from all members, the balance of the mortgage was $25,000, with a monthly payment of $349.90. Fr. Gabriel Abdelsayed and Dr. Lewis Khella signed the property deed. Thanksgiving prayers were raised by Father Gabriel and the congregation on June 26, 1980. The Holy Liturgy was ministered for the first time in this newly owned church by Fr. Gabriel Abdelsayed on June 29, 1980.

Fr. Mousa El-Syriani (HG Bishop Athanasius of Beni Mazar)

HH Pope Shenouda III assigned Fr. Mousa El-Soriany to St. George Church starting in September 1980. Father Mousa was a kind but firm monk who clearly had been aware of the history of the service and the experiences of his predecessors. According to the newly assigned priest, he had heard about His Holiness's visit to Philadelphia in April 1977 and the congregation's issues of concern. He also had an opportunity to meet with Fr. Angelos Boghdadi and had been familiarized with the events and ministerial needs of the congregation and the disruption of spiritual service for over two years. He was under the impression that Father Gabriel had been able to establish solidarity among members of St. George Church. Father Mousa's intention was to build on what Father Gabriel started and to harmonize relations among all members of the congregation.

Fundamental and permanent solidarity is achieved when there is agreement on faith matters, interests, objectives, and standards. It is better expressed by St. Paul when he states, "Bearing with one another in love, endeavoring to keep the unity of the Spirit in the bond of peace." (Ephesians 4:2–3) Even that inspiring call would only be attainable if members of the congregation practiced humility—a virtue of human nature. Humility restrains one's own power, respecting and allowing room for other members to integrate, cooperate, and bear each other in love. Apparently, that was a far cry for some members who were still babes in Christ and who were being fed with, in the words of St. Paul, "milk and not with solid food. For until now you were not able to receive it, and even now you are still not able for you are still carnal. For where there are envy, strife, and divisions among you, are you not carnal and behaving like mere men?" (1 Corinthians 3:2–3)

Father Mousa surely had his share of struggle before his assignment ended in August 1983, but he was able to tackle many issues with compassion and success. He remained a monk and lived an ascetic life. He valued self-discipline but was as strict with himself as he was with others. His monastic life resembled that of a desert ascetic, especially in the absence of remuneration or a monthly stipend. He put some dedicated members to work, spearheaded by Messrs. Nagy Elbardisi, Joseph Hanna, and Nazmy Anton. They, with the help of others, remodeled the building and prepared it for worship according to the designs and traditional style of the Coptic Orthodox Church. The finishing was colorful and warm, decorated with icons of Christ and the Virgin Mary with the child Jesus portrayed by Coptic artist Ms. Nadia Kawakab Shoukry. The church was also decorated with exquisite pictures of the twelve disciples.

The St. George congregation for the first time owned a nice, warm, and pleasant place for spiritual service. Father Mousa cared about children and youth religious education. A committee was formed from qualified educators and dedicated servants, and a special religious curriculum was planned for age-appropriate classes ranging from kindergarten through college.

CHAPTER 18

❖⸱⟨•⸱❳◆❲⸱•⟩⸱❖

One Body, One Spirit, and One Local Church

I will hear what the Lord God will speak.

—Psalms 85:8

*Blessed is the soul who hears the Lord speaking within her,
who receives the word of consolation from His lips. Blessed
are the ears that catch the accents of divine whispering,
and pay no heed to the murmurings of this world.*

—Thomas A. Kempis

St. Mena Church Perspective

The cause that led to incorporating and establishing St. Mena was to resume spiritual service. Service had been interrupted due to the closing of St. George Church after Pope Shenouda III ended the service of Fr. Angelos Boghdadi in Philadelphia. He was transferred to serve with His Holiness from 1978 to 1988 at St. Mary and Aba Ruwees Coptic Orthodox Church. He eventually returned to the United States, where he served from 1988 to 1992 in the state of Colorado. On December 26, 1992, he transferred to St. George Coptic Orthodox Church in Tampa, Florida. In 1997, HG Bishop Youssef elevated him to the rank of hegomen. Father Angelos was welcomed in the Diocese of the Southern

181

United States and served there for nearly twenty years. He was eighty-nine years old when he departed on Friday, December 21, 2012.

In Pennsylvania, Father Mousa followed Father Angelos and was assigned to serve in the newly purchased property in Conshohocken. Although he, Fr. Bishoy Demitri, and other caring priests managed to alleviate the ill feelings of many members, the effects of closing St. George Church and starting St. Mena were devastating, to say the least. The church split distressed believers, caused havoc in the life of a priest and his family, and disgraced the name of Christ.

Looking back, one must acknowledge that the disharmony was partly due to people not feeling welcome because of the strong emphasis on orthodoxy and doctrine of the Coptic Church. The nonorthodox Copts who were new immigrants or who were married to members of other denominations perceived it as a litmus test for belonging. However, it was hard for many of them to see that the priest was the guardian of the church sacraments, and it was not in his authority to deviate from his responsibilities.

That's exactly what the apostle Paul teaches: "Now I urge you, brethren, note those who cause divisions and offences, contrary to the doctrine which you learned, and avoid them. For those who are such do not serve our Lord Jesus Christ, but their own belly, and by smooth words and flattering speech deceive the hearts of the simple." (Romans 16:17–18) It was not easy for many members to forgive and forget and go back to being part of the beloved St. George community of believers. Empathy was key, and some spoke of the importance of seeing things from the other side's perspective, using compassion to get past resentment. This was about recognizing that although the majority felt the facts were on their side, the opposing minority's opinion was understandable as well. In the end, it was agreed to think about it, but most importantly, to pray about it, knowing that the good Lord offered a new beginning to the congregation with the arrival of a new priest.

St. Mena Congregation Perspective

The truly faithful know that churches are hospitals, full of sick and wounded people. They are not clubs full of saints. As Christians, we know that no one is perfect; we are imperfect people, subject to misunderstanding, disagreement, and hurt feelings. As St. George Church opened its doors once again and loving shepherds opened their arms to welcome all and unite the body of Christ, there was no excuse but to join in. Most members of St. Mena's congregation felt the call to reunite and be the one body they always yearned to be. However, many were against the move and objected to joining St. George Church after all their efforts and expenses to establish St. Mena Church.

The final call to members of the congregation of St. Mena was to recognize that buildings come and go, and the church is not just a building made of bricks and stones. The word "church" is a translation of the Greek word *ekklesia*, which is defined as "an assembly." The biblical meaning of church is not of a building, but of people. In Romans 16:5, it says, "Greet the church that is in their house." Paul refers to the church in their house—not a church building, but a body of believers. The body of Christ is made up of all believers in Jesus Christ from the day of Pentecost (Acts 2) until Christ's return. Biblically, the Coptic Orthodox Church regards the church in two ways: as the universal church and as the local church.

Many members showed deep understanding and wisdom by seeing the benefit of once again joining the original church. Most of them were part of the historical establishment of the first church of St. George. Besides, there was only one reason why members of the congregation would consider walking away from the church completely—when members or leaders deviated from or abandoned their faith in key issues like the Coptic Orthodox foundational doctrines or the deity of Christ. That rarely happened in traditional apostolic churches, as the leadership would intervene against any such deviations.

The congregation of St. Mena was adamantly in agreement not to follow the trends of other new Coptic churches in the United States. As discussed earlier, a group in New York, possibly supported by a visiting priest from Egypt, split from the entire Coptic community and their elected representatives. The representatives were duly elected members of the incorporated body of the Coptic American

Association (CAA). They had a long, dedicated history of serving Copts, not only new immigrants to the US but also previously in their homeland, Egypt.

Suddenly and behind the scenes, a group motivated by what may be called Saul of Tarsus blinding zeal incorporated their own group as St. Marcos Church in New York. The split had long-term influence on the process of establishing Coptic Orthodox churches in the diaspora and especially in the United States. It appeared that some church leaders perceived that the new movement was helpful in multiplying the numbers of churches, which was seen as a sign of successful ministry. The split was also thought to be helpful in that it prevented conflict from lingering in the church and disturbing the peace within the church environment.

Establishing a new church and the sense of pride and accomplishment that comes with it is still perceived as a reflection on the priest's successful ministry and the congregation's unity of spirit and love. In reality, that is far from the entire story. Building a church partially depends on the financial means and resources of its members. Among the faithful, some who are considered "elite" because of their financial means to support the church can flex their muscles, threatening to walk away if the priest fails to please them or abide by what they dictate to him even in spiritual matters. Those very "elite," because of their profession, prestige, or popularity, are usually chosen or elected to serve on the board of deacons—a convenient practice that needs to be looked into by the upper echelon of the Coptic Orthodox Church.

The original entity structured by the late Bishop Samuel at the inception of the church in America and Canada, namely the church council, is far better than having a board of deacons. Bestowing the title "deacon" upon someone is not helpful if they cannot support the fundamental principles, duties, and performance that come with the title. First, they are supposedly "deacons," but the majority are not ordained, and many have declined ordination for deaconship. Second, they are deacons but are not allowed to discuss or participate in spiritual matters that are exclusively the priest's right. Third, they are not allowed (in some churches) to interfere with administering church funds—the board's role may be to advise, but they are not to interfere with how the funds are distributed. (A board of deacons, for example, may strongly believe in the need for a second priest, while the priest may strongly believe accumulated funds should be used to build a new and bigger church.)

In the Uniform By-Laws for the Coptic Orthodox Churches in North America (dated Friday, June 4, 2010), Chapter 6, Article II, Section on Board of Deacons, it states that the board is responsible for "financial and administrative aspects only," while the spiritual services are "entirely entrusted to the clergy." Thus, it appears that deaconship, at least according to these bylaws, is not considered to be part of the clergy. That's exactly why it is quite logical to refrain from using the title of "board of deacons" and consider implementing Bishop Samuel's "church council," which better represents the advisory role of the group.

The purpose is to avoid conflict, division, and resentment for what can appear to be overlapping and interfering roles of offices within the board. At times, the board is perceived as a convenient facade to run the business of the church. But when some members of the board adhere to their authorized role to make decisions based on a voting majority, others may feel alienated. In cases of overriding the priest's decision, it may look disrespectable, which can lead to alienation, indifference, separation, and then all-out division. Boards in other denominations have been accused of embezzling funds, resulting in IRS scrutiny and scandal. At all costs, the body of the church must remain united to set an example for Christian living and Christian management of good stewardship. For "every house divided against itself shall not stand." (Matthew 12:25)

Having bylaws that establish a cooperative, integrated relationship between a priest and board of deacons as a "spiritual team," per se, may spring from good intention but unfortunately has not been very promising in the West versus in Egypt. The election of congregation members to the board of deacons—in most cases that I am aware of—has been considered a pain for the priest. He carries an exhaustive spiritual and administrative workload already—he doesn't need to have to deal with defiant personalities and relationships among congregation members. Not only is he a priest; he is also a member of their families, a close friend, a business partner, a consoler, and a counselor to all those who have marital, parental, or financial troubles. Naturally and subconsciously, the priest would only vouch for choosing reasonable, respectable people, not "naggers" or hard-to-please types.

Electing board members was originally done every two years, then three years, but in reality, elections are the last thing the priest wants to be bothered with or even think about for many years.

Divisions within many churches have been a sad reality. Such deviation from a spiritual path was neither acceptable nor promulgated by the late HH Pope Shenouda III. He has written and spoken extensively about it. The following is one of his articles pointing at the dangers of such an unacceptable path, offering practical advice for self-control and harmonious relations among group members.

Division

by
HH Pope Shenouda III

One of the Saints said: If ten thousands of angels gathered together, they would have one opinion. Regretfully, when only a few men get together, they disagree!

Division is a proof that the ego is alive... the ego that works alone away from the spirit of God...that wants to exert its opinion regardless of what the result may be and does not care what disastrous outcomes division causes!

So what are these outcomes? A scholar once said that when two eagles battle for a prey, it ends up in the mouth of a fox. That is why the Lord Jesus says, "Every house divided against itself shall not stand." (Matthew 12:25) It is a verse that the dividers forget.

Often a group acts and causes division, then leaves behind a destructive scene and goes on to its affair as if they have done nothing! The Lord demands avenging for the blood of its disastrous deeds.

Division among brethren is proof of an absence of love.

Division of the young against the elder is proof of rebellion, disobedience, and disrespect for superiors...all are sins. Division also is proof of self-superiority or of dignifying one's ego. Most likely the father of confession is not aware of all that goes on and is out of the loop, not consulted in anything. In the Epistle of St. Paul, he condemned them for division and described them as "still of the flesh" and far from the spiritual unity.

Members of the one body cooperate together for the welfare of the body.

If all feel this unity, they would all work for the good and collaborate together.

Unity requires respect of the opinions of others, or at least learns to deal with other opinions without revolting, and without anger and without destruction.

Try to win the other party without splitting up with him.

Be objective and refrain from personal issues.

Train yourself to team up with the group spirit.

(The above article has been translated into English by the author.)

The Other Opinion: People's Grievances

Other opinions and grievances were also brought to the attention of HH Pope Shenouda III while he was in the United States.

The group presented themselves as learned and quite respectable to the church's teaching and tradition. In a special meeting with the pope, they brought up his words in the book *Liberation of the Spirit* (Arabic *Intelak el Roah*), where he wrote a chapter on the danger of "worshipping men." They asked what they should do in the face of conflict with their priest and his style of leadership. Then they presented some grievances that were mainly focused on disagreement with his style of leadership, service, and relationships.

The following were some of the presented grievances:

- Abouna (a priest is called "father"—in Arabic: *abouna*) surrounded himself with a limited number of people to sing his praises. They communicated his wishes, his desires, and even his disapproval.

- Abouna perceived himself superior and "chosen," thus laypeople had to blindly abide by whatever he said. Case in point: he would solicit input from the young members of the congregation, encourage them to voice their opinion, and attempt to listen to them. Then he would disappoint them by saying, "I heard you, but the final decision is mine," rather than, "I understand your concern. Let us pray about it and seek the Lord's guidance!"

- Abouna rarely engaged in youth meetings or had regular service meetings or monthly spiritual days for the youth and Sunday school children. He considered it interference in his spiritual responsibility.

- When people tried to lighten his burden or understand the language barrier when dealing directly with our youth and their culture, he would get offended. He expressed indirect disapproval if people invited another priest to attend youth meetings, take confessions, and unload their burdens.

- Abouna would speak about being a leader, but he would lose his composure easily under the slightest pressure.

- A respectable spiritual leader should not use inappropriate language and insult his servants.

After listening to sincere people who cared for the church and wanted to restore peace and unity, His Holiness comforted them with these words:

- We always say, if you are unhappy with a church or a priest, do not go to another church and pray. Each one of you, consider your own salvation and inner peace. Know when to distance yourself from disturbing conflicts in the church where you serve.
- Any conflict between a priest and members of a congregation, even if they mean well, does not warrant forming groups and widening the conflict, which only ends in division and destroys the unity of the local church. If you are unhappy where you are, be part of the solution and leave.
- Division within a church has devastating impact on the priest as well as the congregation. Always remember the Lord's words: "Every house divided against itself shall not stand."
- Churches ought to be established based on the needs and number of people who want the spiritual service of a priest. Churches should not be established because of division and separation.
- Under the guidance of bishops and by directly monitoring needs, the central church is in a better position to organize and structure the establishment of new churches.

CHAPTER 19

━━◆━<•••>◆<••>━◆━━

Further Growth of St. George Church

There are troubles and trends, but these are present in every age.
I sometimes like to picture the existence of the
Church as the existence of the moon.
Sometimes it's full, sometimes it's half, sometimes it's a quarter.
But it's there.

—John Cardinal Krol

The Dawn of a New Era

On August 28, 1983, the Very Rev. Fr. Samuel Thabet Samuel arrived to serve the Coptic community scattered in Conshohocken, Philadelphia, South Jersey, and Delaware. To most of the congregation members, the presence of a new priest delegated by HH Pope Shenouda III was the dawn of a new era. Members of St. Mena Church felt the same and were convinced to discontinue worshipping at their church and reunite once again. Most agreed that the establishment of St. Mena Church had accomplished its mission to maintain spiritual service during the time when St. George was closed.

Some members of St. Mena Church objected to the move and didn't think unity with the people from St. George could be achieved. Healing was difficult, and many were overwhelmed by the dramatic experience. So a few families from St. Mena declined to join, prefer-ring to continue worshipping in the magnificent chapel at Eden Hall in northeast Philadelphia, renovating and preserving it as a historical property. To them, it was a far better place of worship than traveling to Conshohocken and worshipping in a 120-year-old "gymnasium." As well, many were convinced that the trauma the preceding three priests had experienced could happen again.

The hope remained that the new priest would be able to win them back, and they would unite with the entire congregation. But it was a dim hope!

The Very Rev. Fr. Samuel Thabet Samuel

Before ordination to priesthood, Father Samuel was an engi-neer by profession. He graduated from the University of Alexandria with a bachelor's degree in civil engineering in 1972. He was born on February 28, 1949, and raised by a devout Christian family. At an early age, he loved the Coptic Church and its monasteries and enjoyed accompanying his father to attend church regularly, espe-cially the vigil services. The young Samuel would spend his summer vacation visiting El-Baramousy Monastery, where his uncle was a monk. At age fifteen, he was ordained a deacon serving the church of St. George in Tanta, the fifth largest city in Egypt. When his family moved to Alexandria in 1960 and joined the church of St. George, Deacon Samuel continued serving at the altar and in Sunday school.

Deacon Samuel was shepherded and monitored by the late Fr. Bishoy Kamel, a prominent and celebrated priest in the Coptic Church. He nominated him for priesthood, and Deacon Samuel was ordained by HH Pope Shenouda III on June 27, 1976, to serve at St. Mary Church in Cleopatra, Alexandria. One year earlier, in 1975, he was married to a well-educated and dedicated servant who had grown up in a priestly family. She was Tasoni Ebtesam El-Neil, who accompanied him to the United States with their two children to serve at St. George Church of greater Philadelphia.

The Heavy Hand of Persecution

Before arriving in the States, this young family had its share of suffering. In September 1981, President Anwar Sadat ordered a massive police strike against his opponents, jailing more than 1,500 people from across the political spectrum. Father Samuel was among the twenty-four priests, eight bishops, and many prominent Coptic Christians who were rounded up and imprisoned on September 3. One prominent Coptic prisoner, Mr. George Abdel Shaheid, author of "A Prisoner's Journal of Black September 1981" published in the *Voice of the Immigrant* newspaper in the United States, stated that prisoners were treated inhumanly. They were cramped in dark, dirty, smelly, insect-infested cells. The cells were cold and crowded, and prisoners were not allowed out of them. Some were terrified, while others were angry and did not know why they had been dragged out of their homes before dawn, terrorizing their families.

The prison was a scary and intimidating environment. There was no medical care, no hygienic facilities or supplies, no exercise allowed, and no connection to the outside world. Newspapers and books were prohibited. There were no beds or chairs; they all slept on barely covered floors. They depended on outside help for food and supplies. The scariest time was when handcuffed prisoners were packed in vans and shuttled to the offices of the secret police. They left the prison at six in the morning and traveled three hours for their interrogation. HG Bishop Benyamin was subject to these trips for three days, but on the third day he returned in an awful shape, pale, shaking, and shivering from cold. The van he and another prisoner were traveling in flipped upside down on the highway, and both were trapped inside for hours in the cold desert until they were rescued.

Praising and Thanksgiving in Prison

In the face of these extreme hardships, the faithful Copts, along with bishops, priests, and consecrated deacons, turned the ugliness of prison into heavenly life by their daily and hourly prayers and Bible studies. The merciful Lord showed His mercy and swiftly extended

His hand to protect, save, and avenge His faithful people. On October 6, a month after their arrest and imprisonment, President Sadat was assassinated by Muslim extremists during the annual military parade held in Cairo commemorating the Yom Kippur War. On November 5, 1981, Father Samuel's wife gave birth to a son, who was named David. "Brother Gerges" was the kind messenger who delivered the happy news, bringing with him cake and flowers. All gathered to congratulate Father Samuel and celebrate the happy occasion. According to Mr. George Shaheid, it was a beautiful day, they laughed much, and Bishop Bishoy divided the cake among them. On February 22, 1982, Father Samuel was released, but the authorities would not allow him to serve in his church.

This period of imprisonment had its impact on Father Samuel's health, and he required medical care in the hospital for quite a while. However, hospitalization revealed the wonders of his gentle soul, his kindness, and his capacity to befriend others of different religions. Even those who belonged to another religion that persecuted and discriminated against his faith had a warm place in his heart. While Father Samuel was in the hospital, he shared a room with El-sheikh El-Telmisani, a devout Muslim cleric, and they developed an intimate friendship that the Muslim cleric spoke about it openly with newspaper reporters. He expressed his gratitude for Father Samuel's love and tender care as he offered the sheikh his service in humility and generosity during their hospitalization.

I attempted to get both Father Samuel and Fr. Bassellious Sedrak to share their prison experience. Father Samuel, with a charming smile, stated that they were poor! He meant that non-Christians are impoverished and deprived of the vitality of enlightenment. Father Bassellious, with a stern voice and fading smile, responded to the question with, "We give thanks to God!" In an interview with Father Samuel on February 22, 1990, Eileen Kenna from the *Philadelphia Inquirer* pressed this very point to discover the circumstances that led him to leave his church in Alexandria and come to the States. Father Samuel responded jokingly, "You have two choices when the pope tells you to go...you go or you go." When she asked about the history of St. George as a local church, he stated, "The local Coptic

Church was established in 1969 and was incorporated in May 1973." He then added, "Several Coptic Orthodox priests served the congregation in churches of other denominations until 1980, when the Conshohocken building was purchased."

The Tenure of Father Samuel

The tenure of Father Samuel started with a shared vision. The board of deacons wanted to listen and learn. They did not see themselves as the anointed ones to run the show or tell others what to do but rather to serve and invite others to join. Father Samuel and the team that assisted him hit the ground running and proceeded with faith and enthusiasm. Whether they were members of the board or other committees, they all had the collective desire to create something new, to foster new relationships with every member in the church, and to sustain unity in the one body.

Members of the Board

The members of the board who were inspired to serve and start a new era in the life of St. George Church were Fr. Samuel Thabet Samuel (president), Mr. Farid F. Mansour (vice president), Mr. Victor Mansour (treasurer), Mr. Sami Faltas, Mr. Farid Samuel, Dr. Ikram Abdou (members), and myself (secretary). For all of us, there was an unwritten mission to fulfill our deepest aspirations of spiritual growth and seek salvation of souls. Father Samuel's priorities were crystal clear; he did not deviate from the goal of the faithful celebration of the Mass. The Mass was started on time, celebrated with love and reverence, and ended at the scheduled time, including a homily that did not exceed fifteen minutes. He visited families at home, catechized the young, and comforted parents. He shared everyone's burden, read the Bible with them, and prayed with them. Father Samuel knew his priorities and did not engage much in nonspiritual ministry but promptly delegated other matters to trustworthy members and followed up with them.

On Sunday after the Holy Liturgy, there was time for the congregation to get together and share a meal. Father Samuel spoke to the congregation while they enjoyed the meal as one family. He also invited others to speak to parents and youth about a variety of topics that enriched their lives and instilled in them a spirit of love, courage, and sense of belonging. There, in this wonderful environment, faith was slowly but surely formed and nurtured. The Word of God and His love was proclaimed in deed rather than words or only in creed. At times, members of the congregation had trouble worshiping in harmony, yet forgiveness was given and received, goodness was affirmed, and the call to respect each other and make peace was heard. It was the same during his meetings with members of the board—it was a time for serious efforts to address issues and ensure that the church remained a vibrant community of faith, where every member was led to a deeper encounter with the One they love most and were privileged to serve.

Board Meetings

Board meetings with Father Samuel were very structured, diligently scheduled on a monthly basis, and followed the bylaws of the church to the letter. The bylaws were established by the Coptic Church for the very purpose of organizing and structuring assigned responsibilities of every leader-servant. At that time, meetings at St. George Church went like this:

1. Each meeting started with a prayer.
2. A printed agenda was distributed to members, and there was follow-up on any assigned tasks.
3. Prepared remarks were presented to the board.
4. The minutes from the previous meeting were reviewed with a formal motion to approve them before officially adding them to the record.
5. Incomplete or unfinished business was reviewed.
6. The date and place for the next meeting was set.

7. All meeting minutes were written in English and kept as part of the church's official records for new generations to emulate should they be called upon to carry the responsibility.

Cutting Expenses

To minimize church expenses, the board brought up the idea of saving on mortgage expenses by paying off the mortgage loan of $21,422.66 to avoid monthly interest. At a meeting on January 11, 1986, the board of St. George Coptic Orthodox Church resolved the following:

1. The congregation was called upon to lend the church the amount, and the balance was paid in full on January 24, 1986.
2. A certificate was issued naming each member and the amount he or she had lent to the church.
3. The sequence and month in which a designated payment would be made to each loan certificate holder was determined by lottery on Sunday, February 16, 1986.
4. Each loan would be repaid in two installments. Each installment would not exceed the sum of $500. Only one installment would be made each month. (See Church Record, pp. 104–105.)
5. The loan was satisfied by returning to each member the borrowed amount he or she had lent the church. Many members offered their share of the loan as a donation to the church.

The money that was saved became seed money for a new project to renovate and modernize the building. Throughout 1987, a central air-conditioning system was installed in the upper level of the church. In the summer of 1988, partitions were installed in the middle of the church behind the priest's office. This project was spearheaded by civil engineers Mr. Farid Mansour, Mr. Afif Abdelmalek,

Mr. Nagi Elbardisi, and others. The anticipated papal visit the following year was a considerable motivation to prepare the church building in the best traditional design possible, but the ultimate goal was to create spaces that met the expanded service of the church. The team worked collaboratively with a hired contractor to modernize the building and preserve its integrity.

A Blessed Family

One of the blessings that enriched the life of the church was the arrival of the Saad family from Alexandria, Egypt. It included Mrs. Madeline Younan with her sons, Deacons Ashraf, Emad, and Shirine. Mrs. Younan immediately took charge of agape services after Sunday Mass and other festival occasions where all shared a traditional homemade meal. Her sons were well-seasoned and well-trained deacons who brought with them the spiritual sense of the traditional Coptic hymns of the mother church. Their tender, touching chanting revitalized the rituals. Hymns are a valuable inheritance that remain unchanged from the apostolic age. While the older son, Ashraf, was busy earning a living, the two younger sons were still completing their education—Emad as a chemical engineer and Shirine as an electrical engineer. Today, they all remain an integral part of services in many churches, serving, teaching, and preaching.

A Papal Visit

On Friday, September, 22, 1989, St. George Church was once again blessed by the historic pastoral visit of HH Pope Shenouda III. This event was celebrated at the Valley Forge Military Academy in Wayne, Pennsylvania. The Coptic faithful flocked to see him, not only from Philadelphia and nearby areas but from all over the country. They all happily welcomed him and joined in the blessed celebration. The pope raised the vesper incense, blessed the participants, and listened to distinguished speakers who warmly welcomed His Holiness. Father Samuel delivered the opening speech that grabbed the attention of all. The following are excerpts from his speech:

> We want to express our hearty love and deep gratitude to the Holy Father. On behalf of the entire congregation of St. George Church in Philadelphia, we thank you from the bottom of our hearts for the support you have given us in countless ways and throughout your visit.
>
> Your inspiring thoughts of love and your words are the treasure, source, and strength that sustain and safeguard us when we hear disturbing news of persecution in our beloved land of Egypt.
>
> While we hold firm to our faith and spiritual atonement, we pray that your Holiness continues to work tirelessly and patiently toward peace and justice for all natives in our homeland and abroad. May God of all might always assist you with His indomitable power and steadfast love particularly in pursuing the elusive goals of peace and justice.

Ecumenical Relations

HH Pope Shenouda III then shared with the audience his message of ongoing ecumenical relations and Christian unity. As bishop, he attended the first ecumenical consultation between theologians of the Oriental Orthodox and Roman Catholic Churches in Vienna in September 1971. The agreed statement included the following words:

> We believe that our Lord and Savior Jesus Christ is God the Son incarnate; perfect in His Divinity, He was not separated from His humanity for a single moment, not for the twinkling of an eye. His humanity is one with His Divinity with-

out commixture, without confusion, without
division, without separation. We, in our common faith in the one Lord Jesus Christ, regard
His mystery inexhaustible and ineffable and for
the human mind never fully comprehensible or
expressible.

His Holiness added that in May 1973, he paid a cordial visit to
Pope Paul VI in Rome. This was actually the first meeting between
an Alexandrian and Roman pontiff since the time of the great schism
of AD 451. Both popes signed a common declaration containing,
among other things, a confession of common faith in the mystery of
the Word incarnate.

After delivering a wonderful educational history lesson, he took
the time to answer questions. One interesting question from the audience asked why it had taken so long to reconcile differences between
the two churches regarding the nature of Christ. His Holiness
answered that it was mainly due to the complicated nature of languages during that era. It was difficult for the theologians involved to
come up with precise comparable words to reach an explanation that
was satisfactory to all.

On Saturday, September 23, 1989, the second day of the visit,
the pope returned to the Valley Forge Military Academy and celebrated the Holy Liturgy. Most of the congregation partook of the
Holy Communion assisted by their Graces Bishops Bishoy, Paula,
and Tadros and Father Samuel. Immediately after the service, the
pope secretly left the building accompanied by Father Samuel,
myself, and security personnel. He wanted to visit John Cardinal
Krol, archbishop of Philadelphia, at St. Agnes Triumph Hospital in
South Philadelphia. The cardinal was recovering from surgery, and
his administration and the hospital had to be notified in advance of
the upcoming visit.

The cardinal welcomed His Holiness the pope, and due to his
fragile health, only Father Samuel and I were allowed in the room,
joined by the cardinal's physician and personal secretary.

With a surprised look, the cardinal asked the pope how and when he had found out about his hospitalization! The pope explained how he was able to interrupt his itinerary to pay him a visit. But then the cardinal had a tougher question, asking how he found the time to be attentive to big and small matters at the same time and how he arranged his priorities. The pope smiled and responded, "God blesses the time, and the needs of the Coptic people are many, not only in Egypt but also abroad." When the cardinal realized that His Holiness had stayed late with the congregation the night before and celebrated the Holy Liturgy earlier that day, he asked the pope when he ever managed to sleep! His Holiness, with a wide and a charming smile, told the cardinal the following story:

> The Coptic populace went one day to meet their patriarch of that time, and it was late at night. The gates were closed, so they knocked at the doors of the papal palace, demanding to meet their pope. The guard answered that he was unauthorized to open the gate after hours. They insisted on getting in and kept knocking, demanding entry. The guard told them not to try, for the pope had already gone to sleep. The people kept knocking, crying out loud, "The good shepherd does not sleep."

The cardinal was utterly amazed, and with an empathetic smile, he told His Holiness, "I hope that the people of this time are more understanding." Then HH Pope Shenouda III wished the cardinal a speedy recovery and they parted with a holy kiss. Thus the Coptic holy shepherd went on his way, reminding us that celebrations, as important as they are, ought not to prevent the faithful from visiting the sick.

Worth Noting

The Very Rev. Fr. Samuel Thabet Samuel is currently the arch-priest of St. Mark Coptic Orthodox Church in Chicago, Illinois. He also has been appointed as Exarch of His Holiness Pope Tawadros II to oversee the Diocese of Chicago.

On Friday, September 22, 1989, before arriving in Philadelphia, HH Pope Shenouda III met with President George H. W. Bush, the forty-first president of the United States. His meeting was at 10:00 a.m. at the White House, and the president welcomed him and his entourage consisting of HG Bishop Bishoy, the Egyptian ambassador Mr. Abdel Raouf Elridi, and Ms. Amal Mansour. The conversation turned to peace in the Middle East and the efforts of President Mubarak of Egypt in pursuing this elusive goal. In response, the Holy Father said to the president, "That peace in the Middle East needs a push from President Bush."

When the president expressed his admiration of the cross the pope carried with him, His Holiness presented it to him as a gift, mentioning that it was made by the sons of the church in Egypt.

After returning to Philadelphia on September 22, the pope went back to Washington on September 23, where arrangements were made for him to open the session of the US Congress on September 25 with a prayer to God for peace in the world and the return of man to the image he was created in...the image and likeness of God.[69]

CHAPTER 20

St. George Parish: A Shining Renewal

*The Perfect man thinks continually on others; on
loving others, on what is good for others,
on the eternal destiny of others, on the sanctity
of others. Himself he places last of all,
or the servant of all.*

—HH Pope Shenouda III

Bidding Farewell to the Shepherd

It may be hard to think about, but it is true that Jesus was raised from the dead with the scars on His body. If He had pleased, He could readily have removed them, but He did not; instead, He showed the disciples His hands and feet. It is a reminder to all that sin is forgiven, not forgotten. When Father Samuel received his transfer decree on July 3, 1990, to serve the church of St. Mark and Anba Bishoy in Chicago, it was not a surprise to many. He had performed well in his ministry at St. George. He was indeed a generous sower, and he sowed on every soil he could find. In his seventh year, he surely was looking for how much crop it had yielded. The crop was plenty, but many wondered if that was all he wanted! Anyway, it was a happy call for him and his family but sad news for many. Some wondered if they could have done anything to keep that wonderful shepherd with them.

The answer was probably not really. "His will be done," but nonetheless, self-examination was warranted, even if the culture to be examined was a church. After all, the faithful all know that a church is not a society of saints but a hospital for sinners. St. George Church was fortunate to have had four wonderful priests and many others who were temporarily assigned. But they all came and went, including two interim priests who served after Father Samuel was transferred, leaving behind broken hearts and inquisitive minds. They were Fr. Shenouda Ghats of Anba Abraam Church on Long Island and Fr. Takla Azmy while on a visit for medical care. Father Shenouda focused his service on the youth, assisted by Deacon Karmy Bekhit (Fr. Mina B. Mina) of St. Mary Church, Newark, Delaware, and Deacon Emad Saad. Both were in charge of Sunday school at the time.

The culture of that era could be described as the "personality" of the church—both its leaders and congregants. One could sense it in every interaction among the worshippers and in the leadership style of the shepherd and those who served with him. It is not only the application of leadership but how it is perceived and interpreted. Regretfully, some negativity within the culture of the church was covert, and some people ought to be left to the merciful Lord to heal if there is no other way, especially if they are not open to change. Regardless, no matter how much time a priest may spend building homogeneous relations within a heterogeneous population, the results may be inconsequential. There is a true saying: "if we ruin the time, it ruins us and our life." Therefore, all who serve in the vineyard of the Lord should carefully monitor their priorities and be diligent in preserving the value of time.

Value of Time

Author Emma Heatherington once said, "Take time for you when you need it. Sometimes time is all we have with the people we love the most. I ask you to slow down in life. To take your time, but don't waste it."

When the pope was visiting the United States, he held meetings with the priests' wives. One of their significant concerns was the time the priests spent away from home and their families. They put it bluntly, saying they were suffering from "lonely marriage" syndrome. Their husbands were seldom caring for their own wives and children. The pope reminded everyone that taking care of one's family is a priority; after all, it is the domestic church. The family had to have a weekly special day uninterrupted by external affairs. The fact is that priests often do not even have time for themselves and their own state of well-being. Studies have found that priests often neglect their physical health and have a carefree attitude to their emotional health. Intellectual pursuits and similar activities are highly revered, often causing imbalanced lives and leading to inappropriate behaviors that trouble the individual and the faith community.

Welcoming a New Shepherd

Bidding farewell to one shepherd and welcoming another is not an easy task. It is best described as a bittersweet experience. It becomes a concerning experience when it happens too many times and one realizes it is bound to happen again. You suddenly have apprehension about the new priest and how he will fit into the congregation. But who are we to intervene in the Lord's higher plan, for His will be done, or as St. Gerard Majella once said, "Here the will of God is done, as God wills, and as long as God wills." Yet the question remains: Will the new priest fare better than his predecessors?

For those who are understandably in doubt, they have to be patient until the typical honeymoon phase is over. After all, Copts are descendants of the great pharaohs who revered priests as gods in ancient times. Therefore, one dares to say it is in the DNA of Copts to be fundamentally unwilling to accept less than perfection. Hence, the Coptic priest ought to be faultless, unblemished, and angelic in nature. It may be difficult for some congregations to accept anything less than this majestic (though unrealistic) expectation.

Copts are taught and led by example, especially when they struggle to emulate the teaching and leadership of the late HH Pope

Shenouda III. He urged and encouraged all to grow toward perfection. He said, "The perfect man thinks continually on others; on loving others, on what is good for others, on the eternal destiny of others, on the sanctity of others. Himself he places last of all, or the servant of all." Of course, Copts surely appreciate these wonderful virtues, but they yearn to see it first and foremost in their priests! Some early Coptic settlers in the States went to Pope Shenouda III and demanded priests similar to Fr. Mikhail Ibrahim, Fr. Bishoy Kamel, and Fr. Tadros Yacoub Malaty. The pope responded, "Because you have seen exemplary priests, it is hard for you to seek others, but God works with all and through all."

The Very Rev. Fr. Roufail Zaki Youssef

Fr. Roufail Zaki Youssef came from Chicago, where he was invited to serve on October 23, 1990, until he left on February 1, 1991. On January 26, 1991, HH Pope Shenouda III delegated Father Roufail to start serving at St. George Church, and his first day at the church was February 2, 1991. Father Roufail was a mechanical engineer by profession. He graduated in 1974 and taught the subject in Minya, Egypt. Later in life, he yearned to take another path and seriously considered the monastic life. His intention was to emulate the lives of the desert fathers and take a vow of poverty, chastity, and obedience. According to Father Roufail, he wanted to devote his life to angelic and heavenly praises and celebrating the Mass, the very heart of the monastic life. It is a life that is mostly isolated from the world to focus on God.

Apparently that was not God's plan, as Pope Shenouda III, the patriarch of the See of St. Mark, called him out of the monastery to serve. Before priesthood, he married Tasoni Suzan and was ordained on Sunday, November 25, 1979. Tasoni Suzan was also a mechanical engineer who graduated from college in 1976. She went on to earn a baccalaureate degree from the El-Minya Theological Seminary (the Eclerikeia) and ranked first in her graduating class. She is an esteemed person, well respected and wise, whose opinions are appreciated by the St. George Church congregation and beyond. Tasoni was raised in a devout priestly family and was fortunate to have a mother who devoted her life to serving humanity and alleviating human suffering. I had the good fortune to meet Tasoni Suzan's mother and her father, the Very Rev. Fr. Bassellious Sedrak, while they visited the States. Tasoni Suzan clearly pursued the identical path of her parents. When she arrived with Father Roufail in Philadelphia on February 2, 1991, they were accompanied by their two lovely young daughters.

Within a couple years of Father Roufail's committed and steadfast ministry, the congregation multiplied. It soon became obvious that the church building in Conshohocken no longer could accommodate the growing congregation. The two-story stucco building at 100 Third Avenue dated back to the Civil War and was drafty and expensive to heat. The sanctuary contained only ten pews, and folding chairs lined every available space. The Sunday school, with an enrollment of about a hundred children, was crowded, and one of the classrooms was wide open except for a partition. During Fr. Samuel Thabet's tenure, members of the congregation wanted to relocate their church to a site on Spring Mill and Cedar Grove Roads in Whitemarsh Township. Plans to build a church were put on hold until approval could be obtained from the township government for the necessary zoning change. However, the preliminary building plan for the new church was opposed by residents in the area and the Whitemarsh board of supervisors. Eventually, the hope for building a church vanished when the priest was transferred, bringing everything to a halt.

With the arrival of Father Roufail, hope was renewed and the matter was placed on the altar. Fervent prayers by the priest and congregation landed them an opportunity that was not short of a miracle. A couple of years before the arrival of Father Roufail, the Evangelical Lutheran Church of the Trinity in Norristown had been for sale, and the asking price was $990,000. The congregation of St. George could not afford to buy it. However, the Alderfer Auction Company placed a new ad in the newspaper to sell the very same church in an auction. Mr. Magdy Gouda handed the ad to the deacon and secretary of the board, Mr. Sami Faltas. The auction was to be held at 1:00 p.m. on Friday, February 25, 1994.

The newspaper ad did not seem promising due to the earlier unaffordable asking price. However, Father Roufail, after celebrating the Holy Liturgy on that Friday, accompanied board secretary Deacon Sami to the auction as a learning experience. They had no intention of actively participating in the process. They did not even think to take a check to pay the 10 percent fee required to participate in the auction. The auctioneer, however, allowed them to participate without advance payment. They never imagined they would be the highest bidder. But they were, and their winning bid got them the huge church property for only $127,000. It was a miracle, an extraordinary turn of events through which God had revealed Himself to them. The Lord always receives glory, showering His blessings on the faithful and for many miracles that He does in the lives of the worshippers.

A Heavenly Gift

Pastor Kim D. Gulser of Evangelical Lutheran Church of the Trinity took Father Roufail and a delegation from the St. George Church for a tour of the newly purchased property. He provided valuable information about the church regarding the previous worshippers, their culture, and the historical and contemporary heritage of the property. Reverend Gulser said he was glad another Christian church had bought the property. Addressing David Stade, a staff reporter from the *Times Herald*, he said, "These are very nice people. They will be an asset to the community."

The new church property consists of three interconnected buildings. The pastor's residence is an independent building. The other two buildings were modified and connected in 1959 and could be considered as one facility. The oldest building was built in 1849 and contains the main sanctuary on the second floor and a small chapel and several rooms on the first floor. The other building, built in 1914, contains offices and a large auditorium on the second floor. Above the auditorium, there is a small suite consisting of two bedrooms, a living room, and a bathroom. A large hall with a kitchen and restrooms are in the basement. The main church sanctuary accommodates more than three hundred people. Adjacent to it on the same level is a large stage. Behind the stage (connected to the sanctuary) are two rooms. One has been devoted to the baptismal font, and the second is used as the deacons' dressing area and contains cabinets for religious books.

Overlooking the church sanctuary is a large balcony that accommodates approximately forty people. Modifications were made to the balcony to create an enclosed section with soundproof glass for mothers with babies and small children so they can tend to the needs of their children while listening to the Holy Mass. Now, prayers, sermons, and scripture reading in the main sanctuary are heard without disruption. The renovation and modernization process was especially welcomed by senior citizens in the congregation, although worshippers of all ages appreciate peaceful churches.

On the first floor close to the main entry, a small chapel was renovated and designed in the traditional Coptic style and named St. Mena and St. Kyrillos Chapel. Behind and down the hall from the chapel are offices for the priests, the church library, a bookstore, and a large meeting room with a kitchenette. There are more than twelve rooms for Sunday school classes. The basement below the office building was completely renovated and is used for refreshments after service and other social activities. It includes a multipurpose hall, a small stage, a large kitchen, a small grocery store for Middle Eastern food supplies, rest rooms, and a storage closet. An elevator services the basement, first floor, and the second floor leading to the main sanctuary of the church.

The church conforms to traditional Coptic style. The altar is screened from the congregation by an iconostasis that was designed in Egypt and shipped to the States in parts. Atop the screen is a picture of the crucifixion of Christ, flanked by figures of His mother, St. Mary, and Mary Magdalene. Below these figures is a large portrait of the Last Supper. Below that and covering the width of the iconostasis are portraits of the twelve apostles. Beautiful illuminated portraits of other Coptic saints hang on each side of the sanctuary walls. Above the congregation, large crystal chandeliers shimmer all over the sanctuary. The church has magnificent stained-glass windows depicting stories of the Bible. Bishop of Durand de Mende (1230–1296) once said, "Stained glass windows, through which the clarity of the sun is transmitted, signify the Holy Scriptures, which banish evil from us and enlighten our being."

Soon after the church was bought, however, some of these windows cracked and required repairs. Cognizant of the windows' value and importance, Father Roufail assigned the work to one dedicated and capable person. Ms. Nadia Shoukry, a member of St. George congregation and a full-fledged artist in the field, was up to the challenge. Supported by the team at her company, she lovingly restored these windows with the original rich color and luster they once displayed. A team of professionals and members of the congregation spearheaded by engineers and architects Messrs. Farid Mansour, Victor Guirguis, Magdy Barsoum, and the late Iskander Saad did a magnificent job getting the work done in a record time. Architect Maged Monir and a team of carpenters came from Egypt to assemble the iconostasis. The church icons were beautifully designed by Mr. Gamil Samuel Abadeer, adding the spectacular and majestic presence of the angels and saints in the sanctuary.

CHAPTER 21

━◆━<••⟩◆⟨••>━◆━

The Pope of Alexandria's Third
Visit to the United States

*The world sees in our conduct, in our behavior, the proof
that we are the real children of God*

—Pope Shenouda III

O nce the renovation and modernization of the new church was
complete, Father Roufail flew to Egypt to meet with the pope.
He presented a detailed report about all the work that was done and
invited His Holiness to the opening ceremony and consecration of its
altar and icons. His Holiness was quite pleased and commended the
priest and the congregation on the good news. The priest returned,
gratefully blessed with anticipation of the pope's third visit to the
United States scheduled for the fall of 1994.

On October 14, 1994, Pope Shenouda III came to Philadelphia
accompanied by his entourage that consisted of Bishop Reweiss
(general bishop), Bishop Sarapion (bishop of social services), Bishop
Missael of Birmingham, UK, and Bishop Karas of St. Antony
Monastery of California. All spent the night at the Hilton Hotel
in King of Prussia. On Saturday morning, October 15, 1994, the
pope, bishops, Fr. Roufail Youssef, his predecessor Fr. Samuel Thabet
Samuel, and other parish priests led the grand opening ceremony.

Many distinguished guests and clergy from other denominations attended this historic event and were warmly welcomed by the joyous members of the congregation. Mr. Jack Salamone, the mayor of Norristown, and Egypt's ambassador in New York, Ms. Souher Salah Zaki, accompanied by members of the Egyptian consulate, all attended the ceremony.

Ceremonial prayers began at 9:00 a.m. and lasted until noon. After the service, all articles, pictures, and the baptismal font were consecrated. Two children were also baptized that day by the hands of His Holiness: Father Roufail's youngest baby daughter, Marina, and a baby girl named Margaret Kamel. His Holiness handed out medals commemorating the occasion to all participants. An official reception was held at the Marriott Hotel in honor of the occasion, beginning with an opening speech by Fr. Roufail Youssef. He thanked the pope, bishops, and dignitaries on behalf of the members of St. George congregation. He also expressed his gratitude for the blessings that the Holy Father, bishops, and priests showered on St. George parish by their presence, prayers, and participation in this historic event.

In his speech, Father Roufail spoke of the pope's spiritual visits to the States that not only helped in establishing many churches but also proclaimed the faith and affirmed the tradition and orthodoxy of the Coptic Church. The mayor of Norristown also spoke, welcoming the pope and announcing October 15 of each year to be the day of St. George Church in the Norristown area. He handed the pope the key to the city as well as a proclamation honoring Fr. Roufail Youssef and the congregation of St. George Coptic Orthodox Church. The proclamation read:

Proclamation to Honor
St. George Coptic Orthodox Church

WHEREAS, The Mayor of Borough Norristown wishes to honor Pastor Roufail Z. Youssef and the congregation of St. George Coptic Orthodox Church on the glorious occasion of the consecration of their church located at 411 DeKalb Street, Norristown, Pennsylvania; and

WHEREAS, The Coptic Orthodox Church is one of the oldest Apostolic Churches in the world and was established by St. Mark the Evangelist in the first century of Christianity, in Alexandria, Egypt; and

WHEREAS, The head of the Church, Pope Shenouda III, the 117 Pope of Alexandria is the successor of the Patriarchs of Alexandria. The Patriarchs were the first to be called "Pope" which means "Father of Fathers"; and

WHEREAS, After many centuries of being segregated to Egypt, North Africa, the Sudan and Ethiopia the Coptic Orthodox Church today has spread to numerous other countries to include the United States; and

WHEREAS, In the Philadelphia area, St. George Coptic Orthodox Church was established in November 1969 and in June of 1980 a building was purchased in Conshohocken and was deeply loved as their church for more than thirteen years; and

WHEREAS, On February 25, 1994, Pastor Youssef participated in an auction on behalf of his congregation and purchased the magnificent building that is being dedicated today; and

WHEREAS, I, Jack Salamone, Mayor of the Borough of Norristown, do hereby proclaim October 15, 1994 as "St. George Coptic Orthodox Church Day" in Norristown and do urge my fellow citizens to join in observance of this memorable day, in gratitude and respect for the significant contribution the Coptic Orthodox Church has made to our community and to all mankind.

IN WITNESS WHEREOF, I have hereunto set my hand and caused the seal of the
Mayor of Borough of Norristown to be affixed
this 15th day of October, 1994.

Mayor Jack Salamone

Dr. Samir Eldaief spoke next, praising the tremendous efforts of Fr. Roufail Youssef and the cooperation of all members of the parish to accomplish this cherished goal. He stated that the enthusiastic support, sacrificial love, and advanced planning for such an outstanding project resulted in its success. Most importantly, the reality of this fulfilled dream was due to fervent prayers and only took place by God's grace and according to His divine plan.

Finally, Pope Shenouda III addressed the congregation. He thanked the Lord for such a gift to his people; he also thanked the mayor, his staff, the visiting dignitaries, and all distinguished guests for participating in this historic event. He commended all who labored tirelessly to create this beautiful church. He also thanked Father Roufail and the congregation for their sincere efforts and dedicated cooperation to finish such a huge project.

The Pope Defending Faith and Human Rights

His Holiness made countless pastoral visits outside of Egypt. As noted, he was the first pope in the history of the Coptic Church to visit the United States. The longest tour took place from August to December 1989, when he made historic visits to all the Coptic churches in the United States after he was released from exile in January of 1985. As a chief defender of the faith and hero of human rights, he was warmly and enthusiastically welcomed by thousands of Copts wherever he went in the United States, Canada, Europe, and Australia. During this trip, he established new churches, consecrated altars, baptized hundreds of children, ordained countless deacons, and taught, preached, and delivered many lectures at seminaries and universities. He opened theological seminaries in New Jersey and Los Angeles.

Most importantly, he shepherded blessed, and supported the Coptic people wherever he went, and they all held "El-Baba Shenouda" in high regard. During his papacy, ordination of deaconesses was resumed after an interval of several centuries. He motivated and encouraged women to be involved in the church and welcomed them into theological seminaries and communal counsels. He said, "We felt a great need for the work of women, and we wanted women to have certain order and service in the church's board, not only to have girls as Sunday school teachers who give a part of their time whenever they can, but we want girls and women to give their whole life to God and serve the church." He also actively invested in the life of the Coptic youth and created a new episcopate for them, appointing HG Bishop Mousa as the first bishop of youth. He said many times, a church without youth is a church without a future.

He also appointed the first bishops for North American dioceses as well as the first Coptic bishops in Europe, Australia, and South America. In 1996, Copts witnessed the installation of the first two diocesan bishops for the United States, one for Los Angeles, HG Bishop Serapion (HE Metropolitan Serapion), and the other for the southern United States, HG Bishop Youssef.

Unfortunately, in the tenth year of his papacy, the pope's relationship with the president of Egypt deteriorated. In September 1981, he was dethroned and banished to Anba Bishoy Monastery by President Anwar Sadat, who formed a "caretaker council" to replace him.

Under his presidency in the early 1970s, President Sadat had embraced Islam and an Islamist agenda. He had been a member of the Muslim Brotherhood, and in the 1971 constitution, he incorporated principles of Islamic sharia into legislation. He freed Muslim Brotherhood leaders from prison, and those who were in exile abroad returned. Feeling newly empowered, Islamists stepped up violence against Copts, and the burning of churches became a daily occurrence in every part of Egypt.

In November 1972, Muslims torched the Coptic church and the Holy Bible Society building in al-Khanka, Qalyubia. Peaceful Coptic Christians were attacked, and no police forces or fire fighters intervened to save the church and keep the peace. Pope Shenouda III ordered some priests to visit the site and celebrate Mass there. His instructions, which were carried out, incensed Sadat. He perceived the pope's action as challenging his authority. It also aggravated some Muslims in the area. After the priests left al-Khanka, attackers burned many nearby apartments belonging to Copts. The incident marked a new era of persecution, discrimination, and vicious attacks on Copts and their properties across the land.[70]

In his writings, Mohamed Hassanein Heikal, a close adviser to President Sadat at that time, encouraged him to resume building churches as his predecessor Gamal Abdel Nasser had done. Sadat, after meeting with Pope Shenouda III and ranking Coptic leaders, pledged to give twice the number of permits Nasser had granted, but he never followed through. Churches were flash points for anti-Coptic sentiment and subjected to continued attacks. The army and police neither intervened to ensure the safety of Copts nor arrested attackers who instigated violence and destruction.

It was reported that Sadat was angered when the pope refused to preside over Easter services in protest of governmental persecution of Christians. Muslim-Christian clashes in Upper Egypt rapidly spread across every part of the country. Copts living abroad opposed the cruel and unjustified action to keep Pope Shenouda III in exile and replace him with a "caretaker council." The Coptic hierarchy and people forcefully stated that "no one can change whom God has anointed." All along, the pope remained the spiritual leader of the Coptic Orthodox Church for more than four decades. He was reinstated by President Hosni Mubarak in January 1985.

From St. George Coptic Orthodox parish, Dr. and Mrs. Rodolph M. Yanney, Mr. and Mrs. Samir Awadalla, Dr. Raef Morcos, and Mr. and Mrs. Samy Atwan spearheaded a relentless battle to defend the pope while he was in exile and championed human rights for Copts around the world. Their tireless work against tyranny, persecution, oppression, and killing of Copts never ceased. Since 2011, hundreds of Christian Copts have been killed, and many churches, businesses, and homes have been destroyed. Another devastating problem is the abduction of Coptic Christian women and girls and forcing them to convert to Islam. Whenever such crimes were committed, authorities failed to respond.

In May 2010, the *Wall Street Journal* reported increasing "waves of mob assaults" by Muslims against Copts, forcing many Christians to flee their homes. Despite frantic calls for help, the police typically arrived after the violence was over. The police also coerced Copts to accept "reconciliation" with their attackers to avoid prosecuting them, with no Muslims convicted for any attacks. *Time* magazine reported on the fears of the Coptic population after the 2011 Egyptian revolution. Many Christian Copts were killed; others were thrown out of their homes, shops, and businesses; and fields and livestock were plundered and torched. Christians lived in terror, anticipating a bloodbath on Friday, April 22, 2011.[71]

When Pope Shenouda III was in exile, these heroes of St. George congregation adamantly demanded his release and defended the human rights of Coptic Christians in Egypt. In 1980, Dr. Rodolph Yanney began publishing *Coptic Church Review*, serving as its editor in chief. Later, he published *Al-Ressala* and *The Bulletin—A Journal for the American Coptic Youth*. Dr. Yanney not only spoke out but defended HH Pope Shenouda III in print while His Holiness was in exile. One of his contributing writers who also championed the cause was his brother Dr. Raef Morcos. Mr. Samir F. Awadalla, the representative of the American Coptic Association (ACA), was another defender of human rights, along with Dr. Shawki Karas, the head of the ACA in Jersey City, New Jersey. Mr. Awadalla published the *Philadelphia Ressala* that defended the human rights of Coptic Christians. He also represented Coptic Americans in Congress and to the White House with other well-known Coptic figures and speakers such as Mr. Magdy Khalil. Mrs. Amal Awadalla, his wife, not only supported her husband but carried the torch to others. She also served in St. George's Sunday school, raising a new generation of Copts who love their faith and country.

Voice of the Immigrant

Mr. Samy Atwan is the editor in chief and chairman of the board of the *Voice of the Immigrant*, the only Coptic newspaper published in the United States. He supervises the daunting task of publishing the newspaper with very limited financial resources and distributes it free of charge! He has shouldered this responsibility for decades, defending the human rights of Coptic Christians in Egypt, in the United States, and around the world. He has written vigorously and extensively about the recent religious tensions rising in Egypt. Mr. Atwan and his team of reporters have communicated with members of Congress and various presidential administrations.

The *Voice of the Immigrant* still provides a bridge to Copts in different communities in the US and Canada, though distribution has been limited. Due to competition from digital media, few Copts read the newspaper anymore. Financial support vanished as subscriptions dwindled considerably. Regardless of changing times, Coptic communities honor and admire Mr. and Mrs. Samy Atwan. He is considered a hero who has spent his life championing a great cause.

Many people felt the *Voice of the Immigrant* published only pessimistic news about killings, rape, and torture that served only to depress readers. That may be true, but avoiding the reality of the situation is not the answer while Coptic brothers and sisters in Egypt continue to be persecuted. History will record that Mr. Samy Atwan is truly a voice for the voiceless as his bold reporting continues to unveil these atrocities. His struggle for the plight of the Copts in modern times will never be forgotten.

One hopes that the voice of Coptic freedom remains powerful in traditional news outlets and cyberspace media. However, the loving faithful ought to refrain from attacking the clergy in the newspaper and online. Not that they are infallible, but it goes against biblical teaching. In every Coptic Mass, the congregation collectively and earnestly prays for their clergy. The Lord says, "For I say to you, that unless your righteousness exceeds the righteousness of the scribes and Pharisees, you will by no means enter the kingdom of heaven. But whoever says 'you fool' shall be in danger of hell fire." (Matthew 5:20, 22) No one, however, would want to forbid a discreet, humble approach to present wrongdoing or offer constructive criticism of inappropriate behavior. Remaining polite and loving is the best path for improvement.

CHAPTER 22

—⟨••⟩◆⟨••⟩—

St. George Parish: A Monument of Divine Grace

The tree grew and became strong; its height reached to the heavens and it could be seen to the ends of all the earth. Its leaves were lovely, its fruit abundant and it was food for all.

—Daniel 4:11–12

St. George parish grew and became a lovely tree. As described in the Book of Daniel, "The beasts of the field found shade under it. The birds of heavens dwelt in its branches and all flesh was fed from it." (Daniel 4:13) St. George's divine influence has been a constant source of strength. His priests celebrate in faith and through teaching, preaching, and inspiring, they impart the power to endure trial, resist temptation, and forgive others.

Father Roufail's stewardship extended beyond St. George parish. For decades, he traveled far and wide to establish other churches in many states and to impart a similar model of worship and leadership. He serves and shepherds those who do not have a permanent priest or an established local church. Wherever he ministers, Father Roufail is unfailingly benevolent and considerate to those he serves.

El-Keraza Annual Spiritual Contest

Over twenty-three years ago, Father Roufail seriously considered reaching out to Coptic youth in every church on the East Coast. The heads of Sunday schools and all servants were very supportive of this unique mission. Hence, the El-Keraza Annual Spiritual Contest was launched in August 1996. The youth of all churches on the East Coast were to compete in their knowledge of biblical, theological, historical, and traditional subjects. A special committee of religious educators was formed to select appropriate subjects and age-appropriate textbooks. The church bookstore ordered these books months in advance and shipped them to participants in every church so they were well prepared for the contest.

The contest started with an early Mass. The church was filled with eager youth representing their congregations, some accompanied by their priests for support and to participate in this joyous day. The hosts and panel of examiners met with each group of contestants in a cordial and warm reception. Then the tests were administered.

The celebration at the end of two days was full of wit and vitality. All participants, regardless of their scores, were celebrated and rewarded according to the degree of their achievement.

El-Keraza Spiritual Contests carry on to this day, and they have proven to be one of the best ways for our youth to learn and grow. The purpose of the contest is to foster the spiritual growth of the youth by testing their knowledge of and appreciation for their Coptic heritage, history, and traditions. They are encouraged to study the lives of Coptic saints and how they lived their ascetic lifestyle and overcame temptation through abstinence from worldly desires. The goal is for them to emulate the desert fathers' virtues, to be humble and loving and refrain from an easy and pleasurable life. Thus, they learn to follow the Lord's commandment to carry the cross daily, walking in His footsteps. The contest's priority is not based on test "accomplishment." What's important is learning to live a pure life that leads them to serve the Lord here and be with Him in the hereafter.

The contest was and still is a wonderful success. Currently, the digital version of the contest is executed by Fr. Mina Shaheid and monitored by Fr. Roufail Youssef.

Family First

Since they came to serve in Philadelphia, Father Roufail and Tasoni have paid special attention to every member of the church family. In addition to Sunday school service, hymn classes were established for young children. Weekly meetings are conducted for servants, youth, and adults. Clubs, retreats, and summer day camps for youth and children are all structured and executed to provide families with engaging ways to spend time together and gain spiritual, emotional, and physical benefits.

Family Education

Spiritual education is fostered by dissemination of literature, recorded CDs, and other media on every subject pertaining to family life. Open forums pertaining to the challenges of children, youth, and parenting are recorded on CDs so parents who are not able to attend family meetings on Saturdays can listen to the "Family First" lectures when it's convenient for them. Through the library and bookstore, rare books, especially on spiritual, emotional, and marital relations, are brought in to motivate families to grow and improve their home lives. Treasures of the desert fathers, the unending source of knowledge and spiritual guidance by HH Pope Shenouda III, and books by well-known professionals in every field are made available.

The Church's Role in Sexual Education

Parents are considered to be the primary educator for sexual health, even though they often feel embarrassed and uncomfortable addressing the issue. At St. George, the newly immigrated Coptic community was neither willing nor capable of dealing with sex education. It became obvious that parents had neither the skills nor the knowledge to do so. Parents complained about sex education materials being given to their children in public schools and their inability to address the issue. The church is quite aware that in the second half of the twentieth century, sexual liberation became a major social trend. The state assumed a greater role in sex education, and this led to widespread unwanted pregnancies and sexually transmitted diseases. Sex education in schools has been considered unacceptable in light of Christian beliefs and values.

This issue was discussed with Father Roufail, and arrangements were made to invest in a well-prepared curriculum that had been taught previously at St. Mary Church in East Brunswick, New Jersey. The program was based on Christian beliefs, traditions, and views of sexuality as a sacred marital relationship between one man and one woman. The program also aimed to have parents as active participants and implement the same educational instructions at home.

Christian-Based Church Curriculum

The inception of the Christian curriculum began with a demand from the congregation at St. Mary Church in East Brunswick more than three decades ago. The aim was to address the "unacceptable" curriculum of sex education in public schools. The late Fr. Bishoy Demitri invited me to address these serious issues with concerned members at his church. The result was to initiate a "Christian-based church curriculum proposal" that contained structured sex education based on Christian belief and traditional Coptic views of sexuality. The intention was to replace liberal sex education programs that were being taught in public schools. Classes were conducted for many weeks and were well attended by both children and parents.

Upon finishing the course, participants were given a certificate of completion that served as an exemption from attending sex education classes at the public school. The same curriculum was taught to children of appropriate age and their parents at St. George Church and was also a great help for parents at home. As it progressed, its popularity increased via word of mouth. As a result, the program was extended to other Coptic churches on the East Coast and was welcomed and supported by other priests and the hierarchy.

In the culture of the new immigrant population, all of this would not have been possible without the open-minded views and support of families and Fr. Roufail Youssef. He took a special interest in this unique sex education program for the families at St. George Church.

One of the churches that welcomed the program, though it designed the curriculum differently, was Archangel Michael and St. Mena Church on Staten Island. Dr. Magdy Bebawi, who was in charge of Sunday school, servants, and youth meetings, planned similar educational programs on a smaller scale. It consisted of a series of lectures for youth and parents delivered in the church and at retreats at beautiful all-inclusive resorts. His idea was to leave behind daily distractions and allow enough time for relaxation and spiritual rejuvenation. Outdoor and spiritual activities were an integral part of these well-planned and well-executed retreats. They were quite beneficial in addressing societal challenges facing Christian families. The objective of the retreats was to strengthen everyone's beliefs and immunize them against temptations in cyberspace and beyond that caused distraction, depression, and anxiety.

St. George's Well-Structured Program

Father Roufail planned the program as part of a weekly spiritual day that began with Mass on Saturday followed by a break for lunch. Presentations were then made to parents and children together, followed by separate question-and-answer forums. It was very hard, though, to enlist many parents to partner with the church in discussing the topic at home. Open and effective communication between parents and children is an important tool when it comes to the subject of sex. Not only were parents embarrassed and quite uncomfortable talking about sex, but the language barrier was also an obstacle for the newly immigrated families. They were neither able nor willing to talk about sex or bear these responsibilities on the home front.

Therefore, sex education was shouldered and mostly facilitated by the church and her dedicated servants. The educational programs at St. George Church would not have been effective without the dedication and support of the late Deacon Youssef Z. Youssef. Despite his enormous responsibility in the medical field, he devoted some of his valuable time to propagate the message at hand.

One may wonder why churches in general avoid speaking loudly and clearly about sexuality and health. Oftentimes, the subject of sexuality is most often linked to sin or immorality. I feel strongly that it is the church's duty to teach about every aspect of family life, not just spiritual life. Both Fr. Roufail Youssef and the late Fr. Bishoy Demitri are considered pioneers in adopting this important aspect of family life. Avoiding this topic (or its complete absence) is not limited to the Coptic Orthodox Church but is common among many other Christian denominations.

Understanding Sexuality

The subject of sex education at St. George Church focused on understanding sexuality and reproductive health. It aimed to enlighten the family with vital information regarding how human beings are created by a wonderful Creator. Sex education for children and adolescents should not be limited to a set of lectures and workshops. Rather, it needs to be an ongoing conversation between parents and children. Effective and open communication is an important tool to help children understand and calm their anxiety about this sensitive subject. Also, such conversations about the facts of life should start early in life. Dr. Miriam Hauffman, an expert in family medicine, stated, "Beginning a conversation about sex early and continuing that conversation as the child grows is the best sex education strategy."

Communication with children about sexuality encourages them to be more open with their parents in discussing other crucial issues, such as alcohol and drugs. Open communication will encourage them to speak about any topic they may fear or feel ashamed to bring up with parents. Also, parents should refrain from lecturing children about sex or presenting it as a serious matter. The conversation could be initiated after watching a movie or a TV episode. It should be discussed around the kitchen table in an easy manner as a fun topic worth exploring and talking about. Attentiveness and listening to children is an art; responding factually with a consoling, not condescending, attitude results in parents earning their children's respect and cooperation.

Discipleship

Finally and most importantly, the congregation will not forget the work of Father Roufail as he strives to mentor others should the Lord call them for priesthood. It is usually a lifetime's work to bring dedicated servants to serve the Lord. Mentoring is a way to nurture the spiritual maturity of servants who possess a desire to humbly and passionately serve others and be a dedicated follower of the Lord Jesus. Many who he took under his wings were ordained priests serving in different states. One in particular Father Roufail groomed several years ago to serve with him in St. George Church and even arranged his lodging and monetary and nonmonetary remuneration. But this ideal choice slipped out of his hands, and he became a monk serving at St. Antony Monastery in California. Apparently it was not God's plan. Little did he know while he was raising lovely daughters that one would marry a priest to be—something that was not prepared or planned for but was heavenly chosen.

CHAPTER 23

The Call

God doesn't call the qualified, He qualifies those He calls.

—Mark Batterson

*Then Moses said to the Lord, O my Lord, I
am not eloquent, neither before
nor since You have spoken to Your servant: but I am slow of speech
and slow of tongue.*

—Exodus 4:10

St. George parish has grown significantly, and the number of attending families has doubled since the purchase of the new church. Fr. Roufail Youssef, who shouldered the responsibilities of serving every member of the congregation alone, finally needed help from another priest. As the church grew, it was clear he would wear himself out trying to constantly be available for a congregation of over two hundred families. It is impossible, even working more than twelve hours a day seven days a week, including emergency calls at night. Even being supported by Tasoni Suzan was not enough.

Father Roufail is the celebrant of the Holy Liturgy at least three times a week. He serves not only as the preacher but teaches weekly Bible studies, officiates at weddings and funerals, and performs other sacraments. His many responsibilities include home visitations and family counseling during the day or late at night. Hospital visitations are constantly on his schedule to pray for healing and anoint the sick. He visits homebound elderly congregants weekly to help them partake in Holy Communions and look after their needs. He accompanies congregation members when they travel around the country and abroad. Father Roufail heads the fundraising committee for charitable causes and meets the church's huge expenses without burdening the congregation with monthly dues and constantly approaching them for donations.

He not only hosts clergy and Copts from other states and abroad, but he and his family also welcome with open arms newcomers to the parish. His home is wide open to congregation members and strangers alike, and he generously looks after those deserted by parents or spouses. Amazingly, he is always available to take confession anywhere at any time at the church, at home, or even during his visits. He brings comfort to people of every age and from every walk of life. He is a unique priest whose prayers and advice have aided people everywhere. A priest of his many gracious gifts has been praying and looking for a chosen vessel to share with him this huge responsibility.

As mentioned, for years, many of those Father Roufail took under his wing were ordained priests who currently serve in different states. One in particular was groomed by Father Roufail several years ago to serve with him in St. George Church, but he privately preferred the monastic life. It was the same path that Father Roufail once passionately wanted for himself, but the Lord did not will it. God chooses, and the faithful have to learn to submit to His divine plan, as proclaimed in the Book of Samuel: "The Lord sees not as man sees; for man looks on outward appearance, but the Lord looks at the heart." (1 Samuel 16:7) His choice is different as well: "For God has chosen the foolish of the world to shame the wise, and he has chosen the weak of the world to shame the mighty." (1 Corinthians 1:27) Besides, some of those who are not chosen today may be preferred for different times according to His divine providence.

Parting the Sea of St. George

Different church members favored different candidates for ordination to priesthood, resulting in disagreement and polarization. But a Moses-like hand swept over the church, and an extraordinary act of God drove a powerful wind strong enough to part the sea for the new priest to walk on dry land and reach his intended destiny. Unfortunately, the wind not only parted the sea of people for the chosen priest to land safely where the Lord wanted him to serve, but it also parted families and friends and disrupted harmonious relationships.

Saddest of all, the wind swept away the congregation's sense of togetherness, shattering the dreams of youth and shaking their faith. They questioned what they had long believed! They wondered what was real, especially when their experience did not match their expectations. In Sunday school and servant meetings, they were taught the goodness of the Lord and appeared to enjoy a close fellowship with Him. Yet in the midst of the storm and their profound struggle, some of them reacted maliciously and disapprovingly. HG the bishop was present to calm the aftermath of the storm and alleviate the pain of the unwilling to yield to election results. He was kind and graciously respectable even to those who did not show respect. It was a disheartening scene and a disappointing outcome. Recall what HH Pope Shenouda III had to say about division:

> Division of the young against the elder is a proof of rebellion, disobedience, disrespect for superiors…all are sins. Division also is proof of self-superiority or of dignifying one's ego, and the father of confession is most likely not aware of all that goes on, is out of the loop, and is not consulted on anything. In the Epistle of St. Paul, he condemned them for division and described them as "still of the flesh" far from spiritual unity.

History Repeats Itself

Philosopher George Santayana captured it best when he observed, "Those who cannot remember the past are condemned to repeat it." Therefore, it behooves every Coptic church not to forget or ignore the lesson. St. Mark Church, the first Coptic church established on the East Coast of the United States, came to existence after extensive efforts to recover from bitter division among "God's people." As I discussed in previous chapters, as the situation within the Coptic community unfolded, there were proper and improper dealings among congregational members, boards, clergy, and laity. Their interaction regarding conflicting issues saw many "standardized barriers to effective communication" and caused confusion and misunderstanding.

Thus, the Coptic community needs to learn from this episode. There must be a high level of transparency at all times based on shared values and facts, circumstances, and data.

On December 3, 1969, HH Pope Cyril VI, in a letter to both conflicting groups in New York, invited them to unite. Through his wisdom and support, he quoted biblical verse: "Now I plead with you, brethren, by the name of our Lord Jesus Christ, that you all speak the same thing and that there be no division among you, but that you perfectly joined together in the same mind and the same judgment." (1 Corinthians 1:10)

In the case of congregational conflict at St. George, Pope Shenouda III's administration acted to further the wishes of the group who opposed the ordination of the newly elected candidate for priesthood. They requested that the new candidate be placed under scrutiny for six months. Father Roufail considered their request a challenge to the results of the congregation's election results as well as to his spiritual leadership. The majority of the congregation sided with him and declined to postpone the ordination any further. Again, the same pattern of communication was set in motion: the opposing group addressed the issue directly and swiftly, dispatching their concern to the upper echelons of the church. As stated earlier, habitual direct communication with the pope has been a strange phenomenon of the Coptic laity in the diaspora.

A bishop in the pope's office in Egypt carried the opposing group's wish to separate and incorporate a new church, thus bypassing the diocese's governing bishop at the time. The words of Pope Shenouda III were crystal clear when he spoke about division and stated that "division is a proof that the ego is alive…the ego that work alone away from the Spirit of God…that wants to exert its opinion regardless of what the result may be and does not care what disastrous outcomes division causes." There was a sense that the upper echelons of the church secretly aspired to expansion and "the more churches the merrier." It would increase the number of churches outside Egypt and prevent further confrontation in the house of the Lord.

Pope Shenouda III visited St. George Church of greater Philadelphia during the tenures of Father Angelos, Father Samuel, and Father Roufail. During the first visit, he did not want to meet the congregation in a rented property in South Philadelphia. Instead, arrangements were made for the reception to be held at St. George Greek Orthodox Cathedral in Philadelphia. During the second visit, the church made arrangements for a grand reception at Valley Forge Military Academy in Wayne, Pennsylvania. The itinerary included a stop at St. George's purchased property in Conshohocken to bless it and consecrate its alter and articles. While His Holiness's motorcade was en route to the church, he realized the purpose of the visit and immediately requested a change at the last minute. The motorcade turned around while in the borough of Conshohocken and proceeded to his official residence in Center City, Philadelphia. No reason was given, and no one apparently dared to ask. It was not for security reasons because security personnel were behind him in the motorcade and honored his request. On the pope's third visit, he welcomed the invitation by Fr. Roufail Youssef after hearing the good news about the purchase of an elegant church property in Norristown, Pennsylvania.

The Sun Shines After the Storm

True Christians well know that regardless how stormy the weather may be and how cloudy it gets, the sun will shine again. The

American Christian televangelist speaker Dr. Robert H. Schuller said once in his weekly *Hour of Power* television program, "No matter how tough times get, you have the potential to achieve the best." That is exactly what happened to members of the St. George congregation of greater Philadelphia. They had their desire fulfilled, and the person they wished to have as a priest was ordained by the hands of HH Pope Shenouda III on November 14, 2009.

The Rev. Fr. Mina Shaheid

He was born on December 12, 1979, in Egypt to devoted Christian parents. The family came to the United States when Mina and his sister were still children. His father, Mr. George Abdel Shaheid, was a pious man, an accountant who occupied a prestigious governmental job in Alexandria and stood up in the face of persecution during the reign of President Anwar Sadat. He was unjustly imprisoned and suffered significantly. In "A Prisoner's Journal of Black September 1981," he described how he and his fellow Christians were violently mistreated for honoring the name of Christ but were blessed by the spirit of glory and of God that rested upon them during these tough times. Having had the honor and blessing of meeting with him and his family, I found them to be godly children who lived by spirit and faith. The Bible describes their experience well: "All who live godly in Christ Jesus shall suffer persecution." (2 Timothy 3:12)

Father Mina was groomed for preeminence, thus fulfilling his father's petition to the Lord while he was in captivity. He earnestly prayed that Mina would be a "pillar in the Coptic Orthodox Church" and his sister an arm of justice and protection to restore fairness and equality. The good Lord granted his wishes. Mina was ordained a priest, and his sister became a high-ranking law enforcement officer in the American justice system. When they arrived in the United States, the family settled in Brooklyn, New York, and attended St. George Church, where the father serves today as a member of the board of deacons. The Very Rev. Fr. Mina Kamel Yanni is the archpriest of the church. Deacon Mina was mentored and nurtured by this noble and loving priest. He was well prepared for priesthood since youth.

It is worth noting that St. George Church of Brooklyn where Deacon Mina grew has been in the news for many good reasons but mainly for the miracle of the blessed Virgin Mary's icon dripping holy oil. The icon was originally housed in the home of Mr. Samir Roshdi Botros. On the morning of March 20, 1994, the icon of St. Mary the Virgin was found dripping significant amounts of oil, and the house was overwhelmed by visitors. Mr. Botros was unable to contain the crowd, so the icon was transferred to St. George Church in Brooklyn. The transfer was broadcast by the media. Bishop Markos, a member of the Holy Synod of the Coptic Church who was visiting at the time, told ABC News that "the miracle is true" and affirmed its validity, adding that similar occurrences happened in Egypt and at St. Mark Coptic Orthodox Church in Houston, Texas.

Before priesthood, Father Mina was married to Shiri Youssef on May 26, 2007. She is a delightful and resilient young woman and, like her husband, grew up in the United States and survived the American cultural mentality of the "me" generation. She proved to be emotionally talented to cope with views that challenged her own Coptic culture. The Lord well prepared her for the role that awaited her to help and support new generations of Coptic youth. She and her husband, Father Mina, adapted quickly to a world undergoing rapid technological change while preserving their heritage of Coptic culture and tradition. Shiri was raised in a devout priestly family and was fortunate enough to be the daughter of Fr. Roufail Youssef and Tasoni Suzan and granddaughter of the Very Rev. Fr. Bassellious Sidrak.

After ordination, Father Mina served his orientation time at the Archdiocese of North America, then was assigned to serve at St. John the Beloved and St. Mary Magdalene Orthodox Church in Randolph, New Jersey. Members of St. George were delighted when a papal decree finally was issued by HH Pope Shenouda III a couple of months later to transfer him to St. George Church, where he was originally chosen. Little did they know that the good Lord planned this path, where he would first serve with HG Bishop David at the

Archdiocese of North America, then at St. John the Beloved and St. Mary Magdalene, where he enjoyed personal autonomy, having the capacity to make decisions and pursue independence.

A Gifted Priest

No doubt Father Mina was groomed for preeminence early in life by his parents, his church, his school, and his own spiritual zeal. The sacrament of the Holy Orders, like that of baptism, confers an indelible character on the recipient. The vocation and mission he received the day of ordination set him permanently on the path of service and sacrificial life. He and those he shepherds continue to pursue the path of discipleship, characterized by denial of self, taking up the cross daily, and following Him. This path understandably begins in the life of the family, the church, the community, and society, but it ends beyond all thinking in the home that is His for evermore. Father Mina is surely a gifted priest and "for everyone to whom much is given, from him much will be required; and to whom much has been committed, of him they will ask the more." (Luke 12:48)

Communicating Knowledge and Skills

Father Mina is quite talented when it comes to church prayers, the general structure of the Holy Liturgy, the different elements of Eucharistic prayers, and reading and explaining the Word. He preaches in a loud and clear voice, and no matter whether it is prayers, readings, teaching, or singing, all are done meticulously. Father Mina is quite cognizant of the different cultures and languages of members of the congregation. He is a trilingual priest, speaking fluent English, Coptic, and Arabic, and communicates well across the cultural and language spectrum.

When it comes to Coptic hymns, he is a maestro, which makes him an excellent teacher. He teaches hymns to different ages and pays special attention to the deacon's choir. The fruits of these efforts paid substantial dividends, as many children and adults have won prizes in hymn competitions throughout the years. Not only does he take his ministry seriously, but at all times he strives to remain current within the fields of his interest.

Continued Education

When Father Mina found a need for supporting members of the congregation with their personal issues and family problems, he went to school and earned a graduate degree in counseling. He clearly showed a strong desire to help people with challenges of daily life based on biblical and spiritual principles. Thus, by the year 2017, he had earned his master's degree in professional counseling from Liberty University, a private Christian university in Lynchburg, Virginia, and one of the largest nonprofit Christian universities in the world. Father Mina is an achiever who is cognizant of the fact that the day he stops learning is the day he stops growing. In 2018, he undertook additional biblical studies, and following that he started on his doctorate degree in congregation and family care in 2019.

To those who still wonder about the purpose of his continued education after earning a master's degree, the answer is simply that Father Mina, a decade ago, recognized the call to serve and to consecrate his life to the church and God's people. After ordination, he has enriched the community with his teaching, preaching, and leadership. In addition, he knew that seeking higher degrees in congregation and family care at a specialized graduate school would empower him and deepen his knowledge. Integration of experience and theological reflection will greatly enrich and enhance his perspectives.

Those who have the pleasure to work with him and witness his career advancement in counseling can easily point to the considerable benefit of his continued education. It furthers his understanding to professionally help others. He has learned to manage conflict without being defensive or personally offended and while always maintaining a smile. Because of his humility, he has subjected himself to learning, growing, and becoming cognizant of his limitations, using them to move forward in life. To his credit, he is a straightforward person, though some may not appreciate his sincerity and tender care. He is unlike many in his position who shield themselves behind the dignity of the priestly robe with an appearance of modesty yet feel and act with a sense of superiority. Thus, they may think there is no need to grow. This is true not only in the Coptic Church but in other denominations as well.

To illustrate the benefit of a loving and caring clergy, *Catholic Faith in Real Life* noted, "Don't put priests on a pedestal." Fr. Donald Cozzens wrote,

> Clericalism is an attitude found by many (but not all) clergy who put their status as priests and bishops above their status as baptized disciples of Jesus Christ. In doing so, a sense of privilege and entitlement emerges in their individual and collective psyche. This, in turn breeds a corps of ecclesiastical elites who think they're unlike the rest of the faithful.

CHAPTER 24

◆—⟨•••⟩◆⟨•••⟩—◆

St. George Parish: Historical Perspective

I. His Grace Bishop Karas

For me, it is essential to have the inner peace
and the serenity of prayers
in order to listen to the silence of God, which
speaks to us, in our personal life
and the history of our times, of the power of love.

—Adolfo Perez Esquivel

At St. George Church once again, history was made. HG Bishop Karas was enthroned by a delegation of bishops appointed by HH Pope Tawadros II on December 2, 2017. The enthronement process was one of the most magnificent celebrations since the opening ceremony at St. George Church during the visit of HH Pope Shenouda III on October 15, 1994. The joy of this event was immense as all the bishops were on hand to witness and attest to the enthronement of Bishop Karas as the bishop of the Diocese of Pennsylvania, Delaware, Maryland, and West Virginia. The diocese of these states was assigned, declared, and officiated on November 11, 2017, by the pope of Alexandria and the Holy Synod in Egypt.

Bishop Karas was born on November 18, 1965. Since a young age, he knew he desired to answer a "calling of God." He joined the

Coptic Theological Seminary in 1983 and graduated in 1987 with a bachelor's degree in theological sciences. After graduation, he spent one year in the Egyptian military and was honorably discharged in 1989. He then served as a consecrated deacon for the Diocese of Tahta and Johaina from 1989 to 1992. Later that year, he joined the monastery of St. Bishoy in Wady El Natroun, Egypt. On June 8, 1993, he was ordained a monk and given the name of Abouna Karas El Orshalimy (Father Karas of Jerusalem). He served in Jerusalem from June 1993 until 1995, and then he returned to the monastery of Anba Bishoy.

On June 7, 1999, he was ordained a priest and served in England at the Diocese of Ireland, Scotland, and North East England with HG Bishop Antony until 2014. During that time, he was elevated to the rank of hegemon on September 10, 2011. He was then ordained a bishop on June 1, 2014, and appointed Exarch of His Holiness Pope Tawadros II of North America on August 2, 2014. HG Bishop Karas is the first bishop enthroned for the newly formulated Diocese of Pennsylvania, Delaware, Maryland, and West Virginia.

Noteworthy: Article I

According to the *Nicene and Post-Nicene Fathers*, as quoted in the uniform bylaws for the Coptic Orthodox Church in North America dated June 4, 2010, chapter 3:

ARTICLE I

The bishop of each diocese is the head of the churches in his diocese and is the one responsible for all the churches, the priests, the monasteries and seminaries in his diocese with the exception of the monasteries and seminaries which belong to the Patriarchate. He is also responsible for all spiritual, financial and administrative matters in his diocese and in all of the churches in his diocese.

His Grace the Bishop

Those who were blessed to meet the bishop, listen to his teaching, or join in celebration of Mass found him a kindhearted shepherd, watchful and diligent in God's service. He is willing to listen to others and cares about their opinion for the love of God. His quiet and solemn demeanor with an occasional sparking smile puts his company at ease. Over the years, he was never seen surrounded by an entourage, nor did he isolate himself from his flock even during formal occasions. He sat among them, sharing a meal and conversing with all. He is a man of few words but with a wealth of wise ideas, emphatically pastoral and practical.

His monastery life shaped his life, engulfed his being, and clothed him with modesty and serenity. His service in Jerusalem, Ireland, Scotland, and England equipped him with a breadth of knowledge and shaped him to deal with the currents of change. His appointment as Exarch of His Holiness Pope Tawadros II of North America provided him with comprehensive experience in leadership and priestly life. Through it all, he presented himself as a stalwart symbol of a leader-servant of faith-filled tranquility, honest realism, and gracious humility. We, the beneficiary of his service, now pray for him with gratitude and great love.

The Office of the Bishop

A bishop, a title derived from the Greek word *episckoes* (overseer), is a direct successor to the apostles. Bishops have, by divine institution, taken the place of the apostles as pastors of the church. The installation of HG Bishop Karas as the first bishop enthroned for the newly formulated diocese was indeed a historic event. The enthronement ceremony, December 2, 2017, is a day that is engraved not only in the minds and hearts of the parishioners but also marked the permanent presence of the successor of St. Mark the Evangelist among them. Almost five decades after establishing St. George Coptic Orthodox Church in Philadelphia, the good Lord has chosen and appointed a superb, sublime, and loving bishop.

HG Bishop Karas is quite popular and loved by the parishioners. Everywhere the bishop goes, members of the congregation flock to take pictures with him. One can easily detect the intimacy and harmony between the shepherd and the shepherded. The way those in the picture lean toward him and touch him, asking for his prayers and blessings, speaks volumes about their connectedness. It is also worth noting that while worshippers rush to take a photo with His Grace, they are happy to capture the occasion and share it with friends and loved ones. Posing in photographs with the bishop reveals a great deal about the loving tradition, closeness, and intimacy of the Coptic community but more importantly about the Coptic respect for their shepherds.

Parents will do well to teach their children that the bishop is an ecclesiastical dignitary who possesses the fullness of the priesthood. He rules the diocese as the chief pastor. It is a tenet of the Coptic faith that bishops are of divine institution. Children learn as such to respect and appreciate those who are in authority over them. Parents not only train children to honor such important principles but also are consistent with their expectations by being themselves models of respect for law and authority. Parents ought to be models for their children whenever there is a disagreement or conflict among family members or the one body. Social media is not the place to address these issues. Social media is a great tool for reaching out to others and even proclaiming the Good News. However, it can also be a liability when it is used as a medium to express anger or to defame.

Shielding Human Dignity

Copts of all ages ought to refrain from using social media as a tool to express their frustration or disagreement about what happens inside or outside the church. Youth especially should think twice before posting anything. When communicating via social media, parishioners ought to read over the tweet or blog post before rushing to act. Using common sense, morals, and good Christian judgment will prevent the hasty from causing trouble for themselves and others. As the Bible puts it, "Whoever guards his mouth and tongue keeps his soul from troubles." (Proverbs 21:23) One can extend this biblical wisdom to avoid unethical communication via any type of media. Practicing moral, ethical communication is important to avoid any appearance of impropriety, disunity, and engaging in harmful relationships. Always remember that nothing is deleted from the internet and becomes what amounts to a permanent record to follow the person's life and hold him or her accountable.

The Bishop's Conceptual Theology

Since enthronement, HG Bishop Karas has been governing with fidelity those entrusted to his care. As a Vicar of Christ, he continues building the church into a sacrament of unity, love, and peace in the diocese and the Christian community at large. His Grace in his leadership role, his homilies, and exhortations has defended the Orthodox faith and its traditional institutional and conceptual structure. The clash between the Gospel's true message and societal culture in this century often forms the Bishop's position and the themes of his homilies. His theology has obviously been influenced by the fathers of the Church. After all, his monastery life shaped his thoughts, engulfed his being, and clothed him with modesty and serenity. The major themes of his conceptual theology are salvation of humankind, biblical theology, and eschatology. Christ Pantocrator is the ruler of the universe, thus our lives are under his protection. There should be no place in the faithful's heart to fear or worry about the world's distractions and influences. As long as the flock remains vigilant following the Lord's commandments, they can show the world there are right and wrong standards for God.

Eschatology: A Paramount Concern

One aspect of theology that appears to concern His Grace the most is the perpetual theme of Christian eschatology. It is a major branch of Christian study concerning death, judgment, and the final destiny of the human soul. His Grace tends to touch on this subject often, focusing his homilies on being prepared and ready to meet with the Lord at any given time. He reminds everyone that the end of time could be at hand any moment. He doesn't necessarily mean that the second coming of Christ and reunion with the Divine is imminent, for that could happen even after thousands of years. However, he says, "If Christ does not come, we may go to Him" in a time not known to anyone.

Praxis of Eschatology

HG Bishop Karas's inspiring word tends to articulate the praxis of eschatology, to seek and save souls before it is too late. Adopting the praxis that he teaches leads to a safe path in this earthly life and keeps the person from indulging in worldly pleasure. There are three core strategies for this praxis that the faithful must do. First, they must "establish" their hearts for His coming. In the words of St. James, "Be patient, brethren, until the coming of the Lord… Establish your hearts, for the coming of the Lord is at hand." (James 5:7–8) Second, they must be watchful and prudent: "But the end of things is at hand; therefore be serious and watchful in your prayers…and to have fervent love for one another, for love will cover a multitude of sins." (1 Peter 4:7–8) Third, the faithful must be cognizant of the reality of the second coming and practice what they have received and been taught, the mystery and doctrine of the orthodox faith.

Always his Grace reminds worshippers everywhere he speaks that the Coptic Church has received the word, traditions, and doctrine of the orthodox faith from Christ and his apostles. Therefore, one ought to listen to the words of Christ and to "hold fast what you have till I come." (Revelation 2:25) His Grace alerts his congregation against false doctrines of those who call themselves Christians who form their own estranged practices and may have strayed from the true path of salvation. "For the time will come when they will not endure sound doctrine but according to their own desires shall they heap to themselves teachers, having itching ears; and they will turn their ears from the truth, and shall be turned unto fables." (2 Timothy 4:3–4)

* * * * *

II. St. George Evangelical Mission

If a church cares about budgets and buildings more than caring for
people and their salvation, such a church should close its doors,
for a church without mercy lives in deception.

—Fr. Tadros Yacoub Malaty

From the very beginning of his service, Father Roufail gave special attention to children and the youth. He focuses on building their spiritual life, monitoring their emotional health, and instilling in them values and social skills that carry them forward to successful adulthood. Youth are the future of the church, and it is very important to educate, guard, and support them at this critical stage. It is also the time when they need to avoid choices and behaviors that will limit their future potential. Parents, families, and the church play a crucial role in helping young people navigate this phase. These spiritual, educational, and service programs are not limited to within the walls of the church but are extended to service in surrounding communities and on university campuses in the area.

Youth, under the guidance and support of the church, formed committees for outreach to catechize and look after those families who needed visitation. They were part of parish youth ministries in colleges, community service corps, and agape camp retreats. Others reached out to nursing homes and volunteered as members in the Office for Youth and Young Adults (OYYA). A youth represented the church at the Interfaith Consortium of Greater Cumberland to serve the elderly and disadvantaged as part of Appalachian Work Camp. Others were selected as participants in the Native American Experience. A number of them went abroad to serve as part of the Mexico Mission Experience, where they taught Sunday and English classes and donated food and clothes. Others went as far as South Africa to serve the Bishopric of African Affairs with HG Bishop Antonious Markos and HG Bishop Paul. Youth also joined missionary trips with the late Fr. Bishoy Demitri and Fr. Mark Hanna to monasteries in Egypt, as well as to Coptic families living below the poverty line in Upper Egypt and wherever they found them. They serve, learn from, and provide financial aid and support to these families. They come back inspired, very appreciative of their mission, and enthusiastic to return and serve again. They serve as goodwill ambassadors inviting Coptic youth in other parishes to join the mission and expand the service. They grow spiritually, emotionally, and cognitively.

A Monastic Experience

Most of the youth took part in retreats at St. Antony Monastery in California. To give the reader a flavor of the spiritual experience and the balance it created in their lives, the following are excerpts from an article titled "A Worthy Expedition" that was written by one participant:

> When I first heard about this trip to California, I was galvanized. To me, this was a chance to discover a new world on the other side of our vast country. It was a chance to see the edge of the largest body of water on the planet. It was a chance to live, for eight days, as one has never lived before.
>
> Three days were spent at St. Antony Monastery; five were spent at various tourist attractions around the state. These included two days at Disneyland, a day at Universal Studios, the San Diego Zoo, and Sea World. As I will show you, it was eight days full of spiritual uplifting and recreation.
>
> The time spent at the monastery was time spent with God. We learned much from the monks and their humble way of life. The monastery was located in an isolated desert encompassed by towering mountains. The night sky was breathtaking. The stars manifested the sky as

bright as great city light, and the sight of the sun setting behind the red snow-capped mountains was astonishing. There is no better place to be close to God than in the midst of his awesome creation.

Each night there was an Ashaya (vespers). Each early morning at four o'clock there was a Tezbeha (praises), and at night there was a liturgy. The Saturday that we were there was also Kiak (4th month in the Coptic Calendar). That day Ashaya lasted from three till seven, we were given a three hour break, and at ten o'clock on Saturday night, Kiak began. (Kiak is the month of the praising of the Virgin Mary during the Advent season.) It was not over until five o'clock Sunday morning. It was immediately followed by a liturgy led by [the late] Bishop Karas.

Sunday night Ashaya was in a church built for St. Moses the Black. It was behind the oil-sleeping tree in which he appeared three times and performed many miracles. After Ashaya, Abouna (Father) Mousa sat and talked with the youth, as he had also done Friday and Saturday. But sooner than we had deemed possible, Monday morning had arrived. So we packed our bags, went to Tezbeha, and left the monastery.

I would have ended the story here but I must give credit where credit is due. There are a few talented people, whose names need not be mentioned, that put this expedition together and kept it together the entire trip. This is no small feat. People are not always easy to deal with, and nobody knows that more than our organizer. Twenty-five people entrusted eight days of their lives to these men, and none of them were disap-

pointed. On behalf of all the excursionists, thank
you. Congratulations for a job well done.

A Teenager's Plight

Among the Coptic youth, there was one who loved to serve and
be part of church life and missionary work. His mission was within
the city of New York, attracting and encouraging other youths to
follow in his footsteps. He surprised his Sunday school teachers by
presenting a challenge to defend Origen (ca. 185–254). Although he
was one of the most prolific and influential of early church fathers,
the Coptic Orthodox Church has yet to consider Origen a saint. He
was one of the most accomplished and distinguished of all theologians of the ancient church, admired for his astounding scripture exe-
gesis. Regretfully, few have been more misunderstood than Origen.

That very Coptic teenager who took upon himself to defend
Origen was named Mina. After a thorough investigation, he concluded that the Coptic Church needs to reconsider his place among
the church fathers.

This teenager surprisingly digested Origen's spirituality and
understanding of scripture, admired his role in the revival of Latin
monasticism, and came to this conclusion to defend Origen. Today,
that very Mina has been serving at St. George Church of greater
Philadelphia as the Rev. Fr. Mina Shaheid. One may predict that
his mission to uphold the place of Origen in the Coptic Orthodox
Church will continue. The late Dr. Rodolph M. Yanney—the
founder and editor in chief of *Coptic Church Review*—in his effort to
have the Coptic Church of Alexandria reconsider its view of Origen
and count him among the saints, wrote to HH Pope Shenouda
III and the members of the Holy Synod in February 2005, asking
them to (1) publish the teaching of Origen among the Copts, and
(2) include Origen in the commemoration of the saints during the
Liturgy because he was a teacher to many, including St. Athanasius
and St Cyril. It was Dr. Yanney's last letter before his departure to
eternal rest.

III. Establishing St. George Mission Church in South Philadelphia

> *I believe that in each generation God has*
> *called enough men and women*
> *to evangelize all the yet unreached tribes of the*
> *earth. It is not God who does not call.*
> *It is man who will not respond!*

—Isobel Kuhn

In 2009, Father Roufail became aware that some families were unable to travel long distances to actively participate in all church activities. Many of them had to take public transportation to attend service at St. George Church in Norristown, so he considered finding a property closer to where they lived in South Philadelphia. Besides, the city has many famous elite colleges and universities. Coptic youth are attracted to these schools, and they come from different parts of the country to pursue their undergraduate and postgraduate education. They, too, needed to find the spiritual and emotional support of the church. Therefore, the caring shepherd spearheaded efforts to find a location in the city of Philadelphia to serve worshippers where they resided. By God's grace, a property was located, a medical building that was bought, renovated, and modernized in October of 2010.

The South Philadelphia location is being prepared as a church with one mission: to eventually evangelize and spread the Good News in the US and abroad. Fr. Mina Shaheid is leading the efforts and is in charge of the evangelizing mission in collaboration with Fr. Roufail Youssef. Father Mina has extended his missionary work abroad accompanied by enthusiastic youth serving at St. Mark Coptic Church in Bermuda. In addition, they've established an online Bible study and participated in the LOGOS-Temple Campus Ministry. On April 17, 2019, both Father Roufail and Father Mina joined HG Bishop Karas to pray and christen the almost four-acre piece of land in preparation for building the newly designated St.

George Church and parish in Plymouth, PA. The project will be completed by the grace of God within the third decade of the twenty-first century.

CHAPTER 25

Pope Tawadros II of Alexandria

The episcopate is a work, not a relaxation; a solitude, not a luxury;
a responsible ministration, not an irresponsible domination;
a fatherly supervision, not a tyrannical autocracy.
It is more important to be proficient in good
works than in golden-tongued preaching.

—St. Isidore of Pelusium

The Lord Heard the Cry

And the Lord said, "I have indeed seen the oppression of My people who are in Egypt, and heard their cry." (Exodus 3:7) So the merciful God chose a righteous man to come to the office of papacy, HH Pope Tawadros II. Despite the recent spilling of blood of hundreds of martyrs in Egypt in the twenty-first century, the Lord acted in His due time. Those who joined the legions of martyrs throughout our Coptic Church history, along with the fervent prayers and fasting of the faithful, moved the hand of God that moves the world. He heard martyrs who "cried with a loud voice, saying, 'How long, O Lord, holy and true, until You judge and avenge our blood on those who dwell on the earth?'" (Revelation 6:10) Thus, the Lord swiftly answered by sending a chosen vessel through which all Copts will glorify the Lord and witness the changing face of history in Egypt and across the world.

God willing, the Copts will see amazing transformations in Egypt during the 118th pope's reign that have not been seen since Joseph and his family fled to Egypt in the first century. God, it is said, sends the world saints when they are most needed—not men and women of "general holiness" but men and women who fit into the pattern of the times and are capable of giving God's tone to their century. The church of St. Mark the Evangelist in the twenty-first century would be "a city that is set on a hill cannot be hidden," and her faithful children will always be "the light of the world." (Matthew 5:14) Tertullian famously said that "the blood of the martyrs is the seed of the church."

A Visionary Pope

In writing this text, I tried to cover significant aspects of Coptic Orthodox Church history in the United States over the last five decades. The intention was to examine and objectively analyze historical events that led to establishing the Coptic Church and extending its roots into the new land. I also attempted to objectively determine the process and pattern by which the Coptic Church expanded outside Egypt. The church was confined for thousands of years within its boundaries where St. Mark the Evangelist founded it in Alexandria. However, it became a global church within approximately the last five decades. Thus, I could have ended the book there. But HH Pope Tawadros II posed a remarkable question and challenged the Copts to find an answer to it while visiting Canada in September 2014.

The pope is known for his pragmatism, wit, and unflappability and wants to set the church on a new path to act proactively instead of reactively. His Holiness uses a big vision as the basis for what the church ought to do. He is motivating Copts to use long-term thinking to create lasting benefits for the church in the twenty-first century. The question posed by His Holiness is more than an inspired call—it is a challenge! He wants the Coptic community to explore and plan the church's catechism activity over the next fifty years. More precisely, Copts need to figure out, through long-term planning, a specific set of goals that outline the path for the church's future and mission.

The Pope's Leadership Style Revealed

His Holiness Pope Tawadros II is the 118th pope of Alexandria and patriarch of the See of St. Mark. He was enthroned on November 18, 2012, at the Cathedral of St. Reweis in Abbassia, Cairo, Egypt. His leadership style and remarkable vision became apparent immediately after his enthronement when he openly stated that the Coptic Church is *not* a "papal church" but a synodical church (Arabic: *Kanisa Magmaeia*) (كنيسة مجمعية). In one of his first homilies as pope, he spoke about healing the paralytic man carried by four men. Since his friends could not get him to Jesus because of the crowd, they made an opening in the roof above Jesus and then lowered the mat the man was lying on.

When Jesus saw their faith, he said to the paralyzed man, "Son, your sins are forgiven." The man, prior to this healing, was dependent on the compassion of those four men, and the Lord was impressed by the faith of his friends. (Mark 2:1–12) Here His Holiness the pope revealed a unique insight about his belief in how the leadership of the church ought to continue, not only by the pope as one leader, but collectively by the whole church. His leadership style was further explained when he compared these four men in the biblical story to the leadership he intended for the Coptic Church. He stated that these compassionate men resemble the role of the church leadership in seeking and saving souls, saying, "They are the bishops, the priests, the deacons, and all the people." This style of leadership requires others, and that implies the collective mission of every member of the faithful. The mission of all clergy and laity together should be to maximize efforts toward the highest goal of seeking and saving souls. That is exactly what the Lord Jesus was sent to do: "For the Son of Man has come to seek and save that which was lost." (Luke 19:10)

The pope genuinely defined his role when he said, "I put myself in the hands of Christ, who is the true leader of the church."

The Pope's Servant-Leadership Style

Pope Tawadros II, while in Alexandria in April of 2019, reiterated his "servant-leader" style, stating, "God has chosen us to serve, and we have conscience, heart, and mind, and service in the church [is] not one [person]; we have the Holy Synod. We in the synod complement each other, and the grace of the Lord and 'His eye sees everything.' We feel that Jesus supports us, and Jesus's grace would not let words or attacks disturb our peace and your prayers also backed us up." His Holiness further explained that the most successful service is "service of love." If you love your service, you reap hundredfold.

Love comes through personal and close connections that form emotional bonds. Those you serve will never leave the church when they feel this love. This is true service that captures people by love through personal connection. Telephone calls are limited to verbal communication and lack the effective presence to truly engage. He compared this to a picture of flowers you send someone, which you can neither touch nor enjoy its fragrance, unlike when you offer them a bouquet. Personal connection is an incarnate expression of love. "In serving," the pope has said, "we need service of love; as such we win souls." All of this is to emulate Christ and be counted among the saints.

The following is his famous quote:

> Love never ends or fails. Love never ends. Everything must be based on love—the relation between two friends, my ministry, my service; the Church services in every field must be based on love. Why? Because God is Love.

Politicization of the Church

For many reasons, the preceding pope of Alexandria adopted a different approach and advocated political views on behalf of the church. The political decision-making process was mainly in the hands of the upper echelons of the church hierarchy. At the same time, certain members of the laity felt quite uncomfortable that the church addressed societal and political affairs single-handedly. The dominant role of the clergy became obvious to government security forces. In turn, they considered the church the voice of the laity and indirectly dictated their demands through the church. That created tension between the laity and the clergy and manifested clearly in protests against the church's stance and its call for restraint.

On New Year's Eve of January 2011, the al-Qiddissin church was bombed, killing at least twenty-one people and injuring seventy others. Ordinary Copts refused to side with the call of the church and President Mubarak to maintain unity and peace. Hundreds of angry Copts clashed with Muslims and police after the bombing. Deteriorating relations between laity and clergy were also evident when many declined to abide by Pope Shenouda's ban on pilgrimages to Jerusalem.[72] The ban was originally put in effect by Pope Cyril VI after the 1967 Six-Day War with Israel. With the loss of Jordanian control of East Jerusalem, Coptic pilgrims visiting the Holy City meant visiting a country that Egypt was at war with.

The 1979 peace treaty between Israel and Egypt should have normalized relations between the two countries. Although the treaty was unpopular in Egypt and the rest of the Arab world, Sadat wanted the Copts to resume pilgrimages to Jerusalem to help normalize Egypt-Israel relations. Pope Shenouda III did not sign on to this plan and decreed a papal ban on visits to the Holy Land. He stated that Copts would only visit Jerusalem hand in hand with their Muslim countrymen. Muslims in Egypt and the Arab world praised the pope, whereas he was sharply criticized by President Sadat and his administration.

According to the *New York Times*, Pope Shenouda's "autocratic tendencies" stifled internal changes in the church. In 1981, he was sent into internal exile by President Sadat because of his strong stance against discrimination, oppressive policies, and deadly attacks by Muslims on Copts. Under Pope Shenouda III, "the church became the de facto political representative of the Copts."[73] With the arrival of Pope Tawadros II, the leadership style has changed, and the church has witnessed a growing Coptic role in community leadership, including Copt representation in Egyptian political parties and parliament. Also, a new generation of youth emerged who struggled during the Egyptian revolution of 2011. They learned to demand their human rights and participate in political parties. Thus, they made themselves responsible for their own affairs, actions, and struggles independent of church interference.

Pope Tawadros II's Views on Politics

When a reporter from *Arab News* met with Pope Tawadros II and tried to get him to reveal his political views, the pope resisted. His response was, "Religion should not interfere with politics." He then added, "The cause of crises in the world is this interference."[74] The reporter felt that the pope's unwillingness to discuss politics was a matter of principle. The fact that he would not express his opinion does not mean he does not have them. Recently, he cancelled his meeting with Vice President Mike Pence in protest of President Donald Trump's decision to move the US Embassy in Israel to Jerusalem on May 14, 2018. The church felt that the decision had failed to "take into consideration the feelings of millions of Arab people."[75]

In his Wednesday weekly meeting in Alexandria on April 17, 2019, Pope Tawadros II addressed the youth with regard to the church's role in politics. He stated, "We are in the twenty-first century, and I am the 118th patriarch. From the days of Mar Morcos [St. Mark the Evangelist] through times covering twenty-one centuries, the church has not been involved in politics. Are we now going to?" He added that we ought not to mix politics and patriotism, for patriotism in the last thirty or forty years has been difficult for many reasons. But in the last four years, "the scale began to counterbalance." Then the pope added, "I have not studied politics, nor did I work in politics." However, he advised the youth to vigorously participate in political activities to gain and hold power in government or to use their vote to influence decision-making.

Youth should learn to reap the rights of being a patriot. "Having your voice and your sister's heard for casting your vote is paramount," said the pope. As for the Coptic Orthodox Church, she does not get involved in politics. It is a patriotic church and remains expressive in her devotion to the country and its land. But youth should never retreat from preserving their civil and political rights or executing their genuine patriotic duty by falsely claiming, "It is not my place," or "There is no use!" As the pope said, "You have not been given a spirit of fear but a spirit of love and sound mind."

The Pope: A Motivator and a Think Tank Vision

A powerful, deep-seated, and enduring motivator is the power of purpose. A motivated person acts with a mission, a feeling of importance, and a sense of significance. Pope Tawadros II is proven to be a motivator who is interested in reform to achieve a better vision and better results. He is already carrying the title of "Futurist Innovator" (to be explained below). Thus, the prophecy of Pope Cyril VI for him is fulfilled. The 116th pope told his mother, who earnestly sought his prayers for her son Wagih Sobhy (the birth name of Pope Tawadros II) in high school, "He will have a great status!" It was something his righteous mother did not understand at the time, but apparently, St. Cyril had seen in her a son who was groomed for preeminence.

As early as sixteen years old, Wagih was fascinated by the adventure of Neil Armstrong, who had just landed on the moon on July 21, 1969. He then wrote to the US astronaut, asking for an autograph. A few weeks later, to the young man's surprise, an unexpected envelope arrived containing a signed color photo of the moon landing. In an interview with an *Arab News* reporter at St. Mark's Cathedral in Cairo, the pope recalled obtaining Armstrong's address from a radio program on Voice of America that motivated him to write the letter. Wagih admired Armstrong not only for his daring journey to the moon but also because he assumed Armstrong's first name was derived from Egypt's Nile River.[76]

I have shared this story to show that Pope Tawadros II, as young as sixteen years old, was interested in the world's affair. By listening to the Voice of America, he clearly sought out multiple sources to get his news. He was not only a listener but a doer, for he was determined to correspond with the astronaut and receive the fruit of his prompt action. In addition, the story reveals his genuine love for Egypt and its River Nile. No wonder when Coptic churches were burned to the ground in Muslim Brotherhood attacks, his popular quote reflected his love for the country: "A nation without churches is better than churches without a nation!"

In his meeting with the youth in Alexandria on April 17, 2019, the pope imparted some of his wisdom as a visionary. He provided advice and ideas on specific economic problems to help youth advance their way of thinking and empower them to explore ways to improve their economic status. Much of it appeared to be relating to his own life as a teenager. The topic of his speech then focused on youth and courage, quoting 2 Timothy: "For God has not given us a spirit of fear, but of power of love and of a sound mind." (2 Timothy 1:7) He related a story about a youth with limited means in a small village who came many years ago to ask him for the address of the French Embassy! The pope recalled that he himself had been interested in writing to a pioneer in a foreign land when he was young, and he did not hesitate to provide the youth the address once he knew his good intention.

The pope explained further that the youth, upon getting the address, went to the French Embassy and showed them a little newspaper advertisement about a French restaurant that offered traditional French dishes, including frog legs. The restaurant was seeking people who could supply them with frogs. The youth explained that in his village frogs were everywhere, and he would be willing to export them. Surprisingly, the restaurant, via the embassy, sent the conditions, and the youth successfully met these requirements. He eventually became a successful businessman. The pope concluded that no matter what our circumstances, God has given us a sound mind to succeed, as well as the power to resist temptation and endure hardness as good soldiers of Christ.

The 118th Pope: A Futurist Innovator

After studying the lengthy manual labor involved in cooking the Holy Myron, the pope decided to make use of modern technology to simplify the process. The Myron is highly sanctified oil in which the grace of the Holy Spirit resides. It is used to sanctify and consecrate to God whatever the Myron anoints. The pope wanted to use modern methods to attain the utmost purity in the oil and at the same time simplify the arduous process for preparing it.

In 2014, His Holiness announced that the Coptic Church would update the process of cooking the Myron. Modern technology, the pope said, "has added value of allowing us to make a bigger quantity of Myron oil since it simplifies the process." The new process, however, did not leave any remains after the extraction process, so people wondered how the baptismal Ghalilaon oil would be prepared. Pope Tawadros II explained that a simple calculation showed that Myron oil ingredients allowed for the preparation of a quantity of Ghalilaon oil that was around 1 percent of the concentration of the Myron oil. "So," he said, "we prepared that portion of Ghalilaon with the same concentration." It was indeed an innovative overdue change that saved time, eliminated manual labor, increased productivity, and improved the quality and purity of the end product. With the help of Fr. Georgious Attala of St. John's in Covina, California, the pope contacted international companies that specialized in the extraction of oils. Father Georgious had been a professor at Cairo University's faculty of science before his ordination to priesthood.

As soon as the pope announced changes in the preparation of the Holy Myron, Coptic fanatics panicked, and regretfully a wave of attacks on social media ensued. The critics include those who believed in the strict, literal interpretation of church tradition and its historical roots. These people erroneously thought of themselves as guardians of the "norm" that had been maintained for generations. In the name of God's creation, they thought, how could anyone dare to let modern technology interfere with their way of traditional thinking and the security of cultural orthodoxy?

New technology always carries with it the fear of the unknown, and in reaction, voices are always raised in objection. It happened when the automobile was invented in the late nineteenth century, yet cars were soon peacefully traversing the roads of the United States and Europe. These days, uncompromising zealots find in social media a window for exploiting the situation with rampant attacks on honorable, dignified, and dedicated spiritual leaders.[77] Despite all these lamenting voices about the history and tradition of the Coptic Church, Pope Tawadros II stayed the course and met all objections with dignified equanimity.

The Pope: An Educational Perfectionist

The 118th pope realized by divine providence early in life that acquiring knowledge and skills via education is essential. The cognitive approach to instruction called "constructivism" asserts that the learner is more important than any other factor and that the learning process should start in early childhood. This constructive view of the learning process calls for problem solving to become the basis of instruction. The learner is the focus and is more important than lessons, teachers, and other external elements. No wonder His Holiness focused on childhood as a bishop and was in charge of the children's committee in the Holy Synod before becoming pope.

Early in his papacy, the pope announced that education in Sunday schools and other Coptic institutions should focus on building an exemplary life and progression toward the state of perfection that the Lord demands of all, as St. Matthew stated: "Therefore you shall be perfect, just as your Father in heaven is perfect." (Matthew 5:48) His Holiness encouraged the establishment of private schools across Egypt with a curriculum designated for the very purpose of building exemplarily lives. He not only focused on childhood education and Sunday school educators, but in the meeting with youth in April 2019 in Alexandria, he called for the creation of an episcopate for children from five to fifteen years old. The youth episcopate is now well established and has been headed by HG Bishop Mousa.

The pope also spoke of his intention to create an episcopate for the Christian family. He established the successful Project of One Thousand Teachers for enhancing the caliber of education over a three-year period. Similar educational services and training will continue that seek to enlighten, edify, and ennoble those who wish to consider monastic life. The Holy Synod committee on monasticism is in charge of developing the criteria for those who wish to begin monastic life when admission is resumed in a year.

The Coptic Institute for Church Management and Advanced Learning

His Holiness spoke about the Coptic Institute for Church Management and Advanced Learning, complimenting the new educational program headed by Dr. Magdy Latif. The mission of the Coptic Institute is to nurture the leadership ingenuity and versatility of bishops, priests, and servants who minister to those they serve. The curriculum includes training in how to manage people effectively, create a vision, set goals, facilitate team dynamics, and manage time. Thus participants are able to help themselves and others to grow and remain accountable. Such newly trained leaders are able to solve problems and encourage harmonious relations among their parishioners. Most importantly, it builds bonds and mutual respect between bishops, priests, and servants and those they serve. The Coptic Institute has already graduated approximately seven hundred successful future leaders of the Coptic Church family.

CHAPTER 26

◆◇◆◇◆

HH Pope Tawadros II's Call: Looking to the Future

Education is the most powerful weapon we can use to change the world.

—*Nelson Mandela*

The 118th pope of Alexandria is a tender, loving father guided by the spirit and adorned with extraordinary prescience and vision. His gentleness, equanimity, and benevolence are native to him. His love and compassionate work for the future of the church is truly empathetic and caring. His heart is open to others—regardless of their intentions—which enables him to face tough times with creativity and resilience. These extraordinary attributes enable him to connect with everyone from statesmen to adversarial people. In the case of the Coptic Church, we can look at his exemplary leadership and trust that he is led by divine providence. For the future of the church, we can look at his paternal leadership and sacrificial love and anticipate how the church will evolve incrementally to new heights of spiritual glory.

HH Pope Tawadros II's Inspired Call!

Most of the pope's audience in Canada noted with pleasure the broad positive response to his call to explore and plan the church's education and catechism activity over the next fifty years. Thus far the church's role has been limited to meeting the needs of the faithful, especially in lands of immigration. It is now time for the church to respond to His Holiness's call for planning ahead through strategic, well-calculated steps into the digital age and beyond.

As the Coptic Church spreads across the globe, an extraordinary commitment to evangelization is urgently needed so that everyone can know and receive the Gospel message and thus grow "to the measure of the stature of the fullness of Christ." (Ephesians 4:13) Therefore, it is strongly urged that all the venerable fathers in the episcopate and all the faithful take the opportunity to proclaim His message. This will ensure it is well received as a map for communities to rediscover the inexhaustible riches of the faith.

A Retrospective Map

As we plan a map for the next fifty years, it behooves all Copts to take a look back. Here, I will only focus on educational aspects and not be concerned so much with the vocational or professional side of the planning process. The general aim of education is obviously to train the whole person—the intellect and the will, not just the mind alone. Knowledge is in the intellect or mind; character is in the will or decision-making. Preferably, a complete education will address the whole person: body, mind, heart, and spirit.

Points of Light Mission to Inspire, Mobilize, and Take Action

When developing a successful program for children that encompasses all aspects of their religious education, the following questions need to be asked:

- How successful is the current system of religious education provided by churches, schools, and Sunday schools in shaping the body, mind, heart, and spirit of the child?
- What is the role of parents in educating their children and instructing them in the faith after baptismal instructions?
- What curriculum and criteria does the church follow for educating parents in disciplining their children and instructing them in the faith?
- What is the role of Sunday school in affirming the fundamentals of the faith and presenting lively models and exemplary teachers?
- What are the qualities, qualifications, and level of commitment of Sunday school servants compared to past generations?
- What is the level of commitment and accountability of Sunday school servants, especially in the West?
- How much do educators still lean on past liturgical practices?
- Children may be taught to pray and participate in the liturgy, but are they taught to pray in their own hearts through contemplation, emulation, and guidance?
- Children may be encouraged to enter the sanctuary more freely, but equally important, have they been taught first how to enter the sanctuary of their own hearts?
- What is the Sunday school system's mission statement that defines its objectives?
- What is the Sunday school system's vision statement? And what is the servants' ultimate goal?

- What are the current incentives other than the label "servant" that motivate and encourage teachers and students to serve, learn, and disciple?
- What measures of accountability and objectives are in place that the head of a Sunday school and the priest can track?
- What types of methods and metrics for accountability are there for both those who serve and those being served? Are they standardized so they can be used in each parish?
- What are the rewards that encourage good behavior and steady attendance in Sunday school?
- What are the rewards that encourage parental support and participation in their child's growth and enrichment?

The Pope's Statement of Priorities

HH Pope Tawadros II, in the early days of his papacy, openly stated his priorities. His goal is to develop scientifically based programs that equip and qualify credentialed servants to instruct new generations in faith and character building. He also wants to build a standardized curriculum that is culturally and age appropriate. The purpose is to serve and monitor the needs of parents and children within their respective communities and cultures.

The Church's Affirming Parental Role

It is worth noting that due to time constraints, the church's role thus far is limited to preaching, teaching, and affirming principles to guide parents in all aspects of family life. However, teaching children begins as soon as they are born, and parents are the primary educators. I believe the church has a role to guide parents whenever possible with the following urgent topics.

Both parents are responsible for controlling noisy children, especially in the house of the Lord. To teach self-control to overactive children, parents must start at home, where they practice sitting still and quiet. A child should be dressed comfortably, and the family should sit together near the back of the church where the kids won't be as much of a distraction. A parent then can take the small one out for a two-minute walk every fifteen minutes if necessary. (The normal attention span of children five to six years old typically is ten to fifteen minutes at a time.) Parents ought to give clear expectations to toddlers and older children before going to church. They can consider bringing very young children later in the service and slowly start coming earlier as they develop and grow. They can also attend the church's special brief service conducted specifically for the youngsters.

It is very important that parents teach children the discipline of waiting in line as a defining feature of modern life. Cutting in line is an impolite, antisocial behavior. Other important skills to teach include getting along with siblings and peers, the art of mediation and harmonious relations, and respect for self and others. Self-respect and respect for public property earns the respect of others.

Proper Etiquette in the House of the Lord

It is the responsibility of parents not only to teach but to practice with their children proper etiquette when attending church services. Here are some ways members of the congregation ought to conduct themselves both in and outside of church.

- External gestures of reverence become a witness to the truths of the faith that members believe and cherish.
- Congregants should genuflect or bow immediately before receiving Holy Communion.
- Partakers in Communion ought to consciously recognize that it is the Lord Himself whom one genuflects or bows to. He is truly present in the Eucharist, in both the body and blood.
- Christian character and conduct outside the church speaks volumes of the new life the faithful not only has adopted but cherishes.
- External appearances of faith without internal conversion is, as St. Paul says, nothing but "sounding brass and tinkling cymbals." (1 Corinthian 13:1)

- External change with internal conversion is the fruit of the Holy Spirit, and charity is an instrument of service and means of penance and reconciliation.
- Although the church does not require everyone to be dressed in their finest every week for Mass, the way one dresses for church is oftentimes a sign of how important the celebration of the Eucharist is to members of the body of Christ. Overly revealing clothing or bare midriffs are never appropriate.
- Churches are meant to be sacred spaces where all can pray and worship. While a cordial greeting is never out of place, carrying on an audible and protracted conversation, especially while standing in line to receive Communion, is never appropriate.
- Spoken and sung responses at Mass are always meant to be done communally, with whatever abilities are bestowed on participants by the Lord.

The Transcendent and the Imminent

In the words of Archbishop John Krol:

> Recent literature on the role of the Church in the world at times draws a sharp distinction between the transcendent and the imminent, between the vertical and horizontal interest of the Church. These are presented as mutually exclusive, as if the Church faced the choice of devoting itself only to heavenly matters or to spending its resources only on the needs of humanity. Some would limit the Church to work in the sanctuary, and to operate in a sphere of other worldliness, irrelevant to the problems of this world.
>
> Others would have the Church immerse itself in worldly problems to the point of losing her proper identity and becoming identified

with other humanist movements. From the very beginning, however, the Church has been concerned with the transcendent and the imminent, the vertical and the horizontal. These two form the cross. The sign and the character stamped upon the Church of Christ.[78]

The Imminent Role

The culture of the twenty-first century has presented more than ever a serious threat to modern religious life. The role of the church is no longer to remain concerned only with the spiritual life of the faithful. The church has no alternative but to immediately follow the lead of HH Pope Tawadros II to plan more ambitious visions and take life-saving action. The purpose of such a move is to preserve and protect the family, especially young children, by meeting the destructive challenges of the digital age and its ability to corrupt the minds and characters of both the young and old.

The traditional theme of facing these challenges via the pulpit and prayer alone—though they are wonderful means—is not enough. The path to meet these challenges is to develop and train the child through a holistic approach that addresses the whole person, including their physical, mental, spiritual, and emotional health, while addressing social factors as well. Thus the focus would mainly pertain to developing the child's cognition from the moment of birth. A well-designed, tailored, and age-appropriate curriculum of education to reach objectives is essential. The curriculum ought to be a comprehensive learning experience that takes into account the nature and development of human intelligence. This is mainly related to the nature of knowledge and how humans gradually come to acquire, construct, and use it.

Proposed Global Executive Educational Entity (GEEE)

Some people strongly claim that spirituality is enough. Yes, it is essential, but it is not enough. Spirituality is an inner sense of relationship with the Creator. This relationship ought to be built and strengthened through the vigilant practice of sacraments instituted by Christ and entrusted to the church. Cognitive development, however, is a progressive reorganization of mental processes resulting from biological maturation and environmental experience. Therefore, in response to the pope's call, I propose that the Coptic Church expediently move to create a scientific team of leading experts in each specialized field called the Global Executive Educational Entity (GEEE). Once established, this entity can eventually have regional branches across the globe.

Proposed Models within a Cognitive System of Human Cognition

The GEEE that I propose would be in charge of developing the cognitive system of the learner to the best of his or her ability, in addition to creating an appropriate curriculum based on cognition and empowering attributes. It should be relevant to each age category and the capability of each individual. The GEEE would oversee applicable standardized and credentialed education. The main policy for Coptic education involves the active participation of the learner in studying and interpreting human experience in the light of faith in order to advance God's glory and the dignity of all people. Through methods appropriate to different age levels and ways people learn, the church would provide opportunities for the learner to explore, reflect, and integrate a Christian understanding of nature, self, society, and God and to manifest this in their lives of love and service. In this endeavor, the church recognizes the learner's dependence on grace to bring human nature to completion.

Based on the mandate of HH Pope Tawadros II to develop scientifically based programs, the GEEE would work to accomplish the following:

- Equip and qualify credentialed servants to teach new generations in faith and character building.

- Form specialized committees to build standardized curriculum that is culturally and age appropriate.
- Serve parents and children within the cultures of their respective communities and countries in which they live.
- Build specialized schools to develop the psychosocial and spiritual child. (Pope Tawadros II has already initiated these schools in Egypt, and a few have been established in the West.)
- Create a cutting-edge scientific research committee to monitor broad anecdotal evidence of progress in these schools as well as apply the most up-to-date scientific findings in the field of educating the whole person.

The GEEE's responsibility would be to formulate programs that include all the deliberate, systematic, and sustained efforts of the church community, in both formal and informal educational settings, to develop the skills, knowledge, and values needed for life. It would help the church, in today's pluralistic society, to harmonize ancient faith with modern human culture and history.

Coptic education sees all knowledge as sacred when human insight is combined with divine revelation in the pursuit of truth, goodness, and beauty. Leadership in this century is generally moving away from traditional models of centralized power and authority at the top. A framework for designing the religious institution's next steps using strategic priorities was clearly pointed out by Pope Tawadros II when addressing the youth in Alexandria on April 17, 2019. The shared vision of the pope and members of the Holy Synod is capable of galvanizing the faithful to generously support building a successful school system in Egypt and abroad. This vision would formulate the educational mission and motivate the experts who are entrusted with planning and executing these revolutionary educational efforts. Now is the time not only to build and expand the Coptic Church to meet worshippers' needs but also to build schools associated with the church to meet the educational future of the Coptic Church in the third millennium.

UNICEF Report on Education

The United Nations Children's Fund, better known as UNICEF, states that education is the most powerful investment in our future. The UNICEF report titled *The Investment Case for Education and Equity* calls for urgent action. It suggests that the UN should allocate more resources to education in the early grades, target resources to the poorest areas and most marginalized children, establish policies and methods that improve spending efficiency, strengthen learning-assessment systems, and implement accountability measures that involve parents and communities. As the report states, "There is no time to lose. Educated children are at the heart of healthy, productive, and prosperous societies. If that is the future we want tomorrow, we must invest today."[79]

In other denominations, parochial schools or education ministries operate nongovernmental school systems. These schools participate in the evangelizing mission of their church, integrating religious education as a core subject within their curriculum. These schools, through a well-designed and well-structured curriculum, focus on the development of individuals as practitioners of their faith.

It behooves the Coptic Church to follow suit in order to preserve its identity in any country across the globe. These schools should maintain a Coptic identity and provide education in regards to life and faith so individuals can develop intellectually, physically, socially, emotionally, and most importantly, spiritually.

Be Aware: The Danger of Government Schools

By the grace of God, I have made extensive efforts to speak at Coptic churches around the United States about the existential importance of keeping our precious children out of the grips of the ideologies that now dominate many public schools. The situation in public schools is getting more frightful every year. All parents, whatever their financial circumstances, must consider keeping their children away from the danger of public schools. These schools present real threats to the souls of their children and even to the country. As activists and authors Mary Rice Hasson and Theresa Farnan explain in their book *Get Out Now: Why You Should Pull Your Child from Public Schools Before It's Too Late*, while education achievement markers have been declining, government schools "have been successful in one area: churning out youthful progressives—growing numbers of men and women in the grips of existential confusion, perpetual victimhood, and political intolerance." In a *Federalist Radio Hour* conversation with host Joy Pullman, Hasson argued that public schools' unavoidable capitulation to transgender ideology is a Rubicon no family should follow them across.[80]

Another Alternative: Homeschooling

Dr. Raymond S. Moore (1916–2007) and his wife, Dorothy, were the authors of *Better Late than Early*, the 1975 book that launched the modern homeschooling movement in the United States. Dr. Moore's educational career began as a teacher, principal, and superintendent of California public schools. After serving in several prominent positions in academia, the US Department of Education invited him to be a higher education program officer. His research about the effects of public schooling on young children convinced him that homeschooling was the way of the future. He and Dorothy spent many years working with legislatures and courts to defend the homeschool movement. They were strong believers in the educational principle of nurturing the seeds of uniqueness within each child.[81]

Why Homeschooling?

Many schools in the United States are plagued with violence. Today's dysfunctional families have contributed to the downfall and delinquency of their children. As such, many children have never known parental love, a peaceful home, and a safe family life. Many Coptic parents in the West have been cognizant of the fact that a child's Christian upbringing at home often vanished once he or she entered public or even private schools. American schools that were known for generations for teaching Christian ethics and moral life adapted a secular mentality, denying the existence of God. Educational institutions have relapsed and bowed down to a false notion of liberty to do whatever seems right. As a result, there are no ethics, virtues, discipline, or decency in most of these secular institutes of education.

According to the National Center for Education Statistics (NCES) and other education researchers, homeschooling has been on the rise in the United States over the last ten years. It has been instrumental in the liberation of children from the suffocating atmosphere of the typical school environment. Children have been receiving educational programs within the walls of their homes under the supervision of parents and volunteers. As homeschooled students, they are not subjected to crime, bullying, drugs, and corruption. I recall a surprising national news segment on ABC about homeschooling that acknowledged how homeschooled children have been accepted in the nation's elite universities.

NCES reports that parents gave a number of reasons for homeschooling their children. In the 2011–2012 school year, 91 percent of parents of homeschooled students said that, more than anything else, a concern about the environment of other schools was an important reason for homeschooling their child.[82]

Conclusion

The driving force behind these educational changes is leadership that believes in empowering and shaping the life of the whole child—body, mind, heart, and spirit. Dr. Moore and his wife started a movement all over the world. As mentioned, His Holiness Pope Tawadros II focused on childhood as a bishop and was in charge of the children's committee in the Holy Synod before he became pope. Now he has been instrumental in initiating a movement where intelligence plus character becomes the goal of true education. His primary purpose is to inspire the educational movement to provide for the fullest possible development of each child and learner—spiritually, morally, creatively, and productively.

The pope is inviting all the faithful to share his insight and fore-sight by asking: How will the church change in the next fifty years? The path to glory via collective minds and willing spirits is wide open. With divine providence, we can revolutionize the educational system in the Coptic Church. We can free learners and their fami-lies from the poisonous and corrupt culture of secular government schools. The mission is to provide parents with ethical educational methods that develop the whole person. Hence, today's children as well as future generations can reach their utmost potential, allowing them to grow "to the measure of the stature of the fullness of Christ." (Ephesians 4:13)

NOTABLE QUOTABLES

Chapter 1: The Plight of the Coptic Christians of Egypt

"The gallant person will always consider the world with a smile of toleration, and his own doings with a smile of honest amusement, and Heaven with a smile which is not distrustful being thoroughly persuaded that God is kinder than the genteel would regard as rational."

—James Branch Cabell

Chapter 2: Immigration Concept: Inexplicable Self-Destructiveness

"The Comedy is always the same. In the first act the hero imagines a place where happiness exists. In the second he strives towards that goal. In the third he comes up short or what amounts to the same thing he achieves his goal only to find that happiness lies a little further down the road."

—James Branch Cabell

James Branch Cabell, a Richmond, Virginia, author, is best known for his controversial *Jurgen: A Comedy of Justice* (1919), one of several ironic fantasies he wrote that took place in Cabell's mythical medieval world of Poictesme (pronounced "pwa-tem").

Chapter 3: Exploring the Unknown

"When you walk to the edge of all the light you have and take the first step into the darkness of the unknown, you must believe that one of two things will happen. There will be something solid for you to stand upon or you will be taught to fly."

—Patrick Overton

Patrick Overton is a PhD, author, educator, community cultural developer, and current director of the Front Porch Institute. He started his work in community cultural development in 1976 as director of Thespian Hall.

Chapter 4: Discerning Insight

"By looking for the unexpected and discerning the surreptitious features in the scenery within us, we apprehend our personality, find out our identity, and learn how to cultivate it. Taking care of our fingerprints will be an enduring endeavor."

—Erik Pevernagie

Erik Pevernagie (born 1939) is a Belgian painter and writer living in Uccle, Brussels, who has held exhibitions in Paris, New York, Berlin, Düsseldorf, Amsterdam, London, Brussels, and Antwerp.

Chapter 5: The Domestic Church

"Those of us who wish to gain understanding must never stop examining ourselves, and if, in the perception of your soul, you realize that your neighbor is superior to you in all aspects, then the mercy of God is surely near at hand."

—St. John Climacus

St. John Climacus, also known as John of the Ladder, was a sixth- to seventh-century Christian monk at the monastery of Mount Sinai. He is revered as a saint by the Eastern Orthodox, Eastern Catholic, and Roman Catholic churches.

Chapter 6: Evaporating Dream

"For the new religious consciousness, the declaration of the will of God is together with this a declaration of the rights of man, a revealing of the Divine within mankind."

—Nikolai Berdyaev

Chapter 7: Saint Mark Emissaries in the United States

"It is the greatest mystery of life that satisfaction is felt not by those who take, and make demands, but by those who give and make sacrifices. In them alone the energy of life does not fail, and this is precisely what is meant by creativeness... If you want to receive, give; if you want to obtain satisfaction, do not seek it, and forget the very word; if you want to acquire strength, manifest it, give it to others."

—Nikolai Berdyaev

Nikolai Berdyaev (1874–1948) was a Russian political commentator and Christian religious philosopher who emphasized the existential spiritual significance of human freedom and the human person. His voice is equally relevant to psychology and psychoanalysis.

Chapter 8: The Harvest Is Truly Plentiful

"We need today more than ever before, precisely a 'band of spiritual firebrands' who can inflame minds and hearts with fire of a loving knowledge of God and Jesus Christ, the Redeemer."

—Fr. Georges Florovsky

Fr. Georges Florovsky (1893–1979) was a prominent twentieth-century Orthodox Christian priest, theologian, and writer, active in the ecumenical movement. His writing is known for its clear, profound style, covering subjects on nearly every aspect of church life.

"A person is humble when he knows that his very being is on loan to him."

—St. Maximus the Confessor

St. Maximus the Confessor (580–662), also known as Maximus the Theologian and Maximus of Constantinople, was a Christian monk, theologian, and scholar. In his early life, Maximus was a civil servant and an aide to the Byzantine emperor Heraclius.

Chapter 9: Christ Ambassadors and Laborers to His Harvest

"Therefore Pray the Lord of the harvest to send out Laborers into His harvest."

—Matthew 9:38

Chapter 10: History Is Made: Coptic Mass Celebrated in Philadelphia

"Yesterday is history, tomorrow is a mystery, today is a gift of God, which is why we call it the present."

—William Keane

William Aloysius Keane (1922–2011), better known as Bil Keane, was an American cartoonist notable for his work on the newspaper comic *The Family Circus.*

Chapter 11: The Law of Supply and Demand

"In our own lives the voice of God speaks slowly, a syllable at a time. Reaching the peak of years, dispelling some of our intimate illusions and learning how to spell the meaning of life-experiences backwards, some of us discover how the scattered syllables form a single phrase."

—Abraham Joshua Heschel

Chapter 12: One Body with Many Members… Why Divided?

"When faith is completely replaced by creed, worship by discipline, love by habit; when the crisis of today is ignored because of the splendor of the past; when faith becomes an heirloom rather than a living fountain; when religion speaks only in the name of authority rather than with the voice of compassion—its message becomes meaningless."

—Abraham Joshua Heschel

Abraham Joshua Heschel (1907–1972) was a Polish-born American rabbi, one of the leading Jewish theologians and philosophers of the twentieth century, and a civil rights activist best known for his writings on ethics and mysticism.

Chapter 13: The Bicentennial Celebration: Historical Perspectives

"A people without the knowledge of their past history, origin, and culture is like a tree without roots."

—Marcus Garvey

Marcus Garvey (1887–1940), born in Jamaica, was a political leader, publisher, and orator for the Black Nationalism and Pan-Africanism movements, to which end he founded the Universal Negro Improvement Association and African Communities League. Garvey advanced a Pan-African philosophy that inspired a global mass movement known as Garveyism.

Chapter 14: Historical Glimpses of the Leadership of HH Pope Cyril VI

"History may record that his greatest act of healing was effected when he healed the fracture between the sister churches of Egypt and

Ethiopia. It has been one of the tragedies of more recent history, possibly one that the present Holy Synod in Cairo will overcome, that festering wound has been left open for some years where Kyrillos the healer brought only blame, but the present tragic divisions (1994) merely emphasize his ministry of agape and Reconciliation."

—Father John Watson

Father John Watson, PhD, FRAS, was an Anglican priest who was very enthusiastic about the Coptic Orthodox Church's history and leadership and has written extensively about her during the last seven years of his life, both in Coptic and international magazines in Europe and the United States. He was chaplain of Sutton Valence School, Kent, England.

Chapter 15: Global Evangelization upon the Return of St. Mary to Egypt

"The most significant event in the patriarchate of Abba Kyrillos was an act of grace. It was a miracle for which no natural explanation is possible. From 2 April 1968 until 29 May 1971, apparitions of Blessed Virgin Mary were witnessed by nightly crowds of up to quarter of a million Christians, Muslims and Jews... The appearances of Our Lady of Zeitoun in Egypt are widely regarded as a seal of approval upon the ministry of Abba Kyrillos."

—Father John Watson

Chapter 16: A Historical Glimpse of the Leadership of HH Pope Shenouda III

"Remember your Leaders who spoke the word of God to you. Consider the outcome of their way of life and imitate their faith."

—Hebrews 13:7

"Blessed are the people whose shepherd is Pope Shenouda III."

—Mar Ignatius Jacob III

Mar Ignatius Jacob III (1913–1980) was the 121st Syrian Orthodox Patriarch of Antioch and all the East.

Chapter 17: A New Start: St. Mena Coptic Orthodox Church

"I stand in awe of the many 'coincidences,' 'chance' meetings, synchronicities, and fateful detours that have impelled and guided me on my life's journey."

—Peter Levine

Peter A. Levine, PhD, is a contemporary psychologist specializing in trauma. He worked for NASA as a stress consultant while the Space Shuttle program was being developed and has shared his expertise while teaching at various facilities throughout the world.

Chapter 18: One Body, One Spirit, and One Local Church

"I will hear what the Lord God will speak."

—Palms 85:8

"Blessed is the soul who hears the Lord speaking within her, who receives the word of consolation from His lips. Blessed are the ears that catch the accents of divine whispering, and pay no heed to the murmurings of this world."

—Thomas à Kempis

Thomas à Kempis (1380–1471) was a German-Dutch canon regular of the late medieval period and the author of *The Imitation of Christ,* one of the most popular and best-known Christian books on devotion.

Chapter 19: Further Growth of St. George Church

"There are troubles and trends, but these are present in every age. I sometimes like to picture the existence of the Church as the existence of the moon. Sometimes it's full, sometimes it's half, sometimes it's a quarter. But it's there."

—John Cardinal Krol

John Cardinal Krol (1910–1996) was an American prelate of the Roman Catholic Church. He was archbishop of Philadelphia from 1961 to 1988.

Chapter 20: St. George Parish: A Shining Renewal

"The Perfect man thinks continually on others; on loving others, on what is good for others, on the eternal destiny of others, on the sanctity of others. Himself he places last of all, or the servant of all."

—HH Pope Shenouda III

HH Pope Shenouda III (1923–2012) was the 117th pope of Alexandria and patriarch of the See of St. Mark. His episcopate lasted forty years, four months, and four days from November 14, 1971 until his death on March 17, 2012.

Chapter 21: The Pope of Alexandria's Third Visit to the United States

"The world sees in our conduct, in our behavior, the proof that we are the real children of God."

—HH Pope Shenouda III

Chapter 22: St. George Parish: A Monument of Divine Grace

"The tree grew and became strong; its height reached to the heavens and it could be seen to the ends of all the earth. Its leaves were lovely, its fruit abundant, and it was food for all."

—Daniel 4:11–12

Chapter 23: The Call

"God doesn't call the qualified, He qualifies those He calls."

—Mark Batterson

Mark Batterson serves as lead pastor of National Community Church in Washington, DC—one church that has seven locations. NCC focuses on reaching emerging generations and meets in theaters throughout the DC metropolitan area. He holds a doctor of ministry degree from Regent University and is the author of ten books, including *The Circle Maker*, *In a Pit with a Lion on a Snowy Day*, *Wild Goose Chase*, and most recently, *All In*.

"Then Moses said to the Lord, O my Lord, I am not eloquent, neither before nor since You have spoken to Your servant: but I am slow of speech and slow of tongue."

—Exodus 4:10

Chapter 24: St. George Parish: Historical Perspective

I. His Grace Bishop Karas

"For me, it is essential to have the inner peace and the serenity of prayers in order to listen to the silence of God, which speaks to us, in our personal life and the history of our times, of the power of love."

—Adolfo Perez Esquivel

Adolfo Pérez Esquivel (born 1931), distinguished as an Argentinian artist, became a human rights activist based on Christian pacifism and was awarded the Nobel Peace Prize in 1980.

II. St. George Evangelical Mission

"If a church cares about budgets and buildings more than caring for people and their salvation, such church should close its doors, for a church without mercy lives in deception."

—Fr. Tadros Yacoub Malaty

Fr. Tadros Yacoub Malaty is a stalwart and vibrant priest, theologian, and spiritual leader in the Coptic Orthodox Church. He is widely published in spiritual, theological, and liturgical studies. All his publications are known for their depth and are characterized by biblical and patristic references. They are an easy-to-understand catechesis intended to transmit the Gospel as the Christian community has traditionally received it, understands it, and celebrates it.

III. Establishing St. George Mission Church in South Philadelphia

"I believe that in each generation God has called enough men and women to evangelize all the yet unreached tribes of the earth. It is not God who does not call. It is man who will not respond."

—Isobel Kuhn

Isobel Selina Miller Kuhn (1901–1957) was a vivacious Canadian Christian missionary to the Lisu people of Yunnan Province, China, and northern Thailand.

Chapter 25: Pope Tawadros II of Alexandria

"The episcopate is a work, not a relaxation; a solitude, not a luxury; a responsible ministration, not an irresponsible domination; a fatherly supervision, not a tyrannical autocracy. It is more important to be proficient in good works than in golden-tongued preaching."

—St. Isidore of Pelusium

St. Isidore of Pelusium lived during the fourth to fifth centuries. He was a native of Alexandria and was raised among pious Christians. He was a relative of Theophilus, archbishop of Alexandria, and of his successor, St. Cyril. While still a youth, he quit the world and withdrew to Mount Pelusium in Egypt, which became the site of his monastic efforts.

Chapter 26: HH Pope Tawadros II's Call

"Education is the most powerful weapon we can use to change the world."

—Nelson Mandela

Nelson Mandela (1918–2013) was a South African antiapartheid revolutionary, political leader, and philanthropist who served as president of South Africa from 1994 to 1999. He was the country's first black head of state and the first elected in a fully representative democratic election.

NOTABLE QUOTABLE THAT SAYS IT ALL

"I have a handful of prayers that I pray all the time… One is that God will put my books into the right hands at the right times. I've prayed this prayer thousands of times, and God has answered it in dramatic fashion countless times. The right book in the right hands at the right time can save a marriage, avert a mistake, demand a decision, plant a seed, conceive a dream, solve a problem, and prompt a prayer. That is why I write. And that's why, for me, a book sold is not a book sold; a book sold is a prayer answered. I don't know the name and situation of every reader, but God does, and that's all that matters."

—Mark Batterson

Mark Batterson is the lead pastor at National Community Church in Washington, DC. He is the author of several books on Christian living, including the bestseller *The Circle Maker: Praying Circles Around Your Biggest Dreams and Greatest Fears.*

Appendix I

Pope Kyrillos VI Publications Certificate of Incorporation and Proof of Publication Notices

E. M. GABRIEL

Commonwealth of Pennsylvania

July 9, 1975

Department of State

TO ALL TO WHOM THESE PRESENTS SHALL COME, GREETING:

Pennsylvania, ss:

I DO HEREBY CERTIFY, That from an examination of the indices and corporate records of this department, it appears that on June 6, 1975, Articles of Incorporation of "POPE KYRILLOS VI PUBLICATIONS"

were approved and filed under, and pursuant to, the provisions of the Non-Profit Law approved November 15, 1972, Act 271.

I DO FURTHER CERTIFY, That no proceedings in dissolution adversely affecting the corporate existence of the foregoing have been subsequently filed.

WHEREFORE, it appears that this corporation remains a presently subsisting corporation as of the date hereof.

IN TESTIMONY WHEREOF, I have hereunto set my hand and caused the Great Seal of the Commonwealth to be affixed, the day and year above written.

C. DeLacey Tucker
Secretary of the Commonwealth

Bucks County Law Reporter
DOYLESTOWN, PA.

Owned and Published by the Bucks County Bar Association

STATE OF PENNSYLVANIA, } ss:
COUNTY OF BUCKS

_____Patrick J. O'Connor_____ being duly sworn according to law deposes and says that he is the editor of the Bucks County Law Reporter, the legal publication designated by the several Courts of Bucks County, Pennsylvania, as the official newspaper for the publication of legal notices in Bucks County, Pennsylvania, which was established in 1951; that the printed notice, a copy of which is attached hereto was published in said paper on the following dates:—

June 5, 1975.

that your deponent is not interested in the subject matter of the notice so published and that all of the allegations of this statement as to the time, place and character of the publication are true. ·

_____
Editor

Sworn to and subscribed before me this

_____6th____ day of ____June_____

A.D. 19_75____

NOTARY PUBLIC, DOYLESTOWN, BUCKS COUNTY
MY COMMISSION EXPIRES OCTOBER 25, 1977

NOTICE IS HEREBY GIVEN THAT Articles of Incorporation have been (are to be) filed with the Department of State of the Commonwealth of Pennsylvania at Harrisburg, Pennsylvania, for the purpose of obtaining a Certificate of Incorporation pursuant to the provisions of the Business Corporation Law of the Commonwealth of Pennsylvania, approved May 5, 1933, P. L. 364, as amended.

The name of the corporation is POPE KYRILLOS VI PUBLICATIONS.
The Articles of Incorporation will be filed on Thursday, June 5, 1975.
The purpose or purposes for which it is to be organized are as follows: To propagate, perpetuate, religious education and teachings in complete accordance with the Faith and Doctrines of the Coptic Orthodox Church of Alexandria. The activities said above would be maintained by means of distributing religious and educational books including all Pope Kyrillos VI Publications. The said corporation does not contemplate pecuniary gain or profit and will be incorporated be incorporated under the provisions of the Pennsylvania Business Corporation

E. M. GABRIEL

No. ....Term, 19....

PROOF OF PUBLICATION OF NOTICE IN THE LEGAL INTELLIGENCER
Under Act of May 16, 1929, P. L. 1784, as amended

COMMONWEALTH OF PENNSYLVANIA, } ss.:
COUNTY OF PHILADELPHIA

............G. Smith............................., being duly sworn, deposes and says that THE LEGAL INTELLIGENCER
is a daily legal newspaper published at 66 N. Juniper Street, Philadelphia, Pennsylvania 19107, and was established
in said city in 1843, since which date said legal newspaper has been regularly issued in said county, that it has been
issued daily since September 4, 1933, and that it was entered at the Philadelphia Post Office under the Postal Laws
and Regulations as second class matter in the United States mails on July 19, 1879; that THE LEGAL INTELLIGENCER
is a daily legal newspaper complying in all respects with the Newspaper Advertising Act of May 16, 1929, P. L.
1784, its amendments and supplements; and that a copy of the printed notice or publication is attached hereto
exactly as the same was printed or published in the regular editions and issues of the said legal newspaper on
the following dates, viz.: ....

....

....March 24 ...., A. D. 19..77

Affiant further deposes and says that she is an employee of the publisher of said legal newspaper and has
been authorized to verify the foregoing statement and that she is not interested in the subject matter of the
aforesaid notice or publication, and that all allegations in the foregoing statement as to time, place and character
of publication are true.

Copy of Notice or Publication

NOTICE IS HEREBY GIVEN THAT
Articles of Amendment to the Articles of
Incorporation of Pope Kyrillos VI Publications, Inc., a Pennsylvania Business Corporation, with its registered office located at
6 Patricia Lane, Levittown, Pa. 19057, have
been filed with the Department of State of
the Commonwealth of Pennsylvania, at
Harrisburg, Pa., on November 17, 1976,
pursuant to the provisions of the Business
Corporation Law of the Commonwealth of
Pennsylvania, approved May 5, 1933, as
amended.
The said corporation is organized exclusively for charitable, religious purposes,
including, for such purposes, the making of
distributions to organizations that qualify
as exempt organizations under Section
501(c)(3) of the Internal Revenue Code of
1954. Pope Kyrillos Publications, Inc., 1128
Gilham Street, Philadelphia, Pa. 19111.
3-24-1

Sworn to and subscribed before me this................28th............day of
............March............ 19....77

Notary Public

Philadelphia, Phila. County
My Commission Expires January 2, 1978

STATEMENT OF ADVERTISING COSTS

....

....

....

To THE LEGAL INTELLIGENCER, DR.

For publishing the notice or advertisement attached
hereto on the above stated dates

Bucks County, ss.

.............Winfield C Sipler............... being duly affirmed according to law, deposes and says that he is the .....Accounting Supervisor.................

(Manager or designated Agent)

of the BRISTOL PRINTING COMPANY, Publisher of the Bucks County Courier Times, daily newspapers of general circulation, printed and published and having its place of business at Levittown, Bucks County, Pa.; that said newspaper was established in 1910; that securely attached hereto is a printed notice which is exactly as printed and published in said newspaper on ....1 June 1975.................

and is a true copy thereof; and that this affiant is not interested in said subject matter or advertising; and that all of the allegations in this statement as to the time, place and character of publication are true.

Affirmed and subscribed to before me this 6th day of June A. D. 1975

Winfield C Sipler
Accounting Supervisor

Josephine C Soares
Notary Public
Commonwealth of Penn.
My Commission Expires
January 8, 1977

APPENDIX II

St. George Coptic Orthodox Church Certificate of Incorporation and Proof of Publication Notices

Commonwealth of Pennsylvania

May 31, 1973

Department of State

TO ALL TO WHOM THESE PRESENTS SHALL COME, GREETING:

Pennsylvania, ss:

I DO HEREBY CERTIFY, That from an examination of the indices and corporate records of this department, it appears that on May 3, 1973 Articles of Incorporation of "COPTIC ORTHODOX CHURCH OF ST. GEORGE" _____

were approved and filed under, and pursuant to, the provisions of the Non-Profit Law approved November 15, 1972, Act 271.

I DO FURTHER CERTIFY, That no proceedings in dissolution adversely affecting the corporate existence of the foregoing have been subsequently filed.

WHEREFORE, It appears that this corporation remains a presently subsisting as of the date hereof.

IN TESTIMONY WHEREOF, I have hereunto set my hand and caused the Great Seal of the Commonwealth to be affixed, the day and year above written.

C. DeLores Tucker

Proof of Publication of Notice in The Philadelphia Inquirer
Under Act No. 587, Approved May 16, 1929

State of Pennsylvania, } ss.:
County of Philadelphia.

.... _M. Bell_ ...., being duly sworn, deposes and says that THE PHILADELPHIA INQUIRER is a daily newspaper published at Broad and Callowhill Streets, Philadelphia County and State aforesaid, which was established in the year 1829, since which date said daily newspaper has been regularly issued in said County, and that a copy of the printed notice or publication is attached hereto exactly as the same was printed and published in the regular editions and issues of said daily newspaper on the following dates, viz.:

....

....

.................................and the__16th_____day of____December_____, A. D. 19_72_

Affiant further deposes that he is duly authorized by Philadelphia Newspapers, Inc., a corporation, publisher of THE PHILADELPHIA INQUIRER, a daily newspaper, to verify the foregoing statement under oath, and also declares that affiant is not interested in the subject matter of the aforesaid notice or publication, and that all allegations in the foregoing statement as to time, place and character of publication are true.

M. Bell

Copy of notice or publication

Sworn to and subscribed before me this____27th_____

day of_____December_____ 19__72_

_____
Notary Public.

My Commission Expires:

Statement of Advertising Costs

To Philadelphia Newspapers, Inc.

For publishing the notice or advertisement
attached hereto on the above stated dates_____ $_____

Affidavit thereto _____ $_____

Total _____ $_____

Publisher's Receipt for Advertising Costs

Philadelphia Newspapers, Inc., a corporation, publisher of THE PHILADELPHIA INQUIRER, a daily newspaper, hereby acknowledges receipt of the aforesaid advertising and publication costs, and certifies that the same have been fully paid.

Philadelphia Newspapers, Inc., a Corporation

No. ....Term, 19....

PROOF OF PUBLICATION OF NOTICE IN THE LEGAL INTELLIGENCER

Under Act of May 16, 1929, P. L. 1784, as amended

COMMONWEALTH OF PENNSYLVANIA,
COUNTY OF PHILADELPHIA } ss.:

..................F. Mahan........., being duly sworn, deposes and says that THE LEGAL INTELLIGENCER is a daily legal newspaper published at 66 N. Juniper Street, Philadelphia, Pennsylvania 19107, and was established in said city in 1843, since which date said legal newspaper has been regularly issued in said county, that it has been issued daily since September 4, 1933, and that it was entered at the Philadelphia Post Office under the Postal Laws and Regulations as second class matter in the United States mails on July 19, 1879; that THE LEGAL INTELLIGENCER is a daily legal newspaper complying in all respects with the Newspaper Advertising Act of May 16, 1929, P. L. 1784, its amendments and supplements; and that a copy of the printed notice or publication is attached hereto exactly as the same was printed or published in the regular editions and issues of the said legal newspaper on the following dates, viz.: ....

December–15 ...., A. D. 19.... 72

Affiant further deposes and says that she is an employee of the publisher of said legal newspaper and has been authorized to verify the foregoing statement and that she is not interested in the subject matter of the aforesaid notice or publication, and that all allegations in the foregoing statement as to time, place and character of publication are true.

Copy of Notice or Publication

NOTICE IS HEREBY GIVEN THAT Articles of Incorporation will be filed with the Department of State of the Commonwealth of Pennsylvania, at Harrisburg, Pa., on Monday, the 15th day of January, 1973, for the purpose of obtaining a Certificate of Incorporation of a proposed business corporation to be organized under the Business Corporation Law of the Commonwealth of Pennsylvania, approved May 5, 1933.
The name of the proposed corporation is Coptic Orthodox Church of St. George.
The purposes for which it is to be organized: Administering the liturgy and the sacraments in Philadelphia, Pa.   12-15-1

....
15th

Sworn to and subscribed before me this..................day of
December ......, 19.... 72

Notary Public

Philadelphia, Phila. County
My Commission Expires January 2, 1974

STATEMENT OF ADVERTISING COSTS

TO THE LEGAL INTELLIGENCER, DR.

For publishing the notice or advertisement attached
hereto on the above stated dates . . . . $...........
Probating same . . . . $...........

Total . . . . $...........

PUBLISHER'S RECEIPT FOR ADVERTISING COSTS

The Founders and the First Board of Deacons of St. George Coptic Orthodox Church in Philadelphia A Signed Letter with All the Names of the First Board Members Submitted to the Commonwealth of Pennsylvania Department of State on May 20, 1973

COMMONWEALTH OF PENNSYVANIA
DEPARTMENT OF STATE
HARRISBURG, 17120

Att. Director

Date: May 22, 1973
Re : Board of deacons

Dear Sir,
    We submit herewith the names of the Church Board Of Deacons in its
first meeting alongwith their signatures , Rev. Mankarious, Awadalla
is the President and shall preside over all Board meeting.
    Following are the: names of the Vice-President, the Secretary
and the Treasurer ELECTED by the Board of Deacons in its first
meeting on May 20, 1973;

    Lewis. Khella   Vice-president
    Esmat M. Gabriel   Secretary
    Nabih I. Abdou   Treasure
In the event that an office held by an appointed member becomes vacant
for any reason, such office shall be filled for the unexpired term ,
by another appointed office by His Holiness the PoPe of Alexandria.
You will be advised same.

                                    very truly yours,

                                    Esmat M. Gabriel
                                    Secretary of the Board

NAME   SIGNATURE

Raafat S. Mishriky
Nabil A. El-Samma
Rodolph M. Yanney
Sidrak F. Wasef
Morris F. Guirguis

———◆—⟨•• ⟩◆⟨ ••⟩—◆———

Pope Shenouda III's Guardianship Letter Regarding Fr. Angelos H. Boghdadi's Two Daughters in the USA

THE HISTORY OF THE COPTIC ORTHODOX CHURCH IN THE UNITED STATES

COPTIC ORTHODOX PATRIARCHATE
CAIRO U. A. R.

<u>TO WHOM IT MAY CONCERN</u>

This is to certify that Reverend Father Angelos Habib BOGHDADY had left the United States on July 3rd, 1977 to serve in Cairo, Egypt for the time being.

He left his two daughters Elham and her sister Eman under the guardianship of Mr. Esmat M. Gabriel and his wife of 1128, Gilham St., Philadelphia, Pa. 19111, U.S.A.

Cairo, November 26, 1977.

Pope Shenouda III,
Pope of Alexandria,
Patriarch of the See of St. Mark.

sm/-

299

NOTES

Preface

1. Daniel Cox and Robert P. Jones, "America's Changing Religious Identity," Public Religion Research Institute, September 6, 2017, https://www.prri.org/research/american-religious-landscape-christian-religiously-unaffiliated/.
2. HG Bishop Shenouda, "The Evangelist: Morcos the Disciple, the Saint and Martyr," *Arabic World Publisher*, p. 19, May 1968.

Chapter 1

3. Sarah Starkweather, US Immigration Legislation Online, University of Washington, Bothell Library, retrieved January 1, 2012.
4. Jennifer Ludden, "1965 Immigration Law Changed Face of America," Special Series, The Immigration Debate, May 9, 2006.

Chapter 4

5. Eva al Masri Sidhom, *Memoirs of an Egyptian American, or the Life Story of the First Co-Ed at the American University in Cairo* (Jasper, AR: Engeltal Press), pp. 77, 88.
6. Dora El-Masri, *Speaking of the Lord's Greatness and His Work through Others* (Sporting, Alexandria: Delta Center Publisher, 1988), pp. 75–78.
7. Sami I. Boulos, *The History of the Early Coptic Community in the USA (1955–1970)* (New Jersey, 2006), p. 45.
8. Ibid, p. 47.
9. Ibid, p. 55.

Chapter 5

10. The Second Ecumenical Council of the Vatican, *Dogmatic Constitution on the Church, Lumen Gentium,* §11; 11 October 1962–8 December 1965.

Chapter 6

11. Boulos, *History of the Early Coptic Community*, p. 67.
12. Ibid, p. 81.
13. Ibid, p. 109.

Chapter 7

14. Catherine Rampell, "Path to United States Practice is Long Slog to Foreign Doctors," *New York Times*, August 11, 2013.
15. Eva al Masri Sidhom, "CAA Records and List of Members, 1965–1970"; Boulos, *History of the Early Coptic Community*, pp. 11–24.
16. Farid Shafik, "Reverend Fr. Hegumen Gabriel Abdelsayed," Coptic Orthodox Church of St. Mark, http://www.saintmark.com, December 2018.
17. Ibid.

Chapter 8

18. "Fr. Bishoy Kamel," St. Abanoub Coptic Orthodox Church, www.stabanoub-dallas.org, retrieved February 16, 2018.
19. Iris Habib El-Masri, *Magnetic Radiation: The Story of Father Pishoy* [sic] *Kamel* (Sporting, Alexandria: St. George Church Bookshop, 1989), pp. 12–14, 16; Tadros Yacoub Malaty, *Pastoral Work in the Life of Fr. Pishoy Kamel* (California: St. Peter and St. Paul's Coptic Orthodox Church, 1979), pp. 6–8, 34–35.
20. "Our Metropolitan," Coptic Orthodox Diocese of Los Angeles, lacopts.org.
21. John H. Watson, "The Transfigured Cross: A Study of Father Bishoi Kamel (6 December 1931–March 1979)," *Coptic Church Review* 23, nos. 1 and 2 (Spring, Summer 2002): p. 23.
22. Habib El-Masri, *Magnetic Radiation*, p. 14.
23. Watson, "The Transfigured Cross," p. 15.
24. Esmat M. Gabriel, *The Exemplary Leadership of Pope Kyrillos VI & Pope Shenouda III* (St. Mina Publisher, November 2013), p. 140.
25. "Fr. Bishoy Kamel," St. Abanoub Coptic Orthodox Church.
26. Watson, "The Transfigured Cross," p. 3.
27. Ibid, p. 22.

Chapter 9

28. Boulos Ayad, "The International Coptic Scholar: Professor Aziz Suryal Attia," *Coptic Church Review* 11, no. 4, (Winter 1990).
29. Ibid, p. 101.
30. Cornelis Hulsman, *Coptic Church Review* 13, no. 3 (Fall 1992).
31. Claremont Colleges Digital Library, Karen J. Torjesen, Gawdat Gabra, and Michael Saad (eds.), ccdl.libraries.claremont.edu, 2006–2007, retrieved December 12, 2018.
32. "The School of Alexandria, Part 1: An Introduction to the School of Alexandria," Coptic Orthodox Church Network, www.copticchurch.net, retrieved September 17, 2017.

Chapter 10

33. Basiliyyus al-Maqari, "Canon Law in the Coptic Orthodox Church," *Arab West Report*, December 27, 2002.

Chapter 11

34. Fr. Tadros Malaty, "The Church in the Land of Diaspora," June 1972, Los Angeles-New York, p. 49.
35. Esmat M. Gabriel, *The Exemplary Leadership*, pp. 58, 59.

Chapter 13

36. Remarks of Gerald R. Ford in Philadelphia, Pennsylvania (Bicentennial Celebration), Gerald Ford Presidential Library & Museum, July 4, 1976.
37. Eleanor Boba, "Treasures of Tutankhamun Exhibit Opens at Seattle Center on July 15, 1978," Essay 20564, HistoryLink.org, May 21, 2018.
38. Ruth Seltzer, "Venerable Egyptian Yacht Plays Host on Delaware River," *Philadelphia Inquirer*, July 20, 1976.
39. Ibid, p. 3.
40. "Isma'il Pasha," Wikipedia, https://en.wikipedia.org/wiki/Isma%27il_Pasha.
41. Zeinab El-Gundy, "El-Mahrousa Yacht: A History Entwined with the Suez Canal," Ahram Online, August 6, 2015, http://english.ahram.org.eg/NewsContent/1/64/136969/Egypt/Politics-/ElMahrousa-yacht-A-history-entwined-with-the-Suez-.aspx.
42. "St. George's the Al-Karma," *The Orthodox Church*, February 1976, vol. VI, no. 66, p. 2.
43. "'Common Declaration' of Pope Shenoudah III, Catholicos Aram I, and Patriarch Paulos, News and Media of the American Orthodox Church, July 22, 2007.
44. "Ethiopian Orthodox Tewahedo Church," Wikipedia, article proposed since November 2018.
45. Esmat M. Gabriel, *The Exemplary Leadership*, pp. 178, 179.
46. Ibid, pp. 103, 104.
47. Pope Shenouda III, "Exemplary Shepherd: Hegomen Mikhail Ibrahim (1899–1975)," Dar El-Alem El-Arabi, pp. 116–120.

Chapter 14

48. Jim Bill and Dave Richardson, "A King's Home," *Time*, September 8, 1952, pp. 33, 34, 37.
49. Iris Habib El-Masri, "The Story of the Coptic Church: History of the Egyptian Orthodox Church, Established by St. Mark the Evangelist," MB Publisher, February 23, 1984, p. 27.
50. Lara Iskander and Jimmy Dunn, "An Overview History of Coptic Christian in Egypt," Tour Egypt, www.touregypt.net, retrieved February 15, 2019.
51. Esmat M. Gabriel, *The Exemplary Leadership*, p. 147.
52. Ibid, p. 19.
53. Ibid, p. 176.
54. Ibid, p. 177.
55. Ibid, pp. 177, 178.
56. Ibid, p. 178.

Chapter 15

57. Esmat M. Gabriel, *The Exemplary Leadership*, p. 179.
58. John H. Watson, "Abba Kyrillos Patriarch and Solitary," *Coptic Church Review* 17, nos. 1 and 2 (Spring and Summer 1996): p. 29.
59. Ibid, p. 18; Edward Wakin, "A Lonely Minority," *New York*, 1963, p. 116.
60. Father Jerome Palmer, OSB, *Our Lady Returns to Egypt* (San Bernard, CA: Culligan Publications, 1969), p. 42.
61. Ibid, p. 24.
62. Ibid, p. 21.
63. Ibid, p. 26.

Chapter 16

64. His Holiness Pope Shenouda III, 117th Pope of Alexandria, Silver Jubilee, November 14, 1996, published by Archdioceses of North America, Los Angeles, CA, and Hawaii; Diocese of Southern United States, p. 2.
65. Ibid, p. 3.
66. Lawrence Joffee, "Pope Shenouda III; Egyptian Spiritual Leader of the Coptic Orthodox Church for More Than 40 Years," *The Guardian*, March 18, 2012.

Chapter 17

67. *St. Mena's Life and Miracles* (Shoubra, Cairo: Pope Kyrillos' Sons, 1982), p. 12.
68. Susie Lloyd, "St. Menas, St. Mina, and Mena—Who All Happen to Be the Same Person (Saint with Funny Names)," *Catholic Digest*, November 16, 2017.

Chapter 19

69. Bishop Mousa, "From the East to the Middle of America," *Elkiraza*, nos. 39, 40 (November 24, 1989): p. 6.

Chapter 21

70. Jamil al-Utafi, "Report on the al-Khankah Sectarian Events," translated and published by *Arab West Report*, January 4, 2009, www.arabwestreport.info/year-2009/week-13/2-report-dr-jamal-al-utayfi-alkhankah-sectarian-event; Mohamed Heikal, *Autumn of Fury: The Assassination of Sadat* (HarperCollins, 1983).
71. Esmat M. Gabriel, "Dr. Rodolph Yanney: The Apostle of Advent—Glimpses of His Life," Society of the Coptic Church Studies, July 15–16, 2011.

Chapter 25

72. Michael S. Saad, "The Modern Period (1952–2011)," *The Coptic Christian Heritage*, Lois M. Farag (ed.), (Abingdon-on-Thames, UK: Routledge), p. 94.
73. Kareem Fahim, "Coptic Pope Dies in Egypt Amid Church's Struggles," *New York Times*, March 12, 2012.

74. Faisal J. Abbas, "The Pope of Hope: Egypt's Tadros II on the Status of Copts, Regional Policies, and Saudi Reforms," *Arab News*, December 4, 2018.

75. Ibid.

76. Ibid.

77. Michael Victor, "New Batch of Holy Myron Oil," *Watani International*, April 5, 2017.

Chapter 26

78. Archbishop John Krol, Sermon at the Consecration of Most Reverend Raymond J. Gallagher, Bishop of Lafayette, Indiana, August 11, 1965.

79. Yoka Brandt, UNICEF Connect, UNICEF.org, January 22, 2015.

80. Joy Pullman, "Why Putting Your Kids In Public Schools Is More Dangerous Than Ever," *The Federalist*, September 26, 2018.

81. Elijah Award, "History of Moore Academy: A Tribute to Dorothy Moore and Court Staff," *The Home School Report*, September/October issue.

82. J. Redford, D. Battle, and S. Bielick, "Homeschooling in the United States: 2012," National Center for Education Statistics, Institute of Education Sciences, US Department of Education, Washington, DC, NCES 2016-096REV.

Other References

* Pope Shenouda III, "Our Teacher Archdeacon Habib Girgis: Pioneer of Religious Education in Modern Times," translated by Saad, Michael Saad.

About the Author

D r. Esmat Messiha Gabriel is an expert in the behavior health-care industry whose accomplishments are well recognized by leading health organizations and medical schools, including Pennsylvania Hospital of the University of Pennsylvania Health System, Thomas Jefferson University Medical College, and Albert Einstein Medical Center.

Dr. Gabriel has received numerous accolades and acknowledgments for his work, including the Ronald Reagan presidential Medal of Merit in 1983. He was elected to the New York Academy of Sciences, is listed in *Who's Who in Gerontology*, and is a member of the editorial board of the *Journal of Coptic Church Review Studies*. Dr. Gabriel is the recipient of the Thomas Jefferson Medical College Golden Pin Recognition Award, the Jessie Smith Noyes Fellowship, and the HH Pope Tawadros II Recognition Award for Devoted Services in establishing the Coptic Church in the United States.

Dr. Gabriel is a clinical researcher who is well published in the field of human behavior. He is a coinvestigator of two national research studies: "The Anxiolytic Effect of Oxazepam in the Treatment of Older Patients Suffering from Neurotic Anxiety" and "The Therapeutic Effect of Serax in Comparison to a Placebo in the Treatment of Insomnia Associated with Psychoneurotic Anxiety." His most recent publications are *Contemporary Leadership Styles Analysis: The Exemplary Leadership of Pope Cyril VI* and *The Exemplarily Upbringing of the Child & Transformational Stages Toward Perfect Maturity.*

CPSIA information can be obtained
at www.ICGtesting.com
Printed in the USA
BVHW082033230221
600893BV00004B/218